ENA

By the same author

Princess Alice
The Great Lock-out of 1926

Gerard Noel

ENA

SPAIN'S
ENGLISH QUEEN

Constable London

First published in Great Britain 1984
by Constable and Company Limited
10 Orange Street London WC2H 7EG
Copyright © 1984 by Gerard Noel
Paperback edition 1989
Set in Linotron Ehrhardt 11 pt by
Rowland Phototypesetting Limited
Bury St Edmunds, Suffolk
Printed in Great Britain by
St Edmundsbury Press Limited
Bury St Edmunds, Suffolk

ISBN 0 09 469230 0

A
XXV
G
with
fondest
love

Contents

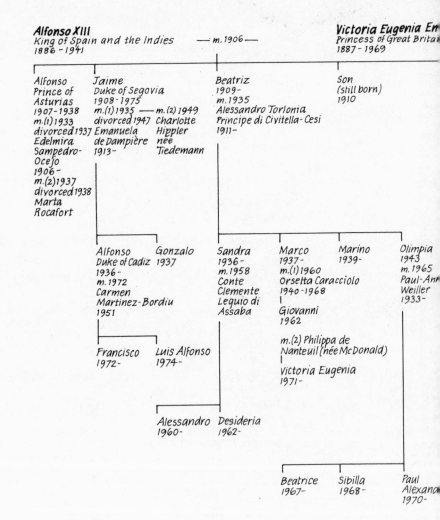

Alfonso XIII
King of Spain and the Indies — m.1906 — **Victoria Eugenia En**
1886 - 1941   Princess of Great Britai
                                                              1887 - 1969

Alfonso   Jaime   Beatriz   Son
Prince of   Duke of Segovia   1909-   (still born)
Asturias   1908-1975   m.1935   1910
1907-1938   m.(1)1935 — m.(2)1949   Alessandro Torlonia
m.(1)1933   divorced 1947 Charlotte   Principe di Civitella-Cesi
divorced 1937 Emanuela   Hippler   1911-
Edelmira   de Dampière   née
Sampedro-   1913-   Tiedemann
Ocejo
1906-
m.(2)1937
divorced 1938
Marta
Rocafort

           Alfonso   Gonzalo   Sandra   Marco   Marino   Olimpia
           Duke of Cadiz   1937   1936-   1937-   1939-   1943
           1936-   m.1958   m.(1)1960   m.1965
           m.1972   Conte   Orsetta Caracciolo   Paul-Ann
           Carmen   Clemente   1940-1968   Weiller
           Martinez-Bordiu   Lequio di | 1933-
           1951   Assaba   Giovanni
                                                        1962

                                                        m.(2) Philippa de
           Francisco   Luis Alfonso   Nanteuil (née McDonald)
           1972-   1974- |
                                                        Victoria Eugenia
                                                        1971-

                    Alessandro Desideria
                    1960-   1962-

                                          Beatrice   Sibilla   Paul
                                          1967-   1968-   Alexano
                                                                     1970-

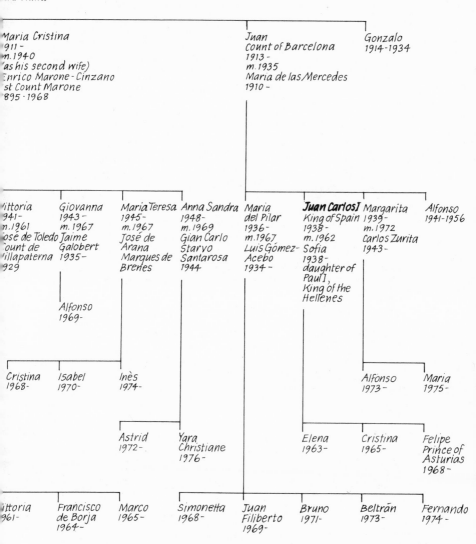

Maria Cristina
1911 –
m.1940
(as his second wife)
Enrico Marone-Cinzano
1st Count Marone
1895-1968

Juan
Count of Barcelona
1913 –
m.1935
Maria de las Mercedes
1910 –

Gonzalo
1914-1934

Vittoria
1941 –
m.1961
José de Toledo
Count de
Villapaterna
1929

Giovanna
1943 –
m.1967
Jaime
Galobert
1935 –

Maria Teresa
1945 –
m.1967
José de
Arana
Marques de
Breñes

Anna Sandra
1948 –
m.1969
Gian Carlo
Staryo
Santarosa
1944

**Maria
del Pilar**
1936 –
m.1967
Luis Gómez-
Acebo
1934 –

Juan Carlos I
King of Spain
1938 –
m.1962
Sofia
1938 –
daughter of
Paul I,
King of the
Hellenes

Margarita
1939 –
m.1972
Carlos Zurita
1943 –

Alfonso
1941-1956

Alfonso
1969 –

Cristina
1968 –

Isabel
1970 –

Inès
1974 –

Alfonso
1973 –

Maria
1975 –

Astrid
1972 –

**Yara
Christiane**
1976 –

Elena
1963 –

Cristina
1965 –

Felipe
Prince of
Asturias
1968 –

Vittoria
1961 –

**Francisco
de Borja**
1964 –

Marco
1965 –

Simonetta
1968 –

**Juan
Filiberto**
1969 –

Bruno
1971 –

Beltrán
1973 –

Fernando
1974 –

Illustrations

Acknowledgements

I am most grateful to various members of the Spanish royal family without whose kindness, candour and courtesy this book could never have been written: first of all to His Majesty, King Juan Carlos of Spain who most graciously received my wife and myself at the Zarzuela Palace and was of enormous help with the information and encouragement he gave me; to HRH, Don Juan, Count of Barcelona, who so kindly received me at his house, Villa Giralda, Estoril, Portugal, and gave me considerable practical assistance; to HRH, the Infanta Beatrice, Princess of Civitella-Cesi, who, at her house in Rome, the Palazzo Torlonia, most generously gave me impressions and information of great interest about her mother; to HRH, the Infanta Margarita de Borbón y Borbón, who spoke freely and affectionately about her grandmother; and to her husband Sr Dr Don Carlos Zurita y Delgado; to Sra Doña Olympia, Madame Paul-Annik Weiller, who was able to tell me much about her grandmother and was very kindly helpful in many other ways.

HRH, Don Juan, the Count of Barcelona, was good enough to give me a letter of introduction to the Head of the Royal Household in Madrid, the Marquis of Mondéjar, whereby I was enabled to gain unhindered access to material in the Royal Archives in Madrid. My thanks in this connection go also to Sr Don Fernando Fuertes de Villavicencio, Director of the Spanish Royal Archives.

I acknowledge with deep gratitude the gracious permission of Her Majesty the Queen to quote from two entries in Queen Victoria's Journal and from those papers in the Royal Archives at Windsor whose references are cited in the notes.

I owe a special debt of gratitude to Sir Anthony Acland, now Permanent Under Secretary of the Foreign Office, for his considerable kindness and help to me when he was British Ambassador in Madrid. For this I am most grateful, as also for the help and hospitality of Sir Richard Parsons, Sir Anthony's successor as British Ambassador in Madrid, whose assistance was invaluable.

A large part of the book is based on information given verbally to the author by those who knew Queen Ena personally at various stages during her life. Some of such persons preferred not to be mentioned or quoted by name but I am equally grateful to all concerned. Their combined and often overlapping evidence enabled me to double check every story and fact of importance. I am no less grateful to the many people who supplied me with invaluable contacts in Spain, Switzerland, France, Great Britain and the USA for the sake of tracing first hand information about the Queen. (In the list of those to whom I am indebted I have, for the purposes of simplicity and greater clarity, used abbreviated and often anglicized modes of address or title.)

I would like to thank in particular: HRH, the late Princess Alice, Countess of Athlone; the Duke of Baena y San Lucar la

Mayor; the late Sir John Balfour; Sr Alfonso Ballestero; the late
Marquis of Bonanza; Mrs T. F. Burns; the Count and Countess
Chrevreu-d'Antraigues; the Revd J. M. Charles-Roux; Sir John
Colville; M. Aldo Corbani; the late Canon Alfonso de Zulueta; Sr
Fernando Diaz-Plaja; Sr and Sra Beltran Domecq; Mr Michael
Dormer; Mr David Duff; Colonel du Parc Braham; the Dowager
Duchess of Durcal; Sr Juan Fernando Finat Walford; Mr Philip
German-Ribon; Sr Javier Gonzales de Vega; Sra Paz de Goma;
Mr Broderick Haldane; the Duke of Huescar; Lady Kelly; the
Duke of Medinaceli; the Count and Countess Mendoza-Cortina;
Baroness Ione von Oppenheim; the Dowager Duchess of
Pastrana; the late General Luis de Camara Pina and Senhora
de Pina; Sra Quiepo de Llano; the Marquis and Marchioness of
Quintanar; the Dowager Marchioness of Quintanar; Srta Luisa
Rich y Paulet; Sra Pepita de Rich; Mr Kenneth Rose; Mme
Jacques Roux; Sra Nenina de Ruiz-Morales; Mrs Teresa Sande-
man; the Marquis and Marchioness of Santa Cruz; the Marquis
of Santo Floro; Srta Marisa de Satrustegui; Sr Mario Solana;
Mr Peter Thwaites; Sra Fernanda de Thynne; Sr Dalmiro de la
Valgoma y Diaz-Varela (Permanent Secretary of the Spanish
Royal Academy of History); the late Lady Mary Walker.

To these and many others I am sincerely grateful and wish
especially to thank my wife who accompanied me on my journeys
to Spain and elsewhere and gave invaluable encouragement and
help to me at every stage in the preparation of the book.

[1]

Jubilee Princess

THOSE close to Princess Ena of Battenberg in her earliest years said that she seemed 'born to be a Queen.' But such things are often said of royal princesses and there were no obvious reasons to justify such a prophecy. There were, however, unusual circumstances surrounding her birth which endowed it with an aura of romance. For it was the first royal birth to occur in Scotland since that of Charles I in 1600, and Ena was the first royal child ever to be born at Balmoral. The date was 24 October 1887, the year of Queen Victoria's Golden Jubilee.

Twenty-five years earlier there had been no celebrations, for the Queen's beloved consort had died only the year before. Many long and painful years had had to pass before she had once more returned to anything like a normal life. Never away from her side during those gloomy years was her youngest daughter, the prop and stay of her morbid widowhood, Princess Beatrice. In April 1884 the Queen and her 'Benjamina' had journeyed to Darmstadt for the marriage of the former's granddaughter, Princess Victoria of Hesse, to Prince Louis of Battenberg. This Prince Louis, father of the future Earl Mountbatten of Burma, had a younger brother called Henry. Henry and Beatrice had met as children but never since. Now, Beatrice, who had hitherto repelled all advances from members of the opposite sex with almost neurotic frigidity—subtly prompted by her mother—fell, for the first and only time, in love.

The attraction was mutual. It was quickly obvious that Henry, the good-looking and charming young officer in the Hessian

Gardes du Corps, was also in love. So it was an elated Princess who returned to England that spring. But in making known her desire to marry the young Battenberg Prince she was reckoning without her formidable mother. The Queen had no intention of losing her companion; but in this particular instance she was unperturbed. By way of reply to Beatrice's romantic disclosure, the Queen made it clear that the question of marriage could not be discussed for some time. Princess Beatrice had thus to wait in suspense for the whole summer. She could not know that her mother was playing a shrewd game to retain her Benjamina's companionable services even after she was married. The Queen's tactics were perfectly timed and when she finally consented to the marriage, it was on condition that the newly-weds should live with her and never, during her lifetime, be allowed a home of their own. There seemed no choice but to accept such conditions and Princess Beatrice was duly married to Prince Henry of Battenberg on 23 July 1885.

Their first child, Alexander, the future Marquis of Carisbrooke, was born in November of the following year and, by the time of the Golden Jubilee, mid-summer 1887, the Princess was pregnant once again. She was not, however, allowed to abdicate her position as principal support to her mother, particularly at a time when the latter was playing the demanding role of the brave widow emotionally facing up to the rigours of the elaborate celebrations. The triumphant Queen enjoyed it all hugely but tried not to show it too much. But Princess Beatrice was exhausted by the time the summer was over. To help her recover her strength Queen Victoria decided to prolong their autumn sojourn at Balmoral. Thus the family were still in residence there when, on 24 October, a baby daughter was born to Princess Beatrice.

It was a very difficult confinement. The Queen recorded in her Journal [1] that she 'was up in the night with my poor Beatrice who was very ill.' She hardly left her until, at four in the afternoon, 'after a terrible [*sic*] long time, the baby appeared to our great joy and relief, a very large, fine girl but she was nearly stillborn.' Had the child been born dead, the country of Spain would have had a very different and perhaps much happier future history. Its royal house would not have inherited the curse of that deadly disease which was to poison the blood of the Spanish Bourbons and destroy the love between Ena and her husband. But, fortunately or unfortunately, for those of every generation, the future cannot be foretold and on that historic day at Balmoral there was thanksgiving and rejoicing.

The proud grandmother went on to note that 'Liko'—the family nickname for her son-in-law Prince Henry—'gave the baby into my arms, wishing me joy of my little Jubilee grandchild.' And she paid special tribute to 'Dr William's dexterity in bringing the Baby safely into the world.'[2] The infant princess was then brought into her mother's sitting-room where Lord John Manners was sitting with Princess Christian of Schleswig-Holstein, more generally known as Princess Helena, Queen Victoria's third, but eldest surviving, daughter. That night a huge bonfire was kindled on Craig Gowan 'as a triumphant signal of the happy event'.[3]

It captivated the imagination of the local highlanders and the happenings inside Balmoral became the chief conversation on Deeside. Though the christening was to be a quiet, family affair, its date was no secret. The castle was serenaded from early in the morning of 23 November and there were cries throughout the surrounding countryside of 'three cheers' for the Queen, the Princess and the new baby. The christening coincided with the first birthday of the Battenbergs' son Alexander, already known in family circles as 'Drino'. The ceremony was to take place at one o'clock in the drawing-room at Balmoral. The font used for the baptism of practically all Queen Victoria's children and grandchildren had been sent all the way from Windsor. Masses of flowers also arrived from there. The officiating minister was Dr Cameron Lees of St Giles' Cathedral, Edinburgh, and the water he used had been specially brought from the river Jordan.

'The christening is on the 23rd,' the Queen had written to the Duchess of Connaught. 'She will be called Victoria (of course) Eugénie Julie Ena (a Gaelic Highland name)'.[4] The first name was chosen to please the aged English Queen, 'the grandmother of Europe'. The second was in honour of the child's godmother the Empress Eugénie de Montijo, the Spanish-born widow of Emperor Napoleon III. She and Queen Victoria had been close friends ever since the Empress had come to spend the years of her exile in England. They called each other 'dear sister' and the Empress's son, the ill-fated Prince Imperial, was rumoured to be a suitor for the hand of Princess Beatrice. The name Julie was that of the baby's paternal grandmother Princess Julie of Battenberg whose natural desire to hold her son's daughter during the baptismal ceremony was thwarted by Queen Victoria who insisted on holding the baby herself. The fourth name chosen, Ena, was to mark the fact that this was the first royal birth in Scotland for so many years, Ena being an old Gaelic name, as Queen Victoria had pointed out.

A long and suitably reverential account of the christening service appeared in the principal local paper[5] which described the ceremony as 'of a strictly private character'. It was carried out in the flower-filled drawing-room with spectacular views of the Craig Gowan heights and attended by not more than a hundred. It was conducted according to 'the simple order' of the Church of Scotland. No prouder man was present at the proceedings than a local musician named Mr John Kirby who had been commanded to attend as conductor of the Aberdeen Madrigal Choir. The choir was installed in the apartment immediately adjoining the drawing-room. As, on the stroke of one, the baby was brought into the room by Lady Biddulph and two nurses, the choir sang a 'Chorale' dear to the heart of Queen Victoria because it had been composed by her husband.

Home life for the infant Ena and her brothers was unlike that of any of Queen Victoria's other grandchildren. For, as already seen, Princess Beatrice and her husband were allowed no home of their own as long as Queen Victoria lived. She did not die until Ena was thirteen. The intervening years were spent in a 'home' that was really a Court. For wherever the Queen went, whether it was Balmoral, Buckingham Palace, Windsor or Osborne, the Battenbergs followed. And each place had the permanent atmosphere of a Court, with ministers, courtiers, official servants and the like, coming and going. Even Osborne, which was the nearest thing to a permanent home that Ena knew in her early years, was overshadowed by Court life. From the children's point of view, such an atmosphere did nothing to produce any fun or excitement. It was just the opposite. The Victorian Court of the last twenty years of the Queen's life stood aloof from the rest of society and, as Bagehot put it, had 'but slender relations with the more amusing part of it'. This was a foretaste of what Ena was to contend with in Court circles in Madrid twenty years later. Now, as then, she was forced to find her own ways of making life more tolerable. Generally speaking she succeeded despite, or perhaps because of, her grandmother's austerity. Ena could see the funny side of it but had the sense to keep her natural rebelliousness within prudent bounds.

It was, of course, the grandmother rather than the mother—Beatrice, the 'shy princess'—who ruled the domestic roost. 'Having been born and brought up in her home she was like a second mother to us,' Ena was later to say, with polite understatement. 'She was very kind but strict with old-fashioned ideas of how children must be brought up; the one she most insisted upon was that children should be seen and not heard.'[6] One of Ena's earliest distinct memories of her grandmother was connected with the improbable subject of baby carrots, which the old Queen happened to like very much. One of her presents to the Battenberg grandchildren was an allotment for the cultivation of flowers and vegetables. Ena, in hers, made a speciality of baby carrots so as to please her grandmother.[7] It was for such reasons as this, small in themselves, that Ena became Queen Victoria's favourite grandchild. Such favour never turned into favouritism but rather

took the form, often involving greater severity than would otherwise be normal, of trying to turn Ena into a perfectionist. The
Queen's admonitions or words of advice would invariably begin
with some such phrase as 'It won't do,' or 'a Princess must
not . . .'[8] In this way did the redoubtable old monarch take over
the Battenberg children as if they were her own. She felt more at
ease with them than she had ever felt with her own children.[9] This
relationship, curiously enough, was to repeat itself when Ena
herself had grandchildren.

Did Ena love her grandmother? Yes—in a certain way. She
looked upon the old lady with a mixture of affection, amused awe
and fascinated curiosity. This was well illustrated by certain
incidents which Ena, with her excellent memory, was able to
recall vividly later on. She remembered in particular such things
as 'the somewhat archaic English' which her grandmother habitually used. This made the grandchildren smile inwardly,
though they were of course much too terrified to show any
outward amusement. One evening, one of Ena's cousins said 'I
think it's time for us to go to bed.' The Queen gave her a fearsome
look and then said, 'Young woman, a Princess should say, "I think
it's time for me to retire".' The recipient of this remark was one of
those thirty or so cousins who had to replace ordinary friends as
playmates in Ena's life. Such cousins were her sole companions—
along, of course, with her brothers Alexander, Leopold and
Maurice.

The brothers were classmates as well as playmates and they all
had most of their lessons together from almost the first day that
Ena's education began. The four of them were near enough in age
to form their own miniature school whose 'co-educational' nature
somewhat made up for Ena's lack of any male company outside
the family circle. Their many nannies supervised the classes when
they were very small. Later there was a succession of governesses,
first French, then German and finally English, with tutors also
arriving, but, unfortunately for Ena, for the boys only. Ena's
father was something of an academic often giving them lessons

himself. He was liberal in his outlook and it was his idea that Ena should not be separated from her brothers in educational activity. Ena's principal interests lay in the direction of the arts, particularly music and the drama. But she was not a fanatic for book-learning and never particularly looked forward to the return to Buckingham Palace or Windsor which she associated chiefly with lessons. Her happiest youthful days were passed during the long summers at Osborne and autumns at Balmoral. The seaside attractions of the former were among the many charms held out by their Isle of Wight home. They were often shared with the Duke of Connaught's children. Of these, the second daughter, Patricia, was Ena's age and was to be, in a certain sense, her rival in the marriage stakes later on.

Balmoral was a specially favoured childhood playground for Ena. It was the place she referred to most frequently and most affectionately in letters written years afterwards to one of her favourite cousins, Princess Mary of Teck who became the wife and Queen of King George V. They were not childhood friends since Princess May, as she was generally called, was twenty years older than Ena. But they became very close friends later on and Ena, as Queen of Spain, wrote frequently to Queen Mary. The first occasion on which they met was when Ena was bridesmaid at the wedding of Mary to the Duke of York, as he then was, which took place in 1893 at the Chapel Royal in St James's Palace. The six-year-old Ena began to talk but was sternly told that one must not speak in church. When the celebrant started his sermon Ena said in a piping voice, 'That man shouldn't be allowed to speak in church.'

That particular wedding had repercussions on the early years of Ena's life for within a year her place as favourite grandchild was usurped by that of the York's first-born child, the future Edward VIII. Ena was later to confess that 'she was at first very jealous of the new arrival, and it was some time before she forgot her old prejudice against the Prince of Wales.'[10] As a boy she found him 'perfectly horrid' and on one occasion told him she wanted nothing to do with rude little boys who did not know how to behave themselves'. Ena had by this time reached the self-important age of sixteen while the future Prince of Wales was a mischievous ten year old. He assured his older cousin that he would mend his ways and then invited her for a walk in the garden at Sandringham where they were both holidaying. Having persuaded Ena to bend down to look into a flower bed he promptly dropped a worm inside the back of her dress. Ena's dignity was greatly outraged.

Despite the freedom and many pleasures of Osborne, their principal home, Balmoral, seemed for the Battenbergs to have everything they could desire such as long days in the exhilarating air, fishing in the lochs, roaming in the hills and pony excursions to local beauty spots. Ena took enthusiastically to riding almost as soon as she could get up on a horse. Riding was also a favourite activity at Osborne where Ena had her first bad fall. It was 1894 when Ena, still only six, was thrown badly when her pony crossed his legs. 'The groom dragged her from under the pony,' wrote Queen Victoria in her journal, 'and mercifully she seemed not much hurt, though she complained very much of her head'.[11] Within a few days Ena was 'getting on very nicely and had her doll in her arms. It is such a blessing . . .'[12] The experience did not deter Ena from riding with as much enthusiasm as ever in the future. She never lost her love for horses—a love which was to bring her much pain when she was forced to sit, with feigned enjoyment, through many a gruelling bullfight in Spain.

For Ena the child, life in a 'home' which was always, in reality, the centre of Court life had both advantages and disadvantages. She met important people, and saw intriguing ceremonies she would never otherwise have witnessed. But life under the same roof as Queen Victoria was never easy or relaxed. The Queen, for one thing, was fanatically against all forms of smoking and visitors had to blow smoke up the chimney if they wanted to try to enjoy a cigar or cigarette in their rooms. Little, however, did the self-centredly complacent old monarch know what what was actually happening almost under her nose particularly as to the activities of her ingenious grandchildren. Ena, who became a heavy smoker later in life, laughed about this in her own old age. She often recounted then how she and her brothers, long before her grandmother had died, enjoyed many a surreptitious smoke behind the bushes. The chief enjoyment was in proving that Queen Victoria, who thought she knew of everything that was going on, was often ignorant of happenings on her own doorstep. Another of the Queen's obsessions was punctuality. Once at Osborne, when Ena was about eight, the Prince of Wales, already over fifty, tried to sneak in unobserved when late for lunch. The Queen sent him away as if he were a boy of ten and would not let him have any lunch at all.

From the age of six onwards, Ena and her brothers were allowed to have meals with the grown-ups. Here again it was the Queen who dominated the dining-table with Prince and Princess Henry sometimes seeming to be as careful of their manners as the children. The Queen had decided that only roast beef or roast mutton and milk pudding were suitable fare for the latter's age group. The basic menus never changed except for the occasional allowance of an Indian curry dish on a Saturday or Sunday. The golden rule for the children at all mealtimes was never to speak unless spoken to. If one of the children broke this rule he, or she, would immediately be swept up in the arms of one of Queen Victoria's famous Indian servants and carried out of the dining-room in one or two long strides. No grudge was borne against the Indian manservants. Despite their turbans and large black beards the children loved them and were never frightened of them. But the worst thing about such meals was the sheer monotony of the food made more unbearable because of the succulent-smelling and delicious-looking delicacies produced by the chef and invariably consumed with relish by the adults. Ena, early in life, showed incipient signs of being a gourmet and in years to come was a voracious enjoyer of good food. Her pleasure, she afterwards confessed, over her first glass of wine—she was about

Ena in the arms of one of her grandmother,
Queen Victoria's Indian servants

thirteen when she had this—was heightened by the sense of guilt. She drank it with a piece of Port Salut but could never afterwards bring herself to admit to her grandmother how much she enjoyed it. She went on adoring Port Salut to the end of her life because of its associations with that moment of 'ecstasy'.[13]

Being so constantly near her grandmother did 'not enormously' influence the future Queen of Spain in later life.[14] The sense of discipline remained but its exaggeration had, in some respects, a counter productive effect. Ena, for example, was never a profoundly religious woman, though the question of the particular Church to which she should formally belong was one day to be of key importance. Her early religious training was of that old-fashioned, fundamentalist variety which was little more spiritually meaningful than the learning of multiplication tables. Ena and her brothers were expected to have scriptural quotations at their fingertips and their grandmother demanded instant answers to her questions about passages from the bible. There was no time even to think. The answers had to come out pat. Ena was once a bit too quick in her desire to give a ready answer to one of the Queen's sudden questions and took the risk of hastily improvising. The Queen had been out for a ride and had barely stepped down from her carriage when she brandished a menacing stick in Ena's direction. With no warning of what was coming next, the old lady shot out the question 'Ena, what were the epistles?' Her granddaughter, in some panic, replied that she supposed they were 'the wives of the apostles'. All nearby waited for the inevitable explosion of fury. But for once the Queen was too surprised to be angry. Ena long remembered the Queen's staring at her in incredulous silence, her white veil beating gently about her shoulders. She then leaned forward to peer at Ena. She seemed to be wondering whether the child was trying to be funny or was just incurably stupid.

Ena's first trips abroad began when she was seven with annual spring visits in the company of her ever-present grandmother to the villa the Queen rented in the south of France. On one trip she

Ena, aged eight at Windsor, with her parents,
Queen Victoria and her brothers, Alexander and Leopold

chanced to meet an English lady who asked Ena, not knowing who she was, where she lived. On being told that the child's home was the Isle of Wight the lady said she had once been there and had seen Princess Henry of Battenberg soon after her marriage. 'She has a little girl now,' the stranger added, 'much about your age. I'm told she's a very sweet child.' Ena, after a slight hesitation, replied, 'She's not always sweet.'

It was through being less than 'sweet' on one occasion that the youthful Ena chanced to become a friend of the ageing Lord Salisbury, Queen Victoria's last Prime Minister. Ena's usual punishment for being naughty was to be sent to her room by her governess. But she invariably escaped. On one occasion, for a more serious misdemeanour which Ena could not afterwards remember[15], her governess tied her hands together with rope and connected the rope to the outside knob of the door. Anyone passing could see the plight of the Princess, humiliated as if 'in the stocks'. The stares of the servants were discomforting enough but Ena's chief terror was that her grandmother would come by. Instead she suddenly found herself face to face with Lord Salisbury on his way to the royal apartment on affairs of state. His remark to Ena stuck in her mind. 'Surely,' he said, 'you must have stolen the Crown Jewels to be punished like this?' All Ena could think of saying was that she supposed she had been impertinent. When asked by the Prime Minister whether this was true she replied, 'I don't know.' Lord Salisbury laughed and liberated the small captive. This set up a comradely sense of complicity between them which became the basis for as close a friendship as time would permit as Salisbury died in 1903, soon after relinquishing office for the last time.

Ena never resented being punished, or, if she did, the resentment did not last long. She early exhibited those powers of resilience and irrepressibility which were to help her and characterize many of her actions later in life. Other characteristics, exhibited early and later developed strongly, were loyalty—to brothers, parents and mentors according to circumstance—and independence of spirit. The latter often showed itself in her attempting all the physical feats engaged in by her brothers. When forbidden to climb one particularly high tree which the boys were scrambling up she would stay sobbing underneath. 'I can *do* it. I can *do* it,' she would lament in frustration. 'And I fall softer than they do.'

Ena also showed certain powers of leadership in the sense of being adventurous and enterprising. She was often the inventor of ways and means to defeat the monotony and austerity of life at Court for normal children. The restrictions occasioned by this became a cause not so much of frustration as of challenge to the young Battenbergs. On wet days, for example, when they were forced to stay indoors, they were not allowed to disturb the ordered tranquillity of the household by playing the piano, singing or making any unusual noise. Instead of dreading such days they welcomed them as the opportunity for one of their favourite games. It was an invention of their own called 'Christian martyrs'. They would prowl round the house looking for each other and, having found someone, would show great cruelty and ingenuity in inflicting as much pain as possible on the victim. The important thing was to make no sort of audible protest. The game proved a rich source for sadistic inventiveness and easily took the place of the most exciting adventure stories.

Naturally the feminine tastes of Ena differed in many respects from those of her brothers. Her lifelong love of jewellery—little short of an obsession—began from the first moment she feasted her eyes on some of the glittering gems possessed by her grandmother. This would happen when the children were allowed, as was considered a great treat, to visit her in her dressing-room. They would there witness the final stages of her preparation for the coming day. It bored the boys but it never bored Ena. The first sight greeting her eyes as she entered the dressing-room was the headband studded with diamonds fastened round the while veil which she almost always wore during the day, exchanging it in the evening for her black 'Spanish lace'. The veil and diadem were kept on a dummy head in the corner of the dressing-room, from where they would be transferred to the head of the Queen. She would then adjust the diadem with infinite care before adding yet another garland of diamonds and topping off the veil with a small crown. Ena's fascination continued as her grandmother selected which of her diamond necklaces and earrings she would wear. Inevitably the impressionable girl came to associate the wearing of such breathtaking jewellery with the wearing of a crown. Did she have any inkling that she might one day be a Queen herself?

Nobody is known to have made any such prophecy to her face. But one prophecy made to her—that she would one day go to Spain*—was made by her father, Prince Henry of Battenberg, who was 'one of the most important factors in his daughter's happiness'.[16] He loved all his children tenderly, with a specially soft spot for Ena. He enjoyed being involved in their lessons and recreations and for this he had more time than would most princes in his position. This very fact had involved considerable sacrifice on his part. For his position was different from others of his kind chiefly because of his agreement to live under the same roof as his mother-in-law as long as she lived. His participation in public affairs was virtually limited to the scarcely arduous job of being Governor of the Isle of Wight. The humiliation of such inactivity for a dashing ex-soldier was made worse by the snubbings to which he was subjected during his early days in England. These reflected that haughty disdain which had been heaped on the Battenberg family ever since it had come into existence under that name earlier in the century.

'If English people think of the Battenbergs at all,' it could be written as late as 1916[17]; 'they still wonder who on earth they were, or content themselves with saying wearily, "Germans of course".' But Prince Henry's German blood came only from the paternal side of his family. His father was Prince Alexander of Hesse, uncle of Grand Duke Louis, the husband of Queen

*See pp. 19–20

Victoria's gifted but ill-fated second daughter Alice.[18] It was on account of his beautiful Polish mother that the Battenberg title was brought out of abeyance after lying dormant for five centuries. It was a romantic story but its romance was not such as to appeal to the snobbery of the day. Prince Alexander was full of fun and charm with few outlets for his exuberance in the strait-laced Darmstadt of the 1840s. So when his prim and proper sister Marie married Grand Duke Alexander, eldest son of the Tsar of Russia, Alexander (of Hesse) accompanied her to St Petersburg. He revelled in the glittering Court life of the Imperial capital and was soon in trouble for attempting to make love to the Grand Duchess Olga. He eventually got himself banished from Russia altogether for eloping with one of his sister's ladies-in-waiting.

The lady in question was the Polish beauty, Countess Julie Theresa von Hauke whose father, though of humble origins, had risen to the rank of War Minister at Hesse-Darmstadt. Prince Alexander married her in 1851 but as she was a commoner the marriage was morganatic. The Tsar, though highly displeased, conferred on her the title of Countess of Battenberg with the qualification of Illustrious Highness. Such things had to be carefully regulated in those days. A few years later she and her children were elevated to the rank of Princes and Princesses of Battenberg and entitled to call themselves Serene Highnesses. The Battenberg title thus came to Ena's father because of his mother for whom it had been specially brought back into existence. But it cut little ice with the haughty royals of Britain and Europe.

Of the first three Battenberg Princes of the first generation, the eldest, Prince Louis, took British nationality and joined the Royal Navy at the age of fourteen. He was First Sea Lord when the First World War broke out but was virtually hounded out of that office by adverse public opinion. The Battenbergs were still 'Germans of course' in the eyes of the Establishment. In 1917 Prince Louis renounced his Battenberg title and assumed

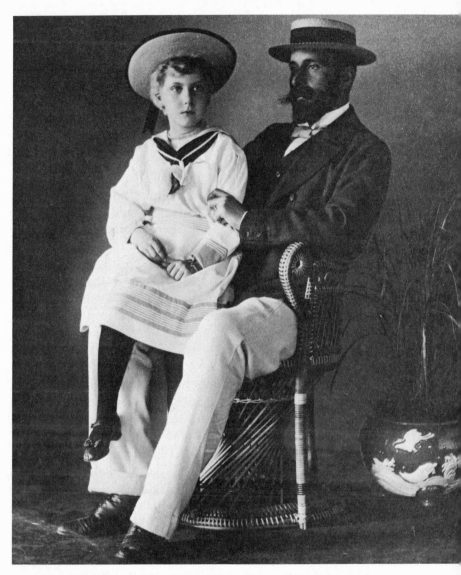

Ena, aged five, with her father, Prince Henry of Battenberg

the surname of Mountbatten. The lifelong preoccupation of his second son, Lord Mountbatten of Burma, was to avenge the humiliations visited on his father. In a certain sense he succeeded. The second brother, Alexander, was made Prince of Bulgaria by the Tsar of Russia but, being insufficiently subservient to his patron, fell into disgrace.

The third brother, Henry, married Princess Beatrice but not without the open hostility of most of the members of his family. As already seen, however, the Queen was willing to have him as a son-in-law strictly on her own terms. But it was not much of a life for Prince Henry. He had nothing to do and nothing in the way of a career to look forward to. Marriage, devoted though he was to Beatrice, brought 'few of the assets of normal married life—a home of one's own, being master of one's own house, being able to start afresh with personal memories and treasures. He had stepped into a routine where every coming and going was pre-ordained, where meals were parades, dress dictated, and the final authority on any problem was the man who had died a quarter of a century before.'[19] Fortunately Henry was less ambitious than most of his relations and he was blessed with boundless tact. In the end, his charm was sufficiently successful with the old Queen to persuade her to relax some of her stern regulations about smoking. His geniality and prowess as a sportsman would have made him popular in any but the extremely closed and ungenerous social circles of his day where snobbery was rife. The more popular Henry became with the Queen and his Princess the less so he became with the jealous circle surrounding the Court. In 1886 he was made ADC to Queen Victoria and a colonel in the Isle of Wight (Princess Beatrice's) Battalion of Rifles. 'It was popularly asserted that the mantle of John Brown had fallen upon the shoulders of this favourite son-in-law, and that the fishing and shooting so long reserved for the exclusive use of the servant were now reserved for the prince.'[20] But this was really only a snide form of criticism on the part of those who disliked Henry and made a point of snubbing him whenever possible. Not long before Ena was born, her father was a guest at a dinner given by the Lord Mayor of London at the Mansion House. The seats were naturally arranged according to precedence and a plan clearly showed where each person was to sit. Some guests at the top table, however, thought they were a bit too crowded so removed one chair. A moment later Prince Henry arrived to take his place but found that it was no longer there. He politely asked his in-laws to move to make room for him but they sat solidly where they were and pointedly ignored him. He was finally inserted into his rightful place by an embarrassed official to whom Prince Henry turned as he sat down to say, 'Thank you; they are very cruel to me.' Many such indignities had to be endured by a man who was ultimately to prove himself far more admirable and patriotic to England than the majority of those who insulted him.

Though Prince Henry's life naturally centred principally on his adored family, he did permit himself one recreation away from them. Every year he went off on a trip on his yacht. He never neglected to send letters to each member of the family individually and always brought back presents. From Seville, after one voyage, he brought back for Ena a fan which could be made larger or smaller and fascinated the child of five. It was her first tangible link with Spain and she kept it always. A subsequent stop off in Spain by Prince Henry had no such happy sequel. It ended in tragedy. In the year 1895, when Ena was eight, the Ashanti Expedition was being mounted and Prince Henry volunteered for service. Queen Ena was later to explain[21] how her father, much as he revelled in family life, somehow felt emasculated with no real job or status beyond, by that time, being Governor of the Isle of Wight. He 'wanted to do something for England. He had been a soldier in the German army before marrying my mother. But then he had to prove himself as an Englishman.' Thus, in 1896, Prince Henry joined an expedition whose object was to turn the long troublesome Ashanti union, in west Africa, into a British protectorate. On the journey out he found himself once more in Spain when the expedition called in at Cadiz. He took the opportunity of sending off a letter, one of his last, to his precious daughter. 'Always be a good girl and love your mother,' he wrote. 'If you do this, when you grow up and are big you too will travel and you will come to this beautiful country. You will see for yourself how much you will like it and how happy you will be there.'

Ena was delighted with the letter and, thinking her father was only on one of his usual voyages, looked forward as much as ever to his return. But Princess Beatrice meanwhile received ominous news. Her husband was seized with fever after reaching Ghana (then the Gold Coast) while on the march to Kumasi. He was put on board the HMS *Blonde* to be brought home, the first message having suggested that the fever might not be serious. But unfortunately it was, and the Prince died after only twelve hours out on the homeward journey. His last message to his wife was, 'In case I die tell the Princess from me that I came here not to win glory but from a sense of duty.' So it was that Ena, by now aged just nine, never saw her father again. One of the last things she had to remember him by was that message from Spain prophesying, accurately enough, that she would one day come to Spain herself but, less accurately, that 'you will be happy here.'

Ena changed greatly after her father died. She became more serious and began to grow up quickly. Her budding good looks matured so that by her middle teens she had blossomed into a striking beauty. She was drawn closer to her mother whose grief over her husband's death took a long time to recede. The Prince had loved, and been loved in, the Isle of Wight wither he was now brought back to be buried in the Memorial Chapel at Whippingham. Princess Beatrice took his place as the island's Governor and became known as 'The Royal Lady of the Isle of Wight.' The Battenbergs went on living with the Queen and their principal place of residence was still the Isle of Wight. Ena and her brothers came to know every part of the island as they explored endlessly with tutors and other companions.

A favourite haunt was Carisbrooke Castle, ownership of which had long been associated with lordship of the island as its ancient 'seat of government'. Ena came to refer to it as 'my castle' as it filled her with an indescribable sensation of freedom and release. It was certainly a place of which dreams can be made and its tangled and spooky past fired Ena's imagination. Her history studies came alive with images from incidents in the life of Carisbrooke: its capture by King Stephen, its attack from France in Richard II's time, its use as a prison for Charles I and his little children after his execution. The Castle was famous for its well which was almost 200 feet deep. The buckets were drawn up by donkeys notorious for their strength and long life. In Ena's young days the donkey on duty was fat and endlessly patient. He was a great pet of Ena's who never failed to bring him a carrot each day in reward for his hard work. For Ena, after the death of her father, it was hard to put away childish things altogether. But then something happened which was to make a final and decisive change in the lives of them all.

To Ena and her brothers Queen Victoria seemed immortal. They could not begin to imagine her ever dying. In January 1901, at Osborne, however, the hitherto indomitable old lady was forced to take to her bed. She who had always enjoyed a hearty appetite could eat nothing and began to grow ominously thin. She appeared to the thirteen-year-old Ena to have lost all interest in life as her health declined day by day. She seemed unmoved by any kind of news, even the worst. On 22 January, all her living children and most of her grandchildren were present round her bed. No one spoke except in a whisper. It was Ena's first experience of witnessing the approach of death. Suddenly she was conscious of the presence of someone old enough to be her father. It was her cousin, Kaiser Wilhelm of Germany, who sat her on his lap. The Kaiser said to Ena in a hoarse whisper and with more emotion than accuracy, 'I am the eldest grandchild and you are the youngest. I hope you, who have always lived with our grandmother, though you are the youngest, will remember her.'

On the other side of the bed from Ena and the Kaiser sat Princess Beatrice. She who had spent scarcely a day away from the Queen all her life now clasped her mother by the hand. The end came at six-thirty that same day. And within a few moments the Victorian era was over.

From this time onwards life was very different for Ena, her mother having, within a short time of the Queen's death, taken up residence in the state apartments of Kensington Palace. Princess Beatrice also inherited Osborne Cottage from her mother, so the children were not cut off from the pleasures of their beloved Isle of Wight. They also began to sample the joys of a new and much freer life in London. The horizons were expanding and Ena began to travel abroad more widely. The family visited Ena's godmother, the former Empress Eugénie, at her villa in the south of France. They also made a long expedition to Egypt. She was allowed to 'come out' prematurely for the celebrations for King Edward VII's coronation but had to return to the less glamorous life of the schoolroom immediately afterwards. In the Isle of Wight one summer, however, she met the young Grand Duke Boris of Russia whose father, the Grand Duke Wladimir, had previously taken an avuncular fancy to Ena. Boris too was smitten since Ena's charm and striking looks made her seem more than her fifteen years. But it was too soon yet to speak openly of romance. Then, early in 1905, Ena and Boris met again in Nice. This time the young Russian Grand Duke did not hold back. He proposed to the now ravishing Princess of seventeen. She almost accepted, but hesitated at the last moment.

Boris agreed to say no more until Ena had been formally launched into society. This happened in the summer of that same year when her uncle, the King, gave for her a magnificent coming-out ball at Kensington Palace. No one enjoyed it more than Ena herself. She was lucky enough not to be shy at this stage in her life; but she was sensitive enough to spot shyness in others. She spotted it in the case of one young man who somewhat awkwardly asked her for the honour of a dance. He was put at his ease by her replying 'Oh, certainly, if you are quite sure you don't mind dancing with someone who is very shy.'

That summer passed in a flurry of dances, balls, dinners and parties. Ena enjoyed herself thoroughly, so much so as seemingly to have forgotten all about Grand Duke Boris. Her most constant companion at this time was her cousin, Princess Beatrice of Saxe-Coburg, who was to cause great grief to her in later years. Ena, thoroughly caught up in the social whirl, told a close friend who had just got engaged, 'I don't think I shall ever marry; life's such fun as it is. Besides I'm quite sure I shall never fall in love.'

But that was before she had met the young monarch who, at that very moment, was causing acute anxiety to his family and ministers. If he did not soon marry a suitable and healthy princess who could stabilize his instincts and inject new blood into his sickly royal line, they feared for the very future of his dynasty and his throne. The young man in question was Europe's most eligible bachelor, the eighteen-year-old King of Spain.

[2]

The King of Spain

MUCH has been written, mostly in praise, of the ill-fated Alfonso XIII of Spain. And much has been written, mostly in over-romanticized form, of his engagement and marriage to Princess Ena of Battenberg. But who exactly was the real Alfonso XIII? And why did it seem crucial to his advisers in 1905 that he should find a suitable and healthy wife as quickly as possible? The answer cannot be attempted without a glance, however brief, at the tangled web of nineteenth-century Spanish history and the extraordinary circumstances of Alfonso's birth.

That he was a 'typically Spanish king'[1] was both his strength and his weakness. The key to his personality and reign must be sought in the Spanish Bourbon line of which he was inordinately proud. But of the heritage and general characteristics of this line he was also a prisoner and ultimately a victim. It had taken a European war and much bloodshed to establish the Bourbon dynasty in Spain. The death in 1700 of the childless Charles II—last of the Spanish Habsburgs—was the end of an era for Spain and for Europe. The dead King had willed the succession to his great nephew, Philip of Anjou, grandson of the still active and belligerent Louis XIV of France. Despite the efforts of England in alliance with Holland and Austria—and the stunning series of military victories of the first Duke of Marlborough—the French King's grandson was finally, as Philip V, recognized as King of Spain. As part of the 1713 (Treat of Utrecht) settlement, England got Gibraltar but her sailors wreaked havoc in the conquered town and destroyed the much revered shrine of 'Our

Lady of Europe'. The crime has always been remembered by Spaniards and never totally forgiven.

The War of the Spanish Succession, which opened the eighteenth century, was followed by pitched battles between Spain and her European rivals. Over half the century was taken up with war on behalf of the Spanish Bourbons. The motives were invariably selfish and dynastic and owed much to the ambition of the Bourbon womenfolk, notably the ruthlessly brilliant second wife of Philip V, Elizabeth Farnese. Spain in the nineteenth century, on the other hand, was plagued by warring of a different kind, namely civil strife. Bitterly opposed factions fought over Spain's bleeding body for possession of her soul as two separate branches of the Bourbon line put forward their rival claims for the Crown.

Thus emerged those 'two Spains' which, drawing on elements long latent in Spanish history, were, in all important respects, diametrically opposed to one another. To say that one Spain was liberal and outward-looking and the other introverted and intensely conservative would be true. But it would also, of course, be a drastic over-simplification. For the two Spains each had their own internal divisions and needed some unifying banner under which to fight. The required banners were provided by the Carlist wars of the nineteenth century which threatened to tear the country apart. The contest was not only over who should sit on the Spanish throne. It was meant to decide which of the 'two Spains' should ultimately prevail.

The seeds of the dynastic side of the contest had been sown with the first Spanish Bourbon, Philip V. From France he had brought the so-called Salic Law whereby no female could succeed to the throne. But in 1789 the then Spanish King, Charles IV, secretly revoked this law. His revocation was not made public until, in 1830, Charles's son, Ferdinand VII, discovered that his fourth wife was pregnant. He was determined that the ensuing child, whether male or female, should be sovereign of Spain and in this he had the backing, for reasons of their own, of the 'liberales', a new political force in the country favouring a thorough going reform of the feudal and clericalist burden with which they felt Spain had been saddled for too long. But Ferdinand had moved too late. His brother, Don Carlos, claimed the throne by divine right unless a male heir should be born to the King. The baby born to Ferdinand and Maria Christina at the end of 1830 was a girl. She was christened Isabel and proclaimed Queen, as Isabel II, on the death of her father in 1833. The claim was immediately disputed by the numerous supporters—traditionalist, conservative and clerical as they were in the main—of Don Carlos. Thus began the first of the famous Carlist wars and a running vendetta which ravaged Spain for a hundred years.

It was much more than a mere law—the Salic Law—which was at stake. For the cause of Don Carlos 'appealed to the mystic, masculine and traditional side of the Spanish genius.'[2] It represented the 'old Spain' with its intense nationalism, militarism, and its nostalgia for the Spain which had expelled the Moorish infidels, established a mighty empire in the Americas and was, through its traditional, almost medieval, concept of monarchy, the greatest single European prop of the one true—Apostolic, Catholic and Roman—Church. 'It was the creed of traditionalist Spain—conservative, masculine, bigoted, unyielding. *Dios, Patria, Rey* were the watchwords of Carlism, and within its ranks were gathered all the die-hard defenders of throne and altar. Its appeal was to the emotions rather than the intellect; it was more of a religion than a political formula.'[3] It was an almost permanent threat to the reign of Isabel II who, though she only came of age in 1843, reigned from 1833 to 1868. Supporting the Queen were the liberals but not because they found in their sovereign a natural ally of their political philosophy. Far from it. Isabel was popular, at least to begin with, because her virtues and vices corresponded to those of most Spaniards. She was generous, self-indulgent and passionate. But she was negatively conservative in outlook because of a mixture of laziness and fear of the Church. By 1868, she had lost the affection of a people by that time disillusioned

[26]

with monarchy, whether Carlist or 'Isabelline'. Her departure from Spain was followed by an imported constitutional monarchy and Spain's first but short-lived experiment in democracy. Then, in 1874, the Bourbon line was restored in the person of Isabel's young son, Alfonso XII.

The liberals, representing the 'new Spain', could trace their ultimate origins to the reign of Charles III. This son of Philip V was the most normal and enlightened of all the Bourbon monarchs. His reign (1759–88) saw the attempt to regenerate agriculture, education and religion by the introduction of 'luces', enlightened ideas. It was part of the whole eighteenth-century European movement in a similar direction and its chief inspirer was of course Voltaire. But the Spaniards came to resent the importation of ideas and culture from France and the liberals were never more than partially successful in their campaign against the excessive power of the Church and the religious orders. The latter were, at certain stages, intensely unpopular among a people who were nevertheless profoundly religious in the ways that really mattered. The Church as such, at all times central to Spanish history, was never either defended or attacked for purely religious reasons. It was defended or attacked because of its stance within a political and social context. Its most rabid supporters were the Spanish equivalents of those 'Ultra-montanes' who favoured a strongly centralized Roman Church and were intensely 'clerical' in outlook. Their strongest allies among the religious orders were the Jesuits who were twice expelled from Spain and whose very name became synonymous with exploitation of the poor. For this reason people came to use the name 'Jesuits' indiscriminately to describe the religious orders in general, all of whom had the same unenviable reputation among ordinary people.

The bitter rivalry of the two nations within one country dominated Spanish history from the early nineteenth century onwards. Among a people prone to extremes, the two Spains came to be looked upon in uncompromisingly irreconcilable forms. One side was considered anti-religious and materialistic while the other was held obstinately to ignore material values and reforms even when they were relevant to what was spiritual. Carlism, under its later guise of 'traditionalism', triumphed with Franco but was violently discredited when, as of 1975, the present King, Ena's grandson, Juan Carlos, took Spain down the firm road of genuine democracy. As even he has found, however, traditionalism in Spain is not yet dead. Certain elements in the Army, with strong backing from the aristocracy, and exploiting working-class disillusionment, would like to see the return of 'strong government'. And this, to many Spaniards, is not compatible with parliamentary democracy as imported from liberal Europe. All the ideological struggles are being fought out over again despite everything that progress and an outwardly well-ordered democratic system have to offer.

This much at least—drastically over-simplified though it be—is the essential minimum on the socio-political side for an understanding of the life and reign of Alfonso XIII. For his long reign takes up the major part of that relatively peaceful period between the second Carlist war in the 1870s and the establishment of Spain's Second Republic in 1931. This period saw an attempt to maintain a precarious balance between the new political forces striving to operate within a constitutional and parliamentary framework. This had been established by the restoration of the Bourbon line with Alfonso XII. He had returned to Spain in a bloodless revolution in 1874 and 'for the first time in a century of revolutions the conquerors did not wreak vengeance on the conquered. There was tolerance and mercy.'[4]

It was an auspicious beginning. A new constitution was drawn up in 1876 whose central provision was that 'the legislative power lies in the Cortes (parliament) with the king.' To make the new system work, however, the politicians devised a system which was too ingenious by half. One of the men most active in deposing Queen Isabel had been a politician called Práxedes Sagasta. The man chiefly responsible for establishing Alfonso XII on the throne was a schoolmaster turned politician called Cánovas del Castillo. The new constitution was largely the latter's brainchild. But to give it life he realized that a civilized system of government and loyal opposition modelled on the British pattern must now be brought into Spanish political life. As leader of the liberal-minded Conservative party he thus got together with Sagasta, as leader of a conservative-minded Liberal party, to ensure that the new scheme worked to their mutual satisfaction and advantage. The resultant system, known as 'rotativismo', ensured that the two parties alternated in power according to a prearranged pattern. Canovas went into bat first and was succeeded by Sagasta in 1881. They changed round again in 1885, 1890, 1892 and 1895. The system even survived press publication of the results of one particular election before voting had actually started.[5]

The whole thing was made possible, even after 'universal' suffrage had been introduced in 1869, by strict manipulation of the votes by local politician bosses known as 'caciques'. Neither Cánovas nor Sagasta looked upon the system as corrupt or dishonest but as a necessary instrument of stabilization after so many years of Liberal–Republican–Carlist strife. 'It was the result (and as such not confined to Spain) of the application of a wide suffrage to a backward society with little interest in or comprehension of national issues ... As a political device in a backward society, it could be defended,' even though 'it was openly recognized as a means of maintaining "the legitimate interests of property".'[6] Such a system, however artificial in origin might, hopefully, give way to something more genuine later on. Or so the optimists liked to think. The one element that was vital was a stable monarchy and this depended on the enjoyment by Alfonso XII of a long and peaceful life and speedy procreation by him of one or more healthy male heirs. This, however, was exactly what did not happen.

Alfonso's reign was beset by personal tragedy almost from its very inception and came to an abrupt and premature end with his death, officially from consumption, in the year 1885. He was only twenty-eight and he died with no male heir. His death produced despondency abroad and panic at home as 'Spain was reduced thereby to a policy of strict passivity while there was reason to fear for the stability of the throne.'[7] This, it was widely feared, might be the moment for the Carlists to strike again; for the Republicans to regroup their forces; for the Basque or Catalan separatists to show their contempt for crudely over-centralized government; for the anarchists even, to say 'a plague on all your houses'. But Spain is like no other country. Alfonso XII, despite his faults, had been a generally popular, even romantic, figure. In happier circumstances he might have become the true friend of his people and they of him. Toward the end of 1885 he happened one day to be standing by the window of the royal palace in Madrid. Outside, in the Plaza de Oriente, he could see a young workman carrying his small son in his arms. The little boy kept pulling at his father's cap and the young King watched them until they disappeared from sight. As he turned away from the window a courtier, seeing how extraordinarily sad his master looked, asked him if anything was wrong. He noticed that the King had tears in his eyes as he answered that he had a presentiment that 'I shall never attain to the joy that workman is having—to kiss my son.'

His presentiment was correct and he died a month before Christmas. The country was stunned. The future seemed black with uncertainty. But with the news of the king's death some other news went out as well: the kind of news calculated, even in the midst of sadness, to make Spanish hearts miss a beat. The King, it was true, had died without a son and was widely mourned. But at the moment of his death his wife was pregnant. Her child was due to be born in May 1886. Thus supplied was the fragile thread on which Spain's continued peace and stability might depend. At this critical and highly delicate moment, Prime Minister Cánovas acted decisively within the context of the bizarre 'system' he had helped to build up. Instead of tightening his hold on the reins of government, he handed them over altogether—to his Liberal 'rival', Sagasta. A general election followed and it was on this occasion that the results were inadvertently announced in a Government-supporting paper before the voting had taken place. Nevertheless no amount of purely political manoeuvring, however astute, could prove decisive on its own. Everything hung on whether the unborn child would be a son and, if so, whether he would be healthy and strong.

The mother of this child on whose health and sex so much depended was Alfonso's second wife, the former Austrian Archduchess Maria Christina. She never lost the austerity of her Habsburg upbringing and found it difficult to win the hearts of her Spanish subjects. Now, on the death of her husband, she became Regent for her five-year-old daughter Mercedes, Princess of Asturias. She, for the time being, was nominally Queen. But if the unborn child should be a boy he would of course be King of Spain from the first second of his life.

Shortly after midday on 17 May 1886, the Lord Great Chamberlain rushed excitedly into the Palace audience chamber where the whole Court was waiting in a barely concealed fever of suspense. The Regent, he announced, had given birth to a son. Almost immediately the waiting cannon crashed out their twenty-one-gun salute. A few moments later, Prime Minister Sagasta came in carrying a silver tray on which lay the infant monarch. It was the first time for five centuries that a boy had been born a king.* Sagasta was fairly bursting with relief and joy.

Would the baby King survive and prosper? He was to have been called Ferdinand according to his late father's wish. But, in spite of superstitious protests, he became Alfonso the Thirteenth 'and an unlucky King he remained all his life'[8]. It was soon observed that he was frail and sickly. His head seemed too big for his rather emaciated body. At the age of four he nearly died. What seemed like an ordinary cold turned to bronchitis. While he was apparently recovering the little King began to suffer from a series of violent

* In the only other comparable case on record, Jean I had been born King of France in 1213 but had died a few days later. Alfonso, for fear he would be born dead, was baptized 'in utero'—while still in his mother's womb.

convulsions. He remained unconscious for some time, reported his almost hysterial grandmother Queen Isabel. He was 'without a pulse, and the heart almost paralysed. The doctors said that if there was another attack as bad, it would be fatal.'[9] His recovery brought such relief that it reunited a family in which some of the old rivalries were beginning to open up again. But Alfonso was never strong despite the sacrificing of his academic education to the strenuous efforts made as he grew up to bolster his physique. What he lacked in stamina, however, he made up for in pluck and physical courage. In these he was never lacking. What he did lack in his young days were sufficient outlets for his restless energy and boyish high spirits. He was brought up by a doting mother in an intensely clerical atmosphere. Until the age of seven he was surrounded by women. Then a priest-tutor took over. He was Fr Montaña, a man of such grotesquely old-fashioned and unimaginative ideas as to put anyone off genuine religion for life. He was succeeded by the Bishop of Sion, chaplain to the Court, who also gave instructions to the King's two sisters. Of the latter old Queen Isabel commented from Paris, 'They never meet men. Who will there be for them to marry but the Bishop of Sion?'

Alfonso was never sent abroad to finish his education which was scrappy and inadequate. But he was frustrated by youthful loneliness, the stuffiness of Court atmosphere and the lack of paternal guidance. He found a father-figure in the person of his military attaché. His principal playthings were toy soldiers and his make-believe world was filled with dreams of military glory. All the greater was his chagrin at the catastrophic events of the year 1898. He was not too young at twelve to be humiliated, as were his Government and Army, by the loss of Cuba, Puerto Rico and the Philippines, almost the last bastions of Spain's once mighty empire.

In that very year of disasters, however, a new Spain was born. Between then and 1931 – when the Second Republic emerged— 'a double process is apparent in Spanish history. The main movement, the one that is most visible to the eye, is the continued disintegration of the various elements that make up the older Spain—administration, Army, Church, the social classes, the links between provinces, which in the absence of any common plan of life turn on one another and attempt to destroy one another.'[10] Alfonso was to find himself in the very thick of this disintegrating process, trying, by a sort of fantastic juggling act, to keep all the old institutions from crashing to the ground. 'The other process, scarcely noticeable at first and never very strong, is a recuperative one, which ends, however, by raising the moral and intellectual level of the country and for almost the first time since 1680 gives Spain the right to be considered as a part (and a valuable part) of modern Europe.'[11] The King himself was not averse to looking abroad, especially to France, for ideas. Unfortunately, however, he was no match intellectually for the brilliant crop of poets, philosophers, scholars and writers who now became an important part of the nation's life. It was part of Alfonso's tragedy that he could never get on to the same wavelength as this new 'Generation of '98' and the men and women whom it inspired in the first third of the twentieth century.

The psychological aspects of Alfonso's Bourbon inheritance provide the best clues of all to his character and life. In between the spurts of physical and nervous energy for which the King became noted in later years came (carefully concealed) periods of total exhaustion. The outward gaiety was balanced by fits of deep depression, often known only to his wife. This is a side of Alfonso's nature of which practically nothing has been written in the past. Queen Ena spoke about it only toward the end of her life to selected friends who, in turn, have referred to it only now that Ena has been dead for some years. What she disclosed puts into perspective the many reports that appeared in non-Spanish newspapers in the early days of their married life but were only discussed in Madrid within very limited circles. What it comes down to is that only those closest to Alfonso knew that, with regard to certain actions and impulses, particularly in the sexual sphere, he could scarcely control himself. And when tragedy hit him early in marriage his Bourbon blood boiled over.

Even when Alfonso was still in his late teens, however, certain grandees of Spain and other Court advisers quickly formed the opinion that the young King should marry as soon as possible. But the choice of wife was important. It was considered vital that the King should, by marriage, inject some new and healthy blood into the Bourbon line. It would be well to look elsewhere than among the often inbred families of southern Europe from whom former marriage partners had been invariably recruited. For, if Alfonso were to die young, as had his father, without leaving behind him a substantially invigorated Bourbon line, there would be grave fears for the future among those without illusions about the Bourbon monarchs of the past. They were classified by one journalist[12] as follows: Philip V, mentally unbalanced and sensual; Ferdinand VI, mad and impotent; Charles III, almost normal; Charles IV, imbecile; Ferdinand VII, excessively sensual, cruel and sanguinary; Isabel II, nymphomaniac; Alfonso XII, tubercular. The writer's judgement was resented at the time not because it was historically untrue but because of being written with such brutal succinctness at the very moment, in 1930, when Alfonso XIII was beginning to lose his grip on the Spanish throne.

Unfortunately this insalubrious aspect of the Spanish Bourbon heritage is all too relevant to the personality and proclivities of the young Alfonso. For his father, Alfonso XII, had died not so much of consumption as of venereal disease. Toward the end of his life he had became recklessly promiscuous. That his death was hastened by sexual excesses was widely recognized and gave rise to many stories, some of which lost little in the telling. Lady Cardigan included in her memoirs an account of Alfonso XII's attachment to the accommodating wife of a young army officer. The latter was inconveniently possessive so the King arranged for him to be sent off for service in Cuba and always to be given the most dangerous missions. He miraculously survived them all and on his return home was told by a brother officer of the real reason for his being kept so long away from Madrid. He was thus waiting at his house, fully armed and seething with vengeful rage, when the King, accompanied by a certain well known Duke, paid his next visit. The loyal Duke quickly drew his sword and killed the jealous husband, the body being spirited away and secretly buried. When Lady Cardigan questioned the Duke about the propriety of his action, his reply was 'It was the quickest way for an interfering husband to be disposed of, Madame.' The author quoting the story commented that in Alfonso XII 'the combination of Bourbon sensuality, tubercular restlessness and marital indifference compelled him to look for distraction beyond the Palace.'[13]

This was true. Nevertheless that particular King had another more compelling and more tragic reason—just as his son was to have a generation later—for his inability to keep his voracious sexual appetite under any kind of control. For Alfonso XII had, four years after becoming King, married his dream Princess, the Infanta Mercedes, daughter of the Duke of Montpensier. The latter was a Carlist supporter and the proposed match caused fearful shivers among legitimist ranks. But the Princess possessed all that was needed to be a natural healer of rifts. She was a radiant Andalusian beauty with an exceptionally sweet disposition. When she married the young King at the age of seventeen it was, on both sides, an idyllic love match such as was rarely known then among royal marriages. The happiness of the young pair was so obvious and spontaneous that it infected all those around them with the intoxicated feeling of pure joy. It would have been difficult to exaggerate how much this blissful couple depended upon one another. The popularity of the lovable girl-Queen with her in-laws helped to heal many residual dynastic rifts and the wholesome and natural delight of royal family life had its beneficial effects on Court and country alike. Within six months of her wedding day, however, this beautiful and infectiously joyful young woman was dead. A sudden attack of gastric fever killed her within days of her eighteenth birthday. The blow of her death was so crushing to Alfonso that authors have been at a loss to find adequate words to describe the depth of his desolation. He never got over it and was never the same again. After his arranged second marriage to the Habsburg Archduchess Maria Christina of Austria he took up his duties again with heavy listlessness and never pretended that he was ever in love with his second wife. He became cynical, disillusioned and increasingly unfaithful. His string of liaisons and passing affairs defied enumeration. His favourite mistress was a dancer called Elena Sanz who bore him two sons. It was Maria Christina's misfortune to fall deeply in love with a husband who, she knew, could never return her love. With conspicuous gallantry she personally conducted Elena Sanz to the King's bedside at the Pardo Palace so that she might say farewell to him for ever.

Copious extra-marital sexual activity, however, had never been the monopoly of the male members of the Spanish Bourbon line. Charles IV had married the formidable granddaughter of Elizabeth Farnese, Maria Luisa, whose reaction to her husband's minimal possession of virility was to take on an impressive array of lovers. The most important and durable was a young guards officer half her age called Manuel de Godoy who later became principal minister of the Crown. Such behaviour by a Queen, openly practised and well known to her husband, was something shockingly novel in the history of Spain. Though extremely plain, Maria Luisa was painted by Goya and never failed to attract admirers. And it was she who introduced into the Spanish Bourbon family that strain of frivolity and unreliability of which, among her descendants, Alfonso XIII was to be the most notable exponent in years to come. Maria Luisa also set an important precedent by her energetic love life. 'It was a long-established usage for kings, especially Bourbon kings, to have mistresses, but queens did not take on lovers.'[14]

It thus came cynically to be said that the abolition of the Salic Law was appropriate now that queens had achieved equality with men in another field as well. Maria Luisa's daughter-in-law,

[36]

Maria Christina of Naples, had what a French statesman called 'le diable au corps' from an early age. The Neapolitan Court from which she came generated the hottest blood in Europe. And this 'royal coquette', as Lord Malmesbury described her after a visit to Naples, bore out the saying that princesses from this fertile stable had to be married as quickly as possible as they would otherwise produce offspring before husbands. Similar inclinations, in the case of Maria Christina's daughter Queen Isabel II, developed ultimately into nymphomania. In extenuation it must be borne in mind that she had been forced, at a tender age, to marry a homosexual. Among her four children by various lovers was Alfonso XII by whom the fiery Bourbon heritage was passed on to Alfonso XIII. Thanks chiefly to Isabel it was passed on not only intact but robustly fortified.

It may seem that disproportionate stress is being put on this particular aspect of Bourbon family history. But its importance has often been underestimated in the past and such underestimation has marred many an otherwise learned attempt to account for the violent vicissitudes of modern Spanish history. The sexual element, so often pushed politely to the periphery, has at almost all times been central to events and of paramount influence thereon. The passionate Bourbon nature, far from being a mere picturesque sideline, has more often than not been the decisive arbiter of affairs. And never more so than in the reign of Alfonso XIII. Its symptoms appeared early in his life and were noted with due apprehension by those concerned for the safety of the throne and the future of the country.

Declared of age at sixteen, Alfonso immediately asserted his independence and an evident desire to control political events. But he evinced other interests as well. Once free of the depressing hothouse in which he had been so over-carefully nurtured his restlessness took over and his eye began to rove. At seventeen his chief interest was centred on a delicious little ballerina called Carmen de Faya. Wherever she was, he wanted to be. One night she nimbly kicked her satin slippers straight at him at San

Sebastian's Concours Hippique. The next day she received an enormous basket of flowers with a card from Alfonso saying 'The loveliest of Spain to Spain's loveliest.' But on the very next day Carmen de Faya was diplomatically spirited away never to be seen by the King again.[15]

It was at this point that certain 'shrewd old grandees' took over and began to plan a visit by Alfonso in the following year to Europe's principal capitals. Enquiries as to a possible future wife for the King were discreetly set in motion forthwith. Alfonso's early display of hot-bloodedness made it obvious that he was very much a Bourbon. But he was also half a Habsburg. And herein lay, for some of those 'shrewd old grandees'—not to mention a lot of other people in Spain—a greater danger still to Alfonso's future. For such people believed implicitly—indeed with almost super-stitious awe—in the existence of something which seems utterly fantastic to late twentieth-century minds. And yet, a hundred years ago, there loomed over Europe, for those steeped in dynastic lore, the spectre of a particularly horrible curse. The supposed curse had special relevance for the Habsburg family as it dated back to the execution of one of its members—the Emperor Maximilian of Mexico—on 19 June 1867. This grisly event ended the ill-fated experiment to establish Maximilian as the ruler of Mexico. Unsuccessful pleadings in Europe for help had already had their effect on his Belgian wife Charlotte. This unhappy Empress had personally beseeched her kinsfolk and supposed friends in Europe to save them from a horrible fate. Their callous indifference to her appeals unhinged her mind and she was never quite the same again.

On the very day that Maximilian died Charlotte pronounced a curse on the three people she held most responsible for his death: the Empress Eugénie for withdrawing the French troops who had been Maximilian's protection; Pope Pius IX for not supporting her pleas to others for help; and the Emperor Franz Josef of Austria (Maximilian's brother) for not sending Austrian troops to replace the French ones. Charlotte, with all the vehemence of a

King Alfonso XIII of Spain in 1905

person demented with despair, summoned the powers of darkness to do their worst to these people and their descendants. Such
powers seemingly answered her imprecations. The Pope was
dispossessed of the last vestiges of his temporal power and
became an isolated and embittered 'prisoner in the Vatican'. At
least he had no descendants to inherit the supposed curse.
Eugénie and her husband lost their throne and their beloved heir,
and only son, the Prince Imperial. For the Austrian Emperor and
his descendants was reserved the heaviest doom of all. His cousin
John was lost at sea. His only son Rudolph died in the famous
suicide pact—if that is what it was—at Mayerling. His favourite
sister-in-law, the Duchess of Alençon, was burned to death and

[39]

her husband died of shock and sorrow a few hours later. His wife, the Empress Elizabeth, was assassinated as was his nephew, the Archduke Ferdinand, at Sarajevo. The latter event led to a war in which 8,500,000 people perished and the mighty Austro-Hungarian Empire was dismembered.

The death of Spain's beautiful young Infanta Mercedes, first wife of Alfonso XII, was attributed to the curse since she was a second cousin of the Emperor Franz Josef. Alfonso's second wife, Maria Christina, was even more closely related to him and through her the curse seemed to continue in her husband's premature death and the sickliness of their posthumous son. When and how would this curse, which had, by the early twentieth century, grown in people's imaginations like some terrible monster, be finally laid to rest? If King Alfonso XIII, having married a robust wife, could emerge as the progenitor of a healthy family blessed with sturdy males then perhaps, as far at least as Spain was concerned, the shadow of the curse could at last be removed.

So much then—so very much—would depend on the person whom Alfonso was successfully to seek out as his future bride.

[3]

Which Princess?

ROMANTIC rumours were flying in all directions even before the King of Spain paid his state visit to England in 1905. He was brought over from France on the royal yacht, *Victoria and Albert*. The crossing from Cherbourg was extremely rough. It was a somewhat shaken Alfonso who arrived at Portsmouth on 5 June in the pouring rain. The rain continued for most of the young King's visit during one of the wettest Junes on record.

Before leaving Madrid, Alfonso had said to the President of the Spanish Cortes (Parliament)—roughly the equivalent of the Speaker of the House of Commons—that 'on my return I shall christen my new yacht and I shall give it the name of my future wife.' On more than one occasion, moreover, the King had said 'I shall marry a Princess who takes my fancy and nobody else. I want to love my wife.'[1] It was now apparent that a certain young Princess *had* taken his fancy. Few doubted that the new yacht would be called after Patricia, second daughter of King Edward VII's brother Arthur, Duke of Connaught. She had visited Andalusia the year before and it was rumoured that she wanted to become a Roman Catholic. Alfonso was said to have fallen in love with her photograph and it was said that he was now in England virtually to claim his bride. The famous charm with which, even at nineteen, he seemed to captivate women had never yet failed him. He felt too that he could be confident of the support of King Edward despite the inevitable difficulties involved in the necessity for the Princess's changing her religion. Certainly it was with great cordiality that the jovial British monarch, dressed as a

Spanish admiral, greeted the King of Spain, dressed as a British general, on the latter's arrival at Victoria Station. Immediately behind King Edward, and the next to greet their royal guest, was the Duke of Connaught.

The two sovereigns were conducted to the state coach by the Duke of Portland and one of their companions in the carriage was the Prince of Wales, the future King George V. The other was the Duke of Connaught who, if all went according to plan, would soon be Alfonso's father-in-law. The six-coach procession to Buckingham Palace was escorted by the Household Cavalry and accompanied by frenzied cheering from the crowds. This was the first visit by a Spanish monarch to British shores for three and a half centuries and, in the Press and among the people, it was to cause no small sensation. The route to the Palace, via Grosvenor Gardens, Piccadilly, St James's Street and the Mall, was festooned at every stage with flags and decorations.

Thanks to scrupulous chronicling[2] every hour of the Spanish King's five-day visit can be accounted for in detail. They arrived at the Palace in mid-afternoon and King Edward suggested that his guest, after such an unpleasant crossing, should rest for a while. Alfonso replied 'Rest! With all London waiting to be explored!' In fact, however, he did rest briefly but after about half an hour he set out to make three calls in the vicinity of the Palace. The most important of these was to nearby Clarence House, the London residence of the Connaughts. He did not, however, meet Princess Patricia on this occasion. The visit was a formal one dictated by duty as were his other two afternoon calls, respectively on the Wales's at Marlborough House and on the King's sister, Princess Helena who lived at Schomberg House in Pall Mall. Alfonso would have to wait until the evening before meeting Patricia but he had also been invited to lunch at Clarence House on the following day.

The climax of Alfonso's first day in London was the dinner party given at Buckingham Palace. Its main significance was that it was a relatively intimate, 'family' occasion, rather than a vast state banquet. Only the close relations of the King and Queen had been invited with thirty-six people in all due to sit down to dinner. Alfonso stood with King Edward and Queen Alexandra in the Throne Room as they received each of the guests. The list of those invited was impressive but confusing to the guest of honour. It was only when the actual dinner was being served, on gold plate, that Alfonso was able to take a closer look at the assembled company. He was impatient to know who was who as only a handful of the guests, notably Princess Patricia sitting nearby, were familiar to him by sight.

The King and Queen sat—as was their custom—not at each end of the long table but opposite each other in the middle on either side. Alfonso was on the Queen's right, his other neighbour being Princess Helena on whom he had called earlier in the day. Alfonso found conversation with Queen Alexandra heavy-going owing to her deafness. It was with relief that he turned to the lively Princess Helena to whom he immediately put a barrage of questions so as to learn the identity of everyone present. They went round the table with Alfonso's flashing eyes eagerly appraising each person as the Princess explained who he or she was. It must have been an amusing sort of 'game' to watch since it was perfectly obvious to all the guests that they were being scrutinized with curiosity by the Spanish King. General conversation became a mere pretence carried on in stilted undertones since all were straining to hear what was being said in the middle of the table. The game went on for quite a time with Alfonso apparently oblivious of the barely suppressed flutterings going on all round him.

When they worked their way round to the very end of the table, on Queen Alexandra's extreme left, Alfonso asked Princess Helena, 'And who is that young lady with the nearly white hair?' The person at whom Alfonso was looking was Princess Ena of Battenberg who, as she later recalled, thought to herself 'Oh God, he's taken me for an Albino!' She was never to forget that moment when she 'blushed shamelessly' causing the Spanish King's gaze to stay fixed on her all the more intently. But then she quickly recollected herself remembering that she was not in the running as a prospective bride. There were others round the table, however—'all my unmarried cousins', as Ena put it—who felt very much in the running, 'and all assumed starched expressions.'³ It was precisely because Ena felt safely out of the race that she behaved more naturally than the others, having, after the blushing incident, recovered her normal composure. After the dinner the King had a short conversation with Ena which consisted chiefly of a series of questions from him to her. Alfonso, as he was later to tell Ena, spoke no English because 'on the occasion of the Spanish war against Cuba he had resolved to forget all he ever learned about the British language' because of its use by Spain's enemies, the Americans. In fact he never had, at any time in his life, more than a very imperfect grasp of English. Ena, at the date of their first meeting, spoke no Spanish, so they conversed in French.

It has sometimes been said that this initial meeting between Alfonso and Ena enabled the King to make up his mind then and there whom he wanted to marry. 'With King Alfonso,' it is claimed, 'it was a clear case of love at first sight and from the moment he first saw Princess Ena he had no other thought but her.'⁴ But this is an over-romanticized version of what happened. Only on their last meeting of the week, as the future Queen of Spain was subsequently to relate in some detail, did Alfonso betray any real interest in the then inexperienced eighteen-year-old Battenberg Princess. It was the events of the week as a whole which were to prove decisive, particularly Princess Patricia of Connaught's reactions to Alfonso's overtures. It would not be until the day after this introductory family dinner that Alfonso would have the chance to test the water in this direction. He had been asked to lunch at Clarence House in order to have ample opportunity to get to know the young lady so heavily tipped to be his first choice as a bride. Alfonso had, after all, threatened to call off his visit to England when, earlier in the year, it had seemed as if the Duke of Connaught was about to cancel his plan to visit him in Madrid on his way back from Egypt. Edward VII had stepped in and told his brother that a visit to Madrid was 'politically absolutely necessary'.[4] There was widespread desire that the King should marry Princess Patricia and the matter had been considered by the British Prime Minister, Arthur Balfour. Thus the Duke dutifully called on the Spanish King and this, in turn, fuelled the rumour that an engagement between his daughter and Alfonso must be in the offing. Balfour consulted the Archbishop of Canterbury who said that religious difficulties would arise if a princess in direct line of succession to the throne were to marry a Roman Catholic monarch. The argument failed to impress the Prime Minister since the Princess was fairly remote from the succession. He felt that all would be well provided the marriage, looked on by so many as highly desirable and even a foregone conclusion, took place in Madrid and was not attended by King Edward in person.[5]

On the Spanish side there was support for a marriage alliance with Great Britain but there were also distinct reservations. Spanish conditions for such a match would have to be met in full. For although Spain at this time was, compared with Britain, a backward and decadent country it was also, especially in the upper reaches of society, a very proud one. Courtiers and upper-class Spaniards were distinctly condescending toward the prospect of their King's becoming engaged to an English and Protestant Princess. Protestantism to them was an evil and a heresy. If the bride-to-be were to abjure her errors all might be well. As for Alfonso's mother, she was much keener that her son should marry into the royal family of some 'traditionalist'—that is, reactionary—country. And she could think of none better than her own Habsburg one.

Alfonso was thus much more nervous than his outward de-meanour showed as he embarked on the second day of his English visit. Significantly enough, moreover, an event occurred on the morning before his luncheon appointment at Clarence House which had not been previously planned and was not subsequently officially recorded. The Spanish King attended a special High Mass at Westminster Cathedral. This engagement had been allowed for in the official itinerary. But after the Mass and its attendant formalities in view of such a distinguished visitor, Alfonso disappeared into Archbishop's House for a private talk with the *de facto* head of England's Roman Catholic community, Archbishop (later Cardinal) Bourne. They naturally discussed the religious implications of an Anglo-Spanish royal marriage at a period of history which knew nothing of the ecumenism of the present day.

Westminster Cathedral itself had been officially opened only two years earlier and had not yet even been consecrated. As a London landmark it was still very much of a novelty that was not necessarily pleasing to everyone. The towering Byzantine campanile had reputedly been a source of annoyance to Queen Victoria as it was all too plainly visible from the windows of Buckingham Palace. The Roman Catholic Church had only acquired legal and 'territorial' jurisdiction in England and Wales just over fifty years earlier. And for many this had been no hierarchical 'restoration', as Catholics themselves called it, but a clear case of 'Papal aggression'. The general climate of English opinion, in other words, was unlikely in the year 1905 to favour the 'conversion' to Rome of a Princess in close line of succession to the throne. Still less likely to be popular would be a marriage alliance with the sovereign of a country known to be 'aggressively' Roman in religion, with a King who was proudly styled 'His Most Catholic Majesty'. Such was the background of the off-the-record conversation that morning with Archbishop Bourne.

Alfonso next paid a visit to Westminster Abbey where, without attending any service, he was received by the Dean and Chapter. A good diplomatic move no doubt, but the morning's events were proving not a little tedious to the fun-loving and romantically minded young King.

At long last he arrived at Clarence House and soon found

himself sitting on the left of the girl he had come to England to marry. He felt within himself that delicious glow that accompanies the awareness of incipient conquest. So much at least was evident to those sitting round the luncheon table. The King's habit of seeming to smile on the right side of his face only was already becoming famous. Many considered it devastating. It seemed to accentuate the roguish, almost arrogant look in his eye which, at such potent moments, had been rumoured to send even strong women off into swoons. Alfonso now focused his most fetching smile upon Princess Patricia.

As the meal wore on, however, it became apparent that something surprising and rather embarrassing was happening. The King, for all his efforts, was making no impact at all on the Princess. For once his normally irresistible charms were failing to impress. At length Alfonso felt impelled to turn in despair to his other neighbour at the table, the dazzling Duchess of Westminster. 'Am I very ugly?', he asked her. 'Because I do not please . . . I do not please the lady on my right.' The luncheon party was thus not an unqualified success.

The King's spirits were very low as he left Clarence House. Dampened by more than merely the incessant rain he was driven later the same afternoon to see part of the Royal Tournament, then held at the Agriculture Hall in Islington. On his way back to the Palace he called at the Spanish Embassy to confer with his Ambassador to the Court of St James, Señor Polo de Bernabé, and his senior colleagues. There was no auspicious news to report and the meeting was rather a stiff and gloomy one. Some of these same diplomats were nevertheless to play a key part in the negotiations for the King's ultimate choice of a bride.

Alfonso meanwhile managed not to be downcast for long. That night there was to be an enormous concourse of guests for a state banquet followed by a late evening reception. This was the biggest and most overpowering occasion to be faced yet by the Spanish King. It was a necessary evil in order that everyone of relevant note could be given the chance to meet, or at least, to see

Alfonso. His retinue of dignitaries and attendants amounted to some dozen persons. Present also were the heads of all diplomatic missions in London, members of the government, former cabinet ministers, Court officials and selected members of the aristocracy. There was little chance of any meaningful private conversation but the various eligible princesses were all on parade, headed by Princess Patricia. Alfonso also spotted Ena but could not remember her name. On his way through from the ballroom where the after-dinner reception was to be held he found himself in the company of Princess Olga, one of the daughters of the Duke of Cumberland. He put to her much the same question as he had put the previous evening to Princess Helena. '"Who is the beautiful blonde Princess?" he asked me as soon we entered the ballroom. These were the first words he spoke to me. My cousin was quite unaware of the impact she had made. She just got on with enjoying the party . . ."[6] Princess Olga gave the King the required information but not without disappointment, being herself, at the age of twenty-two, one of the 'eligible' princesses.

Alfonso had few opportunities to speak to Ena that evening and was crestfallen when told that most of the events fixed for the next few days were 'men only' occasions. When being told of his engagements for the next twenty-four hours, in fact, he asked each day 'Will ladies be present?' With such strong doubts having begun to creep in about Princess Patricia he was anxious to widen his acquaintanceship with the other marriageable princesses who were always present at mixed gatherings in his honour. Prominent among them was the flirtatious Princess Beatrice of Saxe-Coburg, daughter of Edward VII's late brother Alfred, Duke of Saxe-Coburg. Also very much in evidence at each of the mixed social gatherings were the two daughters of Princess Helena, the Princesses Helena Victoria and Marie Louise.

On the following day the Spanish King's spirits were further dampened. He had caught a bad cold but was still faced with a heavy round of engagements, mostly without any attractive female company. A formal visit to the Natural History Museum was

Three marriageable Princesses as bridesmaids in 1905. *Left to right*: Princess Victoria Eugénie of Battenberg, Princess Beatrice of Saxe-Coburg, Princess Patricia of Connaught

followed by a solemn inspection of the Albert Memorial. After this Alfonso managed to escape to do some private shopping in Bond Street. While looking for a present for his sister, the Infanta Teresa, his car caught fire and a crowd quickly gathered. When the King emerged from the shop he was recognized and cheered, all the more so when he remarked, pointing to the burned out

[49]

vehicle, 'Doubtless an anarchist's car, but not one of the right mettle since it waited until I had left it to explode.' His ability to laugh in the face of danger was one of the chief reasons for his popularity in those romantic early days.

The romantic side of this particular visit, however, was not so far going very well. It was beginning to look as if those who had been sceptical about the possibilities of an Anglo-Spanish marriage alliance might be right. The historical precedents were not encouraging. The last such alliance between the countries had antedated the parting of the ways signalled by the trauma of the Spanish Armada during the reign of the first Queen Elizabeth. Elizabeth's elder sister, Mary Tudor, had been married to King Philip II of Spain, the last Spanish monarch to visit English shores. But Philip soon tired of his English bride and went home without her. She herself never even got as far as the Spanish Court. In the time of Spain's Philip IV there had been talk of marriage betwen the young Pretender, Bonnie Prince Charlie, with a Spanish princess. But this would have looked like part of yet another Catholic plot against England, and the idea came to nothing.

Despite such unpromising precedents Alfonso bravely spoke, while in London, of his being received with 'an enthusiasm which reveals that which was evident on the occasion of matrimonial alliances celebrated between Spain and England in past centuries.' The significance of his words was not lost on his susceptible audience. They were used in the course of his reply to addresses of welcome by the Lord Mayor of London and Archbishop of Canterbury. The occasion was a lunchtime banquet at the Guildhall on the same day as the shopping adventures in Bond Street. The Spanish journalist Azorin, in London to cover the visit for the Madrid review *ABC*, called it the most important incident of the whole week. The rain had stopped at last and the banquet was accompanied by the usual ceremonial pomposity. For the Spanish royal family, however, it provided a family joke that is often retold and laughed over even to this day.

Too much was expected of the charming but inexperienced King whose linguistic abilities were not considerable. During his Guildhall speech he departed from his prepared text to refer to the bad cold he had caught since arriving in London. He apologized for his consequently hoarse voice which was due, he said, to his being 'constipated'. (In Spanish the expression 'constipado' means to have a cold.)

It was on the evening of that same day, however, that the turning point of his London visit occurred. He was to be entertained at two of London's grandest houses, both now replaced by modern blocks. The first was the old Lansdowne House in Berkeley Square where his host for dinner was Lord Lansdowne, the Foreign Secretary. This was followed by a reception at Londonderry House, a smaller but even more beautiful building standing until quite recently in what was then the narrow section of Park Lane near Piccadilly. The King was received after sweeping up the magnificent double staircase to the ballroom on the first floor. Most of the royal family, including the inevitable 'eligible' princesses, were present. It was the most glittering occasion yet for the Spanish monarch apart from the entertainments at Buckingham Palace itself. Supper was to be served in the large Adam-style drawing-room on the ground floor. It had been arranged that Princess Patricia was to sit next to the King. Alfonso duly took his place. But there was no Princess. Patricia pointedly remained upstairs talking to a young guardsman. Lord Londonderry, the embarrassed host, went to look for the Princess and insisted on her coming down to supper. She did so; but by now it was too late. Alfonso's as yet unspoken but clearly understood proposal of marriage had all too obviously been turned down. It was a considerable shock to Alfonso but a decisive factor in his final choice.

From now on the Spanish King, in search of an English bride, began seeking out 'the fair one'. On the following evening they met again. The occasion was a gala performance of Gounod's *Romeo and Juliet* at Covent Garden. Now, for the first time, tongues started wagging with a vengeance. Members of the glittering audience were agog with excitement as they strained through their opera glasses to follow what was happening in the royal box. To whom, if anyone, was Alfonso devoting most of his attention? In fact it was Ena though this was not immediately apparent to the onlookers. They did not sit together during the performance but conversed with each other animatedly during the interval. They compared notes on the programme and were obviously at ease in each other's company. Word began to spread around the opera house that Ena, contrary to all original expectations, might be the favoured one. But one rumour was quickly denied by another and the endless gossip remained inconclusive. Alfonso knew he could not yet let his feelings become public knowledge. But he *was*, as it happened, falling in love. Ena began to be aware of it while they were dancing together the following evening at Buckingham Palace. This was at the sumptuous Court ball to say farewell to the gallant young royal visitor. Ena found it difficult to believe she was the object of Alfonso's special favour. A few days previously she would not have believed it remotely possible. A member of her mother's household at Kensington Palace had asked Ena what she thought of the young King. Her reply was cautious. 'I'm glad the people have welcomed him so warmly,' was all she said.

At the final Buckingham Palace ball, however, an entirely new and more intimate note crept into the relationship between Ena and Alfonso. They allowed the music and general hum of conversation to form a barrier against eavesdroppers. For the first time during that momentous week they spoke privately to each other. As they danced and talked Alfonso was rapidly assessing 'the fair one' in his own mind. Here was a girl who was obviously very different from Princess Patricia of Connaught. The latter was prettier in the 'modern' style: slim, tall and elegant, very much the well-groomed debutante. Ena's good looks were more natural, if 'old-fashioned!' Her skin was flawless and her corn-coloured hair was her crowning glory. Her serene good looks contrasted greatly with the appearance of Alfonso. His skin was very white, the thinness of his face being accentuated by the long, somewhat crooked Bourbon nose and prominent chin. His sleeked-back hair and black moustache, slightly turning up at the ends, made him a prototype of those jerkily moving heroes of the early silent films. His dark, restless eyes were easily his most compelling feature as far as the girls were concerned.

The couple, so suddenly all wrapped up in each other, drew attention from all round as they danced. But strain as they might, the onlookers could not hear what Alfonso and Ena were saying to one another. The King asked his partner if she collected post-cards, a hobby much in fashion at the time. Most young girls kept albums of them filled in, between the cards, with watercolour sketches. Such albums were often elaborate affairs, an antidote to the hours of boredom suffered by upper-class girls of that period. Postcards from 'lovers'—usually imagined ones—were generally the most prominent feature of such albums. Ena herself was not an avid collector, but she made a point of replying enthusiastically, 'Yes, yes, I collect postcards.' 'Well,' said Alfonso, 'I shall send you some on condition that you reply.' Ena recalls[7] that 'with his irresistible smile', he added 'I hope you will not forget me.' Ena was taken aback and hardly knew what to say in reply. Her actual answer was more formal than the King had expected. All she could think of saying, rather lamely, was 'It is very difficult to forget the visit of a foreign sovereign.' It was in fact a very characteristic sort of reply for the reserved Ena to make. Had she been the sort of person to say, as so many might have done, 'No, of course, I shall never forget you,' she might also have been the sort of person to hold the mercurial Alfonso's attention and loyalty when things went so badly wrong later on.

Ena's impressions of Alfonso on that fateful evening were that he was 'very thin, very southern, very gay, very charming. He was not handsome at that time, though he improved greatly in this respect later on.'[8] The King did not see Ena again; but she saw him. She was on her way out of Kensington Palace by carriage when she saw him arriving to call on her mother. He left a photograph of himself for Ena. This she naturally prized. It occupied a place of honour in her room and was the object of envy from all the contemporaries among her female cousins. But she was still far from certain that Alfonso had made up his mind in her favour and did not know that he, on his return to Spain, said to his Prime Minister—though the remark was accompanied by a tantalizing laugh—'Don't worry, I've found a name for my yacht.' Even the postcards, which began to arrive almost every week, did not convince her that the notoriously flirtatious King was in love with *her*. The postcards were nevertheless like chapters in a 'love story' as far as Ena's imagination was concerned. They kept coming during all of the eight months that elapsed before they met again. None contained more than two or three sentences. The messages tended to be trivial: descriptions of beauty spots visited by the King in Spain and elsewhere. But sometimes there were souvenirs and odd little mementoes in reply to which Princess Ena never failed to send Alfonso news of herself and her own little world. It was all very exciting for an impressionable young woman but had little or nothing, at this stage, to do with love on Ena's part.

Nevertheless, limited though Ena's world was, the question of her possible marriage to the King of Spain quite soon became a matter of keen discussion among politicians and diplomats. Lord Lansdowne was a friend and admirer of the Spanish King and had, as already noted, been his host at Lansdowne House. He was Foreign Secretary until the end of 1905 and was privy at every stage to King Edward's desire for a Spanish match. It did not matter particularly to the British monarch which of the princesses Alfonso chose and for some time after his guest's departure he still imagined Princess Patricia to be in the running. He was not at first told that Alfonso had almost certainly transferred most of his attention to Princess Ena of Battenberg, a development which involved a highly delicate matter rarely discussed in royal circles.

This was the question of haemophilia about which there was

still considerable mystery. The whole subject was more or less taboo while Queen Victoria was alive. She died in merciful ignorance of the fact that this disease, as far as the British royal family was concerned, had originated with her. Its full impact on the history of modern Spain has been given surprisingly little recognition though it was, in fact, to prove crucial. For, as has been written, 'It is difficult to find a disease which is more dramatic and tragic than haemophilia, or to name a clinical entity (if one excepts tuberculosis, syphilis and insanity) which has influenced modern history more than this hereditary defect. There can be no doubt that the presence of this disease in the royal families of Russia and Spain played a part in shaping the destiny of present day Europe.'[9] It is interesting that the author of the above words happens to mention tuberculosis, syphilis and insanity, all of which had been prominent at one time or another in the history of the Spanish Bourbons. Now, to bring yet further ravagement, might be added the devastating curse of haemophilia. Alfonso was fully warned of the danger but did not of course know the whole story of the disease's penetration into the British royal family.

It had all come about because, behind Queen Victoria's outwardly robust health, there lay concealed a grave physical defect. The deadly malady in question is thought to be older than recorded history even though it was never mentioned by Latin and Greek writers. But the existence of haemophilia is implied by passages in the Talmud relating to the dangers of death from haemorrhage after circumcision. And Albacusis, the great Moorish surgeon of the eleventh century, related that in a certain village were men who when wounded suffered an uncontrollable haemorrhage which caused death, and boys who bled often fatally when their gums were rubbed harshly.'[10] Surprisingly, however, the disease received no medical recognition until the nineteenth century. It cannot be traced in the Hanoverian or Saxe-Coburg-Gotha royal lines but when these two families were united in the persons of Edward, Duke of Kent and Victoria of Saxe-Coburg, the disease made its appearance in the only child of this marriage, the future Queen Victoria. It did so through a spontaneous mutation in the X-chromosomes handed on to her by one of her parents. Which parent? Mutations are known to occur much more often in the germ cells of older fathers and the Duke of Kent was fifty-one when the future Queen Victoria was born while her mother, Victoria of Saxe-Coburg, was thirty-one. Later the Queen spoke of the disease occasionally but was convinced that its origin was 'not in our family'—meaning the House of Hanover. 'This was strictly correct but the mutation almost certainly occurred in a Hanoverian gene and not in the Saxe-Coburg genes Queen Victoria inherited from her mother.'[11] Contrary to what is sometimes believed the disease can be inherited through either males or females though it normally exists in the female in the carrier state only with bleeding characteristics not manifested. The essence of the disease is that the blood fails to coagulate so that even a slight bump or cut can cause enough bleeding, often only internal, to prove fatal. While an affected male has normal sons, all his daughters are potential carriers. It is thus not difficult to see why the disease spread so rapidly in nineteenth century royal circles, with arranged marriages between close relations being an added complication and danger. 'Because cousins have one-eighth of their genes in common, the wonder becomes not so much that so many of Victoria's descendants (at least sixteen in three generations) were affected but that an affected male did not marry a carrier female cousin and produce that rarity of rarities, a true female haemophiliac.'[12]

Of Queen Victoria's daughters, her eldest, the Crown Princess of Prussia, had been a probable carrier. Two of her sons had died in infancy, possibly but not certainly from haemophilia. The second daughter Alice had been a carrier and had transmitted the disease, with fatal consequences, into the Russian Imperial family. But the full impact of this transmission had not become wholly apparent in the year 1905. The youngest daughter, Beatrice, was the other daughter who might reasonably have been expected to be a carrier. The extent to which Alfonso was aware of the danger is disputed. There are those in Spain to this day who maintain that their King was never properly informed of the risk to which he would be exposing his offspring should he marry Princess Ena. As evidence of this they point to the fact that after the birth of the first son Alfonso scarcely spoke to his mother-in-law because he blamed her for not being fully frank about the danger. It is certain, however, that Alfonso was given abundant warning. The key person in the passing of the necessary information was the man who was Spain's Foreign Minister in 1905. This was the Marquis of Villa-Urrutia who was in London with his beautiful wife for Alfonso's visit. King Edward took an early opportunity to ask the Spanish King if Villa-Urrutia might not become Spanish Ambassador to the Court of St James. For the man who was Ambassador at the time, Señor Polo de Bernabé, was not popular with Edward VII for the simple if rather unfair reason that he was extremely ugly. On the other hand, he conceived an immediate liking for Villa-Urrutia after taking one look at his beautiful wife. Thus the Marquis had become Ambassador by the time of Ena's marriage to Alfonso in May of the following year, but not before he had reported back to his fellow cabinet ministers the warnings he received about the haemophilia danger. These warnings came not only from King Edward but also from Princess Beatrice, Lord Lansdowne and Princess Ena herself.[13]

The man, meanwhile, who was the chief go-between in the pre-marriage negotiations was, not the Spanish Ambassador in London, but the Counsellor at the Embassy, the extremely intelligent Marquis of Villalobar. As a protegé of the Empress Eugénie, he was automatically an ally in promoting the cause of a match between Ena and Alfonso, which was the old Empress's dream. He was too shrewd a diplomat to ignore the implications of the haemophilic dangers. But the principal warnings to Alfonso came from his aunt, the Infanta Eulalia, the *enfant terrible* of the family. Eulalia had always been a high-spirited rebel, chafing against the boring and useless life imposed on princesses in her position and against the outmoded and unrealistic attitude of the Spanish Court in which she had been brought up. Her warnings to her nephew about Ena were brushed aside on the grounds that Eulalia was 'always trying to make trouble'. Alfonso, moreover, was disposed to make light of the supposed dangers he would take in marrying the Battenberg Princess. He liked living dangerously and this seemed to him, as far as he ever gave it any prolonged thought, no more risky than exposing himself to the crowds in Madrid, Barcelona or Paris. After all, not all who could transmit haemophilia would necessarily do so and not all of their male offspring would necessarily be fatally stricken by the disease.

For the time being, however, Alfonso did no more than send postcards. Though the messages continued to be 'tame and punctilious', Ena would invariably reply with some such phrase as 'I am thinking of you and I do not forget you.' It seems strange to us that Ena and even Alfonso had to receive permission to exchange such communications. But behind all the sedateness, decorum and diplomatic hide-and-seek, were there the beginnings of deeper and more passionate longings? Many years later Ena was to profess sentiments which few could have guessed at the time. 'I desired with all my heart', she declared, 'to have this Spaniard who was as seductive as fire and as dangerous.'[14] But this was said fifty-five years later at a time when Queen Ena was inclined to over-romanticize certain events in her early life. At the same time, she would not have been human had she not been flattered by the assiduous attentions of the highly eligible King of Spain.

[4]

A Chill to the Heart

SOON after his return to Spain from England Alfonso told his Prime Minister—if only laughingly—'Don't worry, I have found a name for my yacht.' But he would say no more than that and had not, at that point, even bought the yacht on which the name was to be painted. He did, however, confide in his mother and his favourite sister, the Infanta Teresa. 'To his mother he described at length the English girl who had captured his heart, and whom he hoped he might persuade to share his throne.' So wrote Evelyn Graham in the only book ever written about Queen Ena in English.[1] 'From the first,' the same author added, 'Queen Christina entered into his enthusiasm.' This last sentence, however, could hardly be more inaccurate. The book was written at the end of the 1920s when Spain's Queen Mother was still alive. The author was so anxious to praise and please that he wrote a hagiography. Everyone in the book is gallant, sweet, gracious, pious and good. No one is ever depicted as being unhappy, unfaithful or even ill. The less pleasant part of the story was not then fully known. And of such little as was known, none liked to speak. The King and Queen of Spain were still on the throne and Ena had half of her life yet to live.

Queen Maria Christina, in point of fact, was strongly opposed to the idea of her cherished son's marrying Princess Ena of Battenberg. She wanted him to marry an eligible Princess from the ancient, Catholic and intensely traditionalist House of Habsburg compared with whom the morganatic Battenbergs were upstart 'small fry'. Queen Christina's first choice for Alfonso, in fact, was her niece the Archduchess Gabrielle. Such a match would have produced continuity in the Spanish Court, particularly as to its female retinue. Amusing in this connection is the description given at about that time by the Sultan of Morocco's Ambassador to Spain. 'The Court of Spain is perfect in every way,' he wrote to his sovereign. But he made an exception of what he quaintly called 'the harem'. This, he said, was 'very gloomy'.[2]

The Queen Mother persuaded her son to postpone any final decision and meanwhile to meet as many other of Europe's other princesses as possible. So he dutifully went off on his rounds—to Berlin, Vienna, Budapest and—for a second time—to Paris. Ena went on getting postcards about which no one was supposed to know. But in the Madrid of 1905 secrets were hard to keep. At that time the Spanish capital was still a very small town, little more than a 'village', as so many people called it, compared to most of Europe's other capitals. Life was parochial and thrived on gossip. 'Madrileños', the citizens of Madrid, loved nothing more than congregating in cafés, clubs and theatre foyers. The main theme of conversation in the summer of 1905 was supplied by a question that had been asked in the prestigious and unswervingly monarchist magazine *ABC*, 'Who will be the future Queen of Spain?'

To provoke discussion the magazine asked its readers to send in their votes for the candidate they favoured and offered prizes to those making the nearest guesses as to how many votes could be gained by the winning candidate. The 'candidates' were the eight princesses most often mentioned as marriageable in the world's Press. They included three English girls apart from Ena and also the Kaiser's daughter, Princess Victoria of Prussia, even though she was only thirteen.

The 'poll' turned out to be unexpectedly popular and coupons were snapped up in boutiques, government departments, clubs, cafés and even the humblest of shops and offices. Easily topping the bill when the result was announced in September was Princess Ena of Battenberg with 18,427 votes. The King was reported to have read the result with great satisfaction. He was still holidaying at the time at his favoured northern seaside hideaway at San Sebastian, the Palace of Miramar in the Basque country. By now he had bought his yacht and ordered a certain form of lettering to be painted on its bow. There are various versions of the story and its implications. To be preferred is that which the Queen told many years later to a Spanish journalist compiling what he called a 'close-up' of Ena based on interviews at her house in Lausanne.[3]

The form of lettering on the yacht was 'Reina X . . . .' The more romantic but less reliable version of the same story claims that what was written was 'Princess X . .' This, plus the fact that the lettering was allegedly in English, would have told everyone that Ena was the bride-to-be. But the Queen insisted that there were four dots and not two, Alfonso's mischievous intention having been to prolong the mystery. In this he succeeded. No one could think of a likely future Queen with five letters in her name, unless it could be the relative 'outsider' Princess Luisa—as her name was spelt in Spanish—of Orleans. The instinctive feeling of the man in the street was, nevertheless, that Ena was still firm favourite, a fact that seemed to be somewhat 'confirmed' by the absence of any official denial. Press reports, Spanish and foreign, were more or less unanimous that she would be Alfonso's final choice. But none as yet could guess the truth and much of the speculation was still based on supposed political considerations. In fact Alfonso, at this stage, was head over heels in love with the Battenberg Princess. He felt he had been helped by providence to find a girl in a million, the Princess of his dreams. He was daily reminded of her blonde, cool and, to him, tantalizing good looks by the photograph of Ena in a wide-brimmed hat which now had pride of place on his dressing table. He saw in the photograph a girl who was radiant not only with beauty but also with sweetness, health and vigour. What more could possibly be desired?

That the dashing young King of Spain, suspected by so many of waywardness and frivolity, was now—and few have ever doubted it—so deeply and genuinely in love, was a source of great satisfaction to all around him. It helped to dissolve the opposition in some political and clerical circles toward the idea of an English match and to enable the so-called 'Court party' to overcome the ultra-traditional views of many of the stiffer grandees and powerful churchmen. In no time at all rumours began to proliferate. *ABC* carried a fantastic story that Ena was about to travel to Rome to be received forthwith into the Roman Catholic church. She would then, it was asserted, sail to Cap Martin for a romantic reunion with Alfonso at the palace of their 'fairy godmother', the Empress Eugénie. The King made no comment on such stories nor on those which began to circulate in Paris that his engagement to Ena would be announced in Madrid in the following spring.

All in all 1905 was a year of conflicting romantic rumours about the Spanish King. It was also a year which found his country in a hopelessly unsettled political state with no less than four changes of Prime Minister. The orthodox political solution to Spain's continuing unrest, particularly in separatist Catalonia, was 're-volution from above'. In practice this meant little more than tinkering with the existing system and using the language of reform. This being transparently obvious, those, especially the anarchists, preaching 'revolution from below' were gaining in numbers and influence every day. To produce stability and end speculation on at least one front, the Queen Mother finally consented to her son's choice of Ena as a bride. Queen Christina was the sort of woman who more easily commanded respect than affection. And, spoiled though he had been by his mother, Alfonso never lost for her a respect bordering on fear. Her resistance to Alfonso's choice lasted nearly eight months, almost exactly the same time as Queen Victoria had held out against Ena's mother over the question of marrying Prince Henry of Battenberg. But, in January 1906, Queen Maria Christina of Spain finally wrote a long letter to Princess Beatrice of Great Britain and Ireland praising her son, telling of his love for Ena and asking for an unofficial approach to be made to King Edward VII.

A few days later, at Windsor, the family were all together for an official visit of the King of Greece. Ena noticed her mother draw her uncle the King into a small drawing-room away from the main group of family and guests. She immediately sensed what was happening and went out on to the terrace to hide her excitement. Soon the King came out to join her. He patted her cheek as he told her what she already knew, saying 'He's a charming young man. You will be very happy, I'm so pleased. I'm so pleased.'

Few outside the family circle, however, were let in on the secret. There was to be no public announcement for the time being. Princess Beatrice and her daughter left England almost immediately. Their destination was Biarritz for what was ostensibly just a 'holiday'. They travelled by way of Paris where they stayed for a few days. It was noticed with interest that they were seen off from the French capital by the Ambassadors of both Spain and Great Britain. They arrived in Biarritz on 22 January and were driven a short distance outside the town to the north to stay at the beautiful Villa Mouriscot, which was, in those days, an extremely picturesque Basque chalet on raised ground overlooking a small lake. Its attractively wooded perimeter surrounded a large garden with a labyrinth of paths winding their way between the flower beds and lawns.

Ena and her mother were to be the guests of Princess Frederica of Hanover who had represented the Empress Eugénie at Ena's christening. The Press was quickly on to the scent and reporters immediately began infiltrating the area from several countries. The journalists became convinced that a big story was about to 'break' by the conspiracy of silence that greeted all their attempts to get some comment from the Villa Mouriscot. One enterprising reporter, however, caught a glimpse of Ena and excitedly wired to his paper 'I saw the Princess Victoria. It is no ordinary holiday that brings that lovely light to her eyes or that smile to her lips. The King of Spain is to have an enchanting bride.'[4] Two days later one of the Spanish King's chamberlains, the Marquis of Villalobar, arrived in Biarritz from Madrid and had to fight his way into the

Villa Mouriscot through the teeming throng of news-hungry journalists. The next day the King himself was reported to be on his way from Madrid. The news had got out to the local inhabitants. Crowds poured into Biarritz from Hendaye, St Jean de Luz, San Sebastian and other nearby centres. They sensed an historic moment, the betrothal of a Spanish King to an English Princess.

The King had set out to travel incognito but the attempt soon had to be abandoned. He was greeted at each station with loud 'vivas' for himself and his future Queen. At Spain's ancient capital of Valladolid the daughters of the town's senior denizens collected at the station to greet the King with cries of 'Long live the bride.' Alfonso replied 'I haven't got one yet.' The girls shot back at him, 'No, not today. But tomorrow you will.' The King made no demur and turned to a member of his suite to say delightedly 'They will welcome her, you see. Even now they are glad, but when they actually see her . . .' At another station an old woman tossed two deep red carnations into the royal saloon saying 'For your Princess. Tell her they are with the love of your people.' Alfonso saluted the old lady and remarked that this was a good omen as these were his favourite flowers. The King, having got out of the train at San Sebastian, had decided to motor the rest of the way. The Marquis of Villalobar had meanwhile left Mouriscot early in the morning to drive towards the Spanish frontier. At a certain point he stopped his car and behaved in what might have appeared to a passer-by to be a rather odd fashion. He got out of the car and stationed himself in the middle of the road. He was standing on the exact frontier between France and Spain.

Quite soon a powerful car approached from the Spanish side. It was carrying General the Marquis of Pacheco and the King. They stopped to pick up Villalobar and then sped on towards Biarritz and the Villa Mouriscot. The King was greeted at the gates of the villa by Ena's brother Prince Alexander of Battenberg and was accorded a tumultuous reception by the crowd. 'Then there

Alfonso and Ena at the Villa Mouriscot

[65]

followed three days of love-making.' So goes one account,[5] though the proceedings were in no way as intimate as this description implies. Ena was naturally very shy and not a little confused to see Alfonso again. She had only previously met him on five occasions in all and each time in very restricted and formal circumstances. They had only ever had one conversation that could be called at all private. At last, here at Mouriscot, they could be properly alone.

One of Alfonso's first questions was 'Did you know I would not forget you when I left London?' 'No,' replied Ena. 'I did not know but I hoped you wouldn't.'[6] The King went on to ask her if she had been unhappy after he had left. Ena then told him that, 'The last time you came to visit my mother to say farewell, I passed your carriage on its way to Kensington Palace from which I had just emerged. I was going to the marriage of a great friend of mine. Instead of enjoying that ceremony my heart grieved because I had missed you by so little'.

At Mouriscot the betrothal of Alfonso and Ena was celebrated privately even though the English Princess had not yet met Spain's Queen Mother. Ena had never looked more beautiful and it was clear that Alfonso was deeply in love. He had never set eyes on, let alone met, anyone quite like her. Ena, for her part, could hardly believe it was all true. The better she got to know Alfonso, the more fatally she fell victim to his famous charm, without necessarily falling deeply in love. She was not the first woman to go through this paradoxical experience. That she would by no means be the last naturally did not occur to her at this moment when she could think only of the present. The interval at Mouriscot was remembered for ever by Ena. Her romantic nature treasured the memory of the magical days. In the dark years later on she liked to remember Alfonso as he had seemed to her then, 'gay and seductive' in her own words[7] and a brilliant talker who made her laugh. She confessed to having been captivated by him.

Though the engagement had not yet been publicly announced the couple decided to record it for posterity in their own way. On one of their expeditions by car they noticed a tree on which some lovers had carved their initials. 'I see they do that here too,' said Ena, adding that 'The Isle of Wight is a favourite spot for lovers and there are hundreds of trees thus decorated.' When they got back to the Villa Mouriscot Alfonso led his Princess to a tree in the garden and suggested that they too should carve their initials on its smooth bark. Ena began but was interrupted by the King who said, 'Let's write Victoria-Alfonso.' So Ena carved her own name and Alfonso added his directly underneath. 'Later we will come back', he said, 'and see how our names grow.'[8] In another part of the garden they planted two fir trees side by side, and the same day Alfonso gave his future bride a piece of jewellery, something for which, as he knew, she had a passion. It was a heart surrounded by diamonds, originally intended by the King to be opal as this was Ena's birthday stone. But she seemed to mind about the old superstition over opal and had been given a sapphire instead.

Alfonso wanted to prolong the Mouriscot sojourn as long as possible, driving over each day from his San Sebastian home, the Miramar Palace. On arrival at Villa Mouriscot he would be greeted by Baron von Ramingen, Princess Frederica's husband, and Lord William Cecil, Princess Beatrice's Comptroller. After giving them brief, almost brusque, greetings, the King would hurry through to the drawing-room where Ena was invariably waiting. They would go out to stroll. Ena loved gardens and knew a lot about flowers. She pointed out to Alfonso which flowers were which as he seemed to know very little about them. One day she said to him: 'You're not paying much attention. Aren't you interested in flowers?' 'Only in one just now,' the King answered. 'And that?' 'Orange blossom,' he replied, referring to a bloom which he associated, practically identified, with Ena herself. Ena blushed and remembered the night he had first looked at her down the dining-room at Buckingham Palace while asking her aunt who she was.

After spending, as a rule, nearly the whole morning in the

garden, the couple would join their host and hostess and the royal household for lunch. Most afternoons were spent driving out to one or other of the local beauty spots. And then, on one particular day, the King took his fiancée into his own country for the first time. They were accompanied by Princess Beatrice and the Marquis of Villalobar. There was also a fifth person present, the Marquis of Viana, a close friend of the King's and later his principal favourite. Ena thus met for the first time a man who was, in later years, to be the cause of profound unhappiness in her life. Suddenly the car stopped and they all got out. Villalobar said to the English Princess 'Your Royal Highness, you have now set foot on the soil of Spain.' Ena replied with emotion, and a smile directed toward the King, 'I am very happy.'

Alfonso then went on alone to San Sebastian to meet his mother who arrived that night at the Miramar Palace. The next day held out a somewhat unnerving prospect for Ena for she was to meet her future mother-in-law for the first time. The King drove in to Biarritz to bring his fiancée and her mother to meet Queen Maria Christina. Princess Beatrice had been to San Sebastian before. She had gone there with her mother to meet Maria Christina in 1889, a few years after the latter had become Regent. It had been the first time a British sovereign had set foot on Spanish soil.

It has been said that 'from the first moment of their meeting Queen Maria Christina and Princess Ena became sincere friends.'[9] The statement, however, needs considerable qualification. The Spanish Queen Mother, as already noted, had been strongly against the choice of the British Princess as her son's bride. She was by no means reconciled to the coming marriage by the time of this first meeting with her future daughter-in-law but was very correct in her behaviour and extended a welcome to Ena which, though scarcely exuberant, was polite enough. Maria Christina was, at the best of times, a woman who lacked warmth. She had come out of the convent in which she had been an Abbess to marry Alfonso's father and something of the old-fashioned

Reverend Mother, dignified, austere and very grand, stayed with her always. She doted on her son who idolized her. That the three of them would have to live under the same roof in daily intimacy for over twenty years was something that might well have daunted Ena had she realized its full implication at the time of that first meeting.

The journey into San Sebastian, however, was enlivened by cheering crowds as Ena's future subjects got their first glimpse of their Queen-to-be. The royal couple travelled in an open car as young women tossed flowers down from balconies on either side of the narrow streets. Throwing flowers from balconies on passing royalty was a favourite Spanish custom at that time. A red rose fell at the feet of the King. He picked it up, brushed it across his lips and handed it to the Princess who smiled and fastened it to her dress. The crowd roared their approval. The Queen Mother was waiting for them at the front door of the Miramar Palace. Ena, on getting out of the car, advanced to kiss the older woman's hand according to custom. But Maria Christina held out her arms and they embraced each other. The local Press enthused over the grace and charm of the English Princess. 'She is very beautiful,' said the *Voz de Guipuzcoa* newspaper on 29 January 1906. 'Very elegant, very sympathetic. In these three expressions are condensed all the opinions, all the impressions of yesterday.'

Ena's visit was returned the following day. Alfonso drove over as usual in the morning and his mother came over in the afternoon in time for tea. All was outwardly pleasant but agonizingly stiff-backed and formal. It was a considerable ordeal for Ena who came, for the first time, under the baleful scrutiny of two powerful members of the Spanish Court. Such people can, if they so desire, make life hellish for anyone newly 'admitted' into the inner sanctum of Court life. This kind of power is greatly increased if the newcomer happens to be young, inexperienced and foreign. Any such person immediately becomes highly vulnerable unless well equipped to hit back with such weapons as guile, charm and toughness or a combination of them all. Sizing up their possible victim on this occasion were the respective attendants on the Queen Mother and King Alfonso, the Duchess of San Carlos and the Marquis of Viana. The Spanish, like the English, are bad linguists and hate speaking foreign languages. Ena at that time spoke no Spanish. All spoke in somewhat stilted French as Ena had to make most of the conversational running. The Duchess and the Marquis had every opportunity to observe the shy and self-conscious English Princess under the cover of elaborate and obsequious mock courtesy. They did so with malevolent shrewdness.

Alfonso's time in Biarritz and San Sebastian was quickly running out. On 3 February he departed for Madrid to seek and obtain from his Council of Ministers official sanction for his proposed marriage. Ena had meanwhile to undertake a necessary but not wholly congenial task. Before she could become Queen of Spain she had to join the Roman Catholic Church. This fact, when it became generally known in Britain, caused widespread resentment and protest. It had been said that Ena had had a prior attraction to the religion of her godmother the Empress Eugénie but of this there is no evidence. On the basis that 'the Coburgs had seldom hesitated to barter faith for a crown'[10] Edward VII had been anxious to do all he could to smooth the way for Ena to change her religion. His main preoccupation was that the necessary procedure should, after the manner of a dubious operation, be got over with as quickly and as quietly as possible. Princess Beatrice was accordingly advised to keep Ena quiet somewhere, such as Osborne, and not to bring her to London as the feeling was particularly strong there. There were many outraged letters to the Press mostly from clergymen of an excessively 'Protestant' outlook. King Edward neatly extricated himself from the problem by declaring that Ena was a Battenberg and therefore a German rather than a British Princess. He conveniently forgot that Prince Henry of Battenberg had become a naturalized Briton on his marriage and died in the service of the Crown. As a further precaution he insisted that Ena's instruction in the Roman

Catholic faith should be conducted abroad. For this purpose France was chosen and a few days after Alfonso left San Sebastian for Madrid, Ena and her mother travelled to Versailles. There the future Queen was given a crash course by Mgr. Robert Brindle, the Catholic Bishop of Nottingham. It was quite a shrewd choice since Bishop Brindle was somewhat unusual among the English Catholic clergy of that period. He came from an English rather than Irish background and from the class generally associated with recusancy. He had been born the year Queen Victoria came to the throne, that is only a few years after 'Catholic emancipation'. He became one of the first Catholic army chaplains and the first ever to receive a state pension for such a post. Having been decorated for his service with the Army in Turkey and Egypt he became Bishop of Nottingham soon after his retirement from the army chaplaincy in 1899. Having seen something of the world he was as tactful as possible in initiating the bewildered Ena into the intricacies of Roman Catholicism. But he had only two or three weeks to try to impart what many people never learn properly in a whole lifetime. It has been claimed that the Bishop 'was surprised as well as pleased to find how much his royal pupil already knew concerning the matters of his faith.'[11] In fact, however, Ena had little chance to do more than scratch at the surface of a highly systematized and dogmatic religion profoundly different at that time from the rather fundamentalist and evangelical approach to the Christian faith to which she had been previously accustomed.

The Bishop's inevitably English approach to his religion, moreover, did little to prepare Ena for Spain's very different, more ostentatious and emotional brand of Roman Catholicism, overladen as it was with much mysterious symbolism and not a little superstition. But she never had been and was never to become particularly religious. Her change in allegiance from one church to another was based on necessity rather than conviction. She always remained more Protestant than Catholic in outlook and never lost the uncomfortable feeling of having betrayed the faith of her family, forefathers and friends. She was never willing, in later years, to discuss the details of her 'conversion' and would invariably draw a veil over what was ever an unhappy memory. What little she did eventually say contradicts the version of events accepted earlier and committed to writing by biographers and historians when Alfonso was still alive. In describing, for example, her actual reception into the Catholic Church, it is stated that 'Owing to the exquisite tact of Queen Christina, who desired at all costs to avoid anything that might hurt British Protestant susceptibilities, the ceremonial was of the utmost simplicity and entirely private.'[12] The word 'private' as used to describe the ceremony is distinctly relative. It took place, it is true, in a 'private chapel', that of the Queen Mother at the Miramar Palace in San Sebastian. The date was 7 March 1906. But there was nothing secluded or intimate about such 'private chapels' in those days. They were, by normal standards, ornate and sizeable churches. All in all, in Ena's own words, 'It was made as unpleasant for me as possible.'[13]

What Ena particularly resented was the humiliating way in which she was made to 'abjure' her previously 'heretical' beliefs. She also had to undergo fresh baptism in case the first ceremony had not been valid in the eyes of 'the true Church'. Though the ceremony was not 'public' it was public enough 'to make one suffer'. She had, after all 'been baptized in my grandmother's house. It could not have been more solemnly done. Nevertheless they made me get baptized again.' In those days (from the Roman Catholic point of view) 'to be a Protestant was the same as to be a Jew.' In either case you were outside the 'one true Church' and could probably not therefore be saved without submitting to that Church.

The Spanish idea of keeping Ena's reception ceremony 'private' was to limit the number of courtiers present to twenty-three. But the Prime Minister of the day, Sigismondo Moret, was also there with his family, as well, of course, as the King, the Queen Mother and their relatives. The eighteen-year-old English Princess was without a single member of her own family. She had never in her life felt more entirely alone than at that moment. She was dressed entirely in white with no jewellery and wore a white veil. The Bishop of Nottingham was assisted by two Spanish Bishops, those of Vitoria and of Sion. Bishop Brindle placed a Bible on the ledge in front of where the Princess knelt and recited the 'Come Holy Spirit.' He then handed her a small booklet from which she read the following paragraphs:

I, Victoria Eugénie of Battenberg, holding before my eyes the Holy Scripture, which I touch with my hand, and recognizing that no one can be saved without the faith which the Holy, Catholic, Apostolic and Roman Church upholds, believes and teaches, against which I deeply regret having transgressed, in that I have maintained and believed doctrines contrary to its teachings, do now, by the help of God's grace:

Declare and profess that I believe in the Holy, Catholic, Apostolic and Roman Church, which is the one and only true Church established on earth by Our Lord Jesus Christ, to Whom I submit with all my heart.

I believe firmly all the articles which she proposes for my acceptance and I renounce and condemn all that she renounces and condemns, being ready to obey everything that she commands.

I profess in particular that I believe:

In one God, in three divine Persons, each of them distinct and equal: that is to say, the Father, the Son and the Holy Ghost.

The Catholic doctrine of the Incarnation, Passion, Death and Resurrection of Our Lord Jesus Christ and the personal union of His two natures, divine and human. The divine maternity of the Blessed Mary, leaving her virginity intact, and equally her Immaculate Conception.

[73]

The true, real and substantial presence of the body of Our Lord Jesus Christ, as well as His soul and divinity, in the most Holy Sacrament of the Eucharist; Penance; Extreme Unction; Holy Orders and Matrimony.

I believe also in Purgatory, the resurrection of the body and life everlasting.

The supremacy, not only in honour but also in jurisdiction, of the Roman Pontiff, successor on earth of Saint Peter, Prince of the Apostles, Vicar of Jesus Christ.

Veneration of the saints and their statues, the authority and apostolic traditions of Holy Scripture which we must not interpret for ourselves but understand only in the sense laid down for us by our Holy Mother the Catholic Church to whom alone belongs the competence to judge its meaning and inter-pretation. And, finally, all other matters decided upon by the Sacred Canons and General Councils, particularly the Holy Council of Trent and the Ecumenical Council of the Vatican.

With a sincere heart and therefore with genuine faith, I renounce and abjure every error, heresy and sect which opposes the truth of the Catholic, Apostolic and Roman Church.

May God be my guide as well as these Holy Scriptures which I now touch with my hand.

At this, her second, baptism, Ena took the additional name Christina in honour of the Queen Mother who was her sponsor. That same evening the Princess received the Bishop of Notting-ham who heard her confession, and the next morning she received her 'first Holy Communion'. It was also arranged that a telegram should be sent to the Pope of the day, Pius X, in Princess Ena's name, saying, among other things, 'I offer myself with all my heart as your most faithful daughter.' All this was widely publicized in the papers and Ena was very nervous about what the reactions might be when she got back home to England. She never got over a painfully nagging worry of what her friends really thought of her for leaving the Church in which she had been brought up, in order to become a Queen. She even thought that some of them had put a curse on her for doing so. Certain it is that her lively sense of loyalty was put under almost intolerable strain when she was called upon to abjure—particularly in such vehement terms—the faith of her childhood. At certain moments of tragedy in future years she was to record her stricken belief that this curse was indeed operative and that such tragedies had come as a punishment for her apostasy. If, moreover, Ena's 'conversion' was gone through as a matter of form only, forced upon her by extraneous circumstances and not embarked upon by her with full consent of the will, it was arguably invalid. This in turn could be used as evidence that there was, in Roman Catholic eyes, a canonical impediment to her subsequent marriage rendering it null and void in the eyes of the Church. The hypothetical question involved would be put to the test only if an annulment to the marriage were to be sought from the 'Sacred Roman Rota'.

Meanwhile the question of Ena's conversion was so crucial that no announcement of the engagement could be made until it had been completed. As soon as it was, the engagement was officially announced in London and Madrid. In Britain the furore which Ena had feared, chiefly because of her change of religion, broke out with a vengeance. It was greater than the King had imagined and he had to write hastily to his Foreign Secretary, Sir Edward Grey, pointing out that he had not yet formally given consent in council to his niece's marriage.[14] He nevertheless wished the alliance to go through and stated that it was absolutely necessary that 'Princess Eugénie of Battenberg should sign a paper formally renouncing her succession to the English throne, having become a Roman Catholic.' To smooth the way further and to get himself out of any embarrassment the King went on to stress that no public grant would be sought on the Princess's behalf but that she

The official engagement photograph

would receive, as a 'private affair', a certain sum from her mother. All of this reflected the mean and rather petty side of Edward's character and he even, at this point, seemed to regret that he had ever created Ena a Royal Highness. In his letter to Grey, however, the King grudgingly added that 'she would have in any future

[76]

official document to be styled thus.' These provisions were included in the ultimate marriage treaty which secured Ena 450,000 pesetas a year during their marriage and 250,000 pesetas a year during her widowhood as long as she did not remarry.

All in all the spring of 1906 was thus a period of severe trial for the still inexperienced Princess Ena. Her main consolation was the knowledge that she was loved for herself by the King of Spain for, at that stage in the story, this happy fact was very much in evidence. She was greatly flattered if not yet deeply in love. Her happiest memory of the otherwise distressing interval in Versailles, while being instructed in the Roman Catholic faith, was of a gift sent to her by Alfonso. During her earlier stay at San Sebastian Ena had remarked how much she liked the luscious oranges which appeared at every meal. They had been specially sent, she learned, from the south of Spain. This gave Alfonso his idea for a surprise present for his fiancée in Versailles. While she and Princess Beatrice were there the King telegraphed the Spanish Embassy in Paris with instructions to meet a certain train which would be carrying oranges destined for the English Princess. An official duly arrived at the railway station with enough baskets, as it was supposed, in which to transport the oranges to the Princesses' hotel. Instead he had to cope with a fully-grown tree in a tub, its branches heavy with the golden fruit which Ena had so much enjoyed. She was so delighted with Alfonso's typically dashing and extravagant present that she kept the tree long after it had been plucked bare of oranges and its branches had become withered.

Ena and her mother came back to England immediately after the ordeal of the 'conversion' ceremony in San Sebastian. To distract herself from the protests against her change of religion she plunged herself into a hectic programme of preparation for marriage. A month later her fiancé came to England for a private visit of just under four weeks. He spent most of the time in the Isle of Wight in Ena's company. She gave the King his first golf lesson. Together they explored the delights of the grounds at

Osborne and the charms of the island as a whole. There were far less inhibitions and restrictions than there had been in Biarritz. Ena's confidence and happiness were fully restored. The occasion was avidly treasured; an interlude made infinitely precious by momentary absence of cares and worry.

These, however, tended to creep back when, after nearly three weeks, they all went up to London. They stayed at Buckingham Palace and wandered hand in hand through the rooms in which they had first got to know one another a year earlier. Alfonso's exuberance buoyed Ena up when sneaking fears for the future began trying to force themselves to the surface. For the Princess 'was going out as a stranger into a strange land, and leaving much that was dear to her behind her.'[15] Fortunately the Spanish King's high spirits were infectious. When visiting Kensington Palace he showed his *joie de vivre*—and enabled the cabman to enjoy some of it himself—by paying the fare with a golden sovereign. He visited Madame Tussaud's waxworks with Ena where they admired the newly made likenesses of themselves. Alfonso stretched out his hand to touch them as if unable to believe they were not real. When walking on the grass in Kensington Gardens he was reprimanded by a vigilant keeper—much to the amusement of Ena. He rode in the park with the Princesses for one last time and left for Spain on 3 May.

It was clear that the young Spanish monarch was 'quick-witted, precocious, something of a prodigy. His charm was exceptional . . .' But on closer acquaintance one came up against his failings: 'his wilfulness, his imperiousness, his determination to get his own way.'[16] Was King Edward VII beginning to have doubts about the wisdom of having allowed his niece to marry a Spanish Bourbon? He did not say as much to Ena in so many words. Having constitutionally smoothed the path for her to marry Alfonso he contented himself with giving her a warning. She was not, he said, to come back whining to England if things went wrong.[17] The words brought a sudden chill to Ena's heart as she contemplated the future.

Alfonso arrived home on 4 May. On 24 May it was Ena's turn to set off for Spain. She arrived at Victoria Station on the arm of her uncle, King Edward. She was confronted not only by her own family and friends but by almost all the leading members of the Spanish colony in London. In their eyes she was now 'one of them'. It was an unnerving feeling for someone who could scarcely greet her new 'compatriots' in their own language. Her sense of being 'taken over' was accentuated by a new experience. For the first time, members of the staff of the Spanish Embassy, headed by the Counsellor, the Marquis of Villalobar, were to travel in her suite. But she was also accompanied to Spain by her mother and two younger brothers, Leopold and Maurice. Her eldest brother Prince Alexander of Battenberg joined them outside Paris.

Similar scenes were meanwhile being enacted in Spain. Alfonso, in the uniform of a General of Artillery, had arranged to meet the English group half-way. He was seen off from the station in Madrid by his mother, aunts and sister, as well as by the Prime Minister, Señor Moret, and a large crowd of the usual hangers-on. Their destination was Irun at the Spanish frontier with France. The border station, now a large and busy junction, was then quite small. It was practically submerged for the occasion by mountains of flowers and copious displays of the Spanish and British colours. Locals were amazed to see the King accompanied, as a guard of honour, by the famous Halberdiers, who normally never left the Royal Palace in Madrid.

Sir Maurice de Bunsen, the British Ambassador to Spain, had accompanied the King from Madrid to the Northern Spanish border. Leaving the King in Irun he now crossed to Hendaye on the French side of the border to greet the British royal party. In a long letter to Lord Knollys, then a member of King Edward VII's household, Sir Maurice described his 'journey of extraordinary interest with King Alfonso to meet Princess Ena at the frontier.'[18] The welcome given to the English Princess by the people of Spain was, he said, overwhelming. It was kept up unabated all the way to

Madrid. Ena heard for the first time the rousing cries of 'Viva la Reina'. The 300 mile journey to the capital, taking the whole day, was one long triumph. The demonstrations, according to de Bunsen, 'grew in intensity as the train proceeded and at the large centres of Burgos and Valladolid the scenes presented by the densely packed crowds beggar description . . . Greater enthusiasm, and more evidently spontaneous and unorganised, I never saw. There was a touch of romance in the story of the King's love match which fired the people and gave zest to their applause . . . King Alfonso desired me to assure the King that the popular joy had in it a large element of pro-English feeling apart from the sentiments excited by the charms and character of the future Queen of Spain.' Such wishful thinking may or may not have been shared by King Edward.

On arrival at Madrid, Ena was whisked off to the beautiful Palace of El Pardo about nine miles outside the capital to the north-west. It was in those days linked with Madrid by a private road going through beautiful parkland which was all royal property. To drive there, Ena and her mother entered a carriage drawn by mules while the King and certain of his courtiers rode at the side. The King galloped and so did the mules. 'On the way, Queen Maria Christina, if she was able to find breath, may have told the Princess that it was at El Pardo that she herself spent the interval immediately before her marriage to Alfonso XII in November, 1879.'[19]

The Pardo Palace is of fairy tale beauty and charm and looks at its best in the month of May. It is square, low and spreading, with walls of snow white stone. Its interior at that time was probably the most ornate and exquisitely furnished of all Spain's royal palaces. Practically every room was covered with tapestries specially made for it at the Royal manufactory from designs by Goya, Bayeux and Teniers. Every ceiling was sumptuously frescoed. Every window commanded breathtaking views of the landscaped gardens, evergreen oaks, cork trees and cistus shrub. In the park beyond roamed deer and wild boar. The whole was encircled by a sixty-mile wall which enclosed what was virtually a world apart. Despite its relative vastness it had a compelling intimacy of its own. It stood as an oasis of ordered beauty amidst the rugged, virile landscape leading to the Guadarrama mountains in the distance. For centuries it had been the favourite residence of the Spanish kings and queens. But it had also known sadness and was to know it again within the lifetime of Queen Ena.

From this vantage point, so typically Spanish, so unimaginably different from Balmoral or Osborne, the bewitched but bewildered Ena was to make her first excursions into Madrid, to have her first meetings with the citizens of a toylike capital city which would be her home for many—who knew how many—years. 'But this was to be only the beginning of her adventures. She did not guess that while those around her saluted her radiant youth with homage, and her lover welcomed her with love, another element of Spain was planning that her wedding day should be that of her death.'[20]

[5]

The Brush with Death

KING ALFONSO XIII of Spain married Princess Victoria Eugénie of Battenberg on the last day of May 1906. It was one of those beautiful, clear early summer days which, it is said, only Madrid can produce. The Princess at the Pardo Palace was awake by dawn. Her bridegroom had adhered to an ancient Spanish custom and arranged for a guard to keep watch outside her bedroom on this last night before her wedding. One of the three men chosen for this assignment was the Duke of Lecera, scion of a very old Castilian family and, ironically, a man destined to play an important role in the Queen's life much later on.

Alfonso arrived at the Pardo at half-past six in the morning wearing an Admiral's uniform. In England it would have been considered a bad omen for the bride to meet her bridegroom on the day of the wedding but before the actual ceremony. Ena and Alfonso attended Mass together before the latter returned to Madrid. At a quarter to eight the bride and her mother set off to motor to the old Marine Ministry building where Ena was to dress for the wedding. Here another old Spanish custom was brought into play. The wedding dress she was to wear was a present from her husband-to-be. It was made of white satin bordered with silver and trimmed with rose point. The lace flounce was half a yard wide and the whole gown was hung with festoons of orange blossom. The four-yard-long train was of cloth of silver embroidered with fleurs-de-lis in seed pearls and edged with the same kind of lace that was on the dress. When Ena had been finally decked out with the help of Miss Minnie Cochrane, Lady William

Cecil and two English ladies' maids, the Queen Mother placed an Alençon lace veil over her head. She had worn the same veil at her own wedding and it was now Ena's to pass on to her own daughters when they came to marry.

Madrid was a blaze of colour and was playing host to more foreign princes and notabilities than at any time in its previous history. The Spanish capital, as already noted, was, at this time, little more than a glorified village compared with the other capitals of Europe. There was only one hotel, the Hotel de Paris in the Puerta del Sol. There was virtually nowhere for all the foreign guests to stay except in the houses of the nobility all over the city. Etiquette demanded that, in order to give pride of place to the bridal pair, no other crowned head should attend the ceremonies. This was convenient from the British point of view since it had already been deemed inappropriate that King Edward should attend for religious reasons. He was represented by his son and daughter-in-law, the Prince and Princess of Wales, at whose own wedding Ena had been a bridesmaid. Other foreign royalty were similarly represented, mostly by heirs to their respective thrones. From Vienna came the Archduke Ferdinand; from Rome, the Duke of Aosta; from Brussels, the Count of Flanders, later the brave and popular King Albert of the Belgians; and from Berlin, the German Emperor's brother, Prince Henry of Prussia. 'Like so many institutions in the course of history monarchical Europe made its bravest show in the last years of its existence.'[1] Envoys came also from the Vatican and the Sublime Porte, from Sweden and Siam, from Persia and Peru. All such visiting princes had been present, with the Knights of the Golden Fleece, at El Pardo to witness the King sign the marriage contract. Now they prepared to join the great procession of coaches to Madrid's church of San Jeronimo. This had been chosen by the King partly because of its associations with Spain in its 'golden century'. The church in question, otherwise of minor importance, stands on the site of a very famous old Gothic church, a few traces of which still remain. A more practical reason for the choice was that Alfonso wanted as many people as possible in Madrid to observe how happy he was and how beautiful was his bride when seen in real life.

Hence the choice of a church so far from the Palace. The planned route between the two would enable practically everyone in the capital to have a close-up view of the royal couple. It would take in a large number of streets such as the then new, broad and imposing thoroughfares of the Paseo del Prado, Calle de Alfonso XII and the Calle de Alcalá, as well as the old Gran Via. And when the wedding was all over the procession would make the second stage of its journey along the old and narrow Calle Mayor, Madrid's ancient 'high street' linking its central plaza, the Puerta del Sol, with the approaches to the Royal Palace. The total length of this route was about four miles, marking out as it did a wide circle within the central area of the city.

While the bride was engrossed in the process of getting dressed, a young man with a trim beard and neatly manicured hands, dressed all in black, was presenting his press ticket at the church of San Jeronimo. His name was Mateo Morral. He had procured the ticket the night before from an American journalist who found that he had been directed to another part of the church. The ticket turned out to be valueless and Morral was refused admission. But the last-minute change of seating arrangements gave rise to much uneasiness. It was symptomatic of the haphazard preparations that had been going on in anticipation of the great day. Court and government officials in Madrid had never had to cope with anything on quite such an enormous scale before. The casualness of the arrangements was remarked on by many of the English visitors, some of whom felt that their security was at risk. They had noticed for several days how freely the crowds had been moving about, jostling the cars of foreign royal visitors, and how unsuccessful the police seemed to be in carrying out such minimal security regulations as had been decreed. Among these had been a prohibition against the throwing down of bouquets on the royal procession. This, however, was an old established and popular custom and no one expected the prohibition to be taken seriously or properly enforced.

One of those to be surprised about the casualness of the pre-nuptial preparations and precautions was another of Edward VII's nieces, Princess Alice. She gave an account of that day's events to this author no less than seventy-four years later but with as much clarity as if it had all happened the week before. Two years before Ena's wedding she had married Prince Alexander of Teck, later Earl of Athlone. On the morning of the Spanish royal wedding day she happened to arrive early at the Royal Palace with her husband to join the other guests to be taken to the church. This was just before nine o'clock in the morning. The King had got back from El Pardo and had already changed into the Captain-General's uniform in which he was to be married. As soon as he saw Princess Alice he came over to talk to her. He seemed to her to be surprisingly relaxed and nonchalant despite the portents and warnings that had been making their appearance, to say nothing of the several attempts already made on the King's life. A few days before the marriage was due to take place some words had been carved with a knife on one of the trees in Madrid's Retiro Park. The words were 'Alfonso XIII will die on his wedding day.' And on the morning of the wedding itself a warning was received at the Palace from a worried couple who said that their son intended to kill the King that day. The Tecks heard of this threat from Alfonso himself who told them of it quite casually.

They wondered, between themselves, if the King's apparent nonchalance was a form of bravado to conceal his nervousness. It seemed more like a form of foolhardiness bordering on dangerous irresponsibility. The thought was still preoccupying them as they entered the church. They were immediately struck by the building's strange narrowness and by the fact that there were no aisles. They could not throw off a clammy feeling of claustrophobia accompanied by the realization that if anyone were to explode a bomb inside a church such as this, all present would almost certainly be entombed with little hope of escape. They were naturally unaware that this was exactly what would have happened had Mateo Morral been able to get into the church an hour or so earlier. The circumstances resulting in his being refused admission have been explained in some detail by the principal person affected by the last minute change of seating arrangements.

This was Princess Maria del Pilar, the fifteen-year-old cousin of King Alfonso. It had originally been planned, as she was to recount,[2] that she should take her place officially in the body of the church with other members of the royal family. But a question had arisen as to where the infant heir apparent to the throne was to sit. This was the four-year-old Infante Alfonso Maria, son of the King's eldest sister, Mercedes, wife of Don Carlos of Bourbon-Sicilies. The boy, styled for the time being Prince of Asturias, would continue to be heir to the Spanish throne until Alfonso XIII had a son. A last minute decision was made that he was too young to sit in the main part of the church as he was certain to get restless during a long ceremony. Pilar's mother, the Infanta Paz, suggested that one of the tribunes overlooking the nave, previously reserved for a section of the Press, should be taken over to accommodate Prince Alfonso, and that her daughter, Pilar, should sit with him to keep him as quiet as possible. The ticket Morral had obtained was for the very tribune in question. The eleventh hour switch, claims Princess Pilar, 'by saving the life of everyone in the church, prevented an appalling disaster unexampled in history.'

Meanwhile the long line of carriages began, from nine o'clock onwards, to wend its way from the Royal Palace toward the San Jeronimo. It presented a scene of pageantry such as had never been seen since in Spain and will never be seen again. The royal stables were famous for carriages which were individual works of art and supreme craftsmanship. Among them were the ebony coach made at the end of the seventeenth century; the tortoiseshell coach, also seventeenth-century; and the gilt state coach made a hundred years later. A separate procession, centred on the bride, formed up at the Marine Ministry building. Princess Ena, Princess Beatrice and the Queen Mother travelled together in the very fine early nineteenth-century mahogany state coach. There was also a coach which, on this magnificent but fateful day, was to play an unexpectedly important part in the proceedings. This was the state coach, relatively plain except for its gold panels, which served as the 'carriage of respect'. This is the carriage which is always kept empty and takes its place in the procession immediately in front of the coach of the King.

Finally, and most magnificent of all, there was the Crown coach, surmounted by two golden globes supporting the crown and emblazoned with the arms of Spain and Naples. The latter was the native country of the wife of Ferdinand VII, the coach's first user. It was this coach which took the King to the church and was intended to bring the newly married couple back for the reception at the Palace. Scarcely less impressive than the King's own coaches were those of the nobility, particularly such rich and powerful grandees as the Dukes of Medinaceli, Alba, Arion, Fernan-Nuñez, Hijar, and many others.

The King was the last to leave the Royal Palace and was accompanied by the infant Prince of Asturias and his father, Alfonso's brother-in-law, the Infante Carlos. The bride's procession had been due to join up with the main one near the Chamber of Deputies, that is not far from the Church. The bride, however, was delayed and the King arrived at the church some time before the Princess. Not knowing why she had been held up, Alfonso was visibly nervous as he waited at the altar. The time now was about half-past ten. All the nonchalance observed in the King a short time earlier by Princess Alice had suddenly disappeared. For all his dashing demeanour and superficial urbanity, Alfonso was still a boy at heart, and often a very frightened one. He usually managed to hide his fear. But when really nervous, as on the platform at Irun awaiting Ena's arrival a few days earlier, he could never conceal the fact. He could not do so now as he waited inside the church. To be ignorant of the reason for the lateness of the bride's procession was an agony. He had no way of knowing that the Prime Minister, Moret, had been half an hour late in arriving at the Marine Ministry, from where he was to escort the bride to the church.

To Alfonso the delay seemed interminable and each minute excruciatingly long. He had not told Ena about the threats against his and possibly her life, those threats which he had tried to laugh off earlier in the day. One of the anonymous messages he had received had actually been accompanied by a picture of Morral and said that an attempt was going to be made to prevent the marriage occurring or of killing the King and the bride. After more minutes of waiting he called to his side one of the attendant grandees, the Marquis of Benalua, to find out what was delaying the other procession. For by now the King was afraid that an attempt had already been made on Ena's life. The Queen Mother had received the same anonymous message and before leaving her, earlier that morning, Alfonso had said to her in urgent tones, 'Protect my fiancée. Protect her!' To this his mother had replied 'I promise.'[3]

The period of waiting at the altar was thus a long and terrible one for the King Alfonso, who hated to show his fear. In the ancient church of San Jeronimo 'amid the tapestries, the banks of flowers, and the perfumed denseness enriched by the coloured sunlight that pierced the stained-glass window',[4] he seemed for the moment a lonely and forlorn figure. Intense was his relief when he heard the British national anthem being struck up. This was the prearranged signal for the arrival of the bride.

Princess Ena, walking under a glittering baldachino, carried a wreath of orange blossom. Perhaps Alfonso was reminded of their conversation in the gardens of the Villa Mouriscot. Ena looked radiant, even if slightly pale, and could be seen to be clasping the Queen Mother's hand very tightly in her own left hand. The salutations of the foreign Princes, Ambassadors and other dignitaries were accompanied by a murmur of admiration for the bride's beauty. The couple had barely taken their places on the chairs prepared for them when the King, as a reaction to his relief from the pent-up fears of the last half hour, impulsively bounded out of his place and passing behind his bride's chair, went over to his mother and, bowing low, kissed her hand. Ena, taking her cue from Alfonso, went over to embrace her own mother which brought tears to Princess Beatrice's eyes. She knew that after this marriage nothing would ever be the same and that, while she herself had never had any married life independently of her mother, her daughter would now be lost to her almost completely.

The religious ceremony then began. It was due to last for three hours. The Primate of All Spain, Cardinal Sancha, Archbishop of Toledo, sumptuously vested in pontifical robes, handed his crozier to the Master of Ceremonies and bade the royal couple to declare if there be any impediment to their marriage. He then, after they had exchanged the nuptial promises whereby they conferred on each other the Christian sacrament of marriage, pronounced them man and wife. As Ena joined her hand in Alfonso's her lips trembled. She turned toward her mother who was openly in tears by now as she returned the loving look of the new Queen of Spain. In her daughter's face Princess Beatrice could read exhaustion as well as deep emotion. But there was no time to be tired. The day was not yet half over. The procession back to the Royal Palace would take an hour. The route was packed at every point with crowds impatient to get as close as possible to their King and his new Queen. Princess Alice of Teck was in the first carriage to leave the church. She and her husband were accompanied by Princess Frederica of Hanover, Ena's hostess during the courting days at Mouriscot. It was now just after two in the afternoon. The sun was still shining brilliantly and Princess Alice had never heard such cheering before in her life. It was like great breakers crashing one after another on the shores of an ocean. But the Princess was troubled by the restless unruliness of the crowds. There seemed to her to be little or no supervision of their movements. No one, as expected, was paying any heed to

The wedding ceremony

the prohibition against the throwing of flowers. Bouquets, recalled Princess Alice, bounced on top of their carriage and she remarked to Princess Frederica how potentially dangerous it all was.

Ena was extremely nervous but outwardly maintained an expression of almost exaggerated calm. The royal carriage was the very last one in the long procession. It was separated from those in front by the empty carriage of respect. The procession was soon heading for the heart of Madrid, the Puerta del Sol. This is a semi-circular open space, the centre of the city in every sense. It is the Spanish capital's Piccadilly Circus or Times Square on a smaller and more sedate scale. The crowds at this point were at their densest and the cheering so loud that those inside the carriages could not hear each other speak. Madrid was letting itself go in a manner few, if any, present on that day could ever remember. It was now about twenty to three and the homeward journey was nearing its completion. The line of glistening coaches had only one more street to pass along before making its final sweep into the courtyard of the Royal Palace. This street was the Calle Mayor, the principal thoroughfare of old Madrid. Long and straight, it is something like the Via Condotti in Rome or a narrower version of London's Bond Street.

The pavements on each side were jammed with excited men, women and children, cheering wildly and at certain points pressing dangerously near to the carriages which only just had room to pass. The height of the houses and narrowness of the street intensified the noise of the cheering and higher up, to left and right, the numerous balconies, like boxes at the opera, were crammed with shouting spectators. The cascade of flowers was now reaching a crescendo. The people on the balconies had for the most part been in the houses since early morning. Many had arranged parties and all seemed in the highest of spirits. Now, at long last, their pent-up emotions broke loose.

Some of the English onlookers, however, were, like Princess Alice, getting distinctly uneasy. They were unused to such unruly scenes on royal occasions. One of them was Miss Minnie Cochrane, Princess Beatrice's lady-in-waiting. She was riding with Lord William Cecil in a carriage not far up the line from the royal one. As soon as they entered the Calle Mayor her attention was attracted to the balconies bulging with frenzied viewers. But quite soon, as she said afterwards, 'I noticed one occupied by one man dressed all in black. At the time I thought it curious that he should have a balcony all to himself . . .'[5] The man was Mateo Morral. After being turned away from the church of San Jeronimo that morning he had made his way back to 88 Calle

Mayor where he had been staying for several days. Number 88 was a lodging house and Morral's room—with a balcony over-looking the street—was on the third floor. There were many such lodging houses in the Calle Mayor of that day, most of them rather drab and down at heel. The street as a whole looked nothing like what it does now. It then had few if any of the elegant and expensive shops for which it is famous today. There would have been little scope for such shops in a 'provincial' capital of only just over half a million inhabitants.

Earlier in the afternoon, Morral had been behaving in a strange fashion. Amazingly, however, he had attracted no adverse atten-tion from anyone, least of all such security men as were in the vicinity. He had, as it seemed, been amusing himself by 'throwing oranges into the street and marking the exact spot where they fell. A silly sort of game apparently; perhaps he had nothing better to do.'[6] In fact of course he was calculating how long it took for an object thrown from as high as the third floor to reach the ground. To hit a moving target would call for split-second timing. (What Morral's tactics would have been had he gained admission to the church is a mystery that died with the man.)

Just opposite 88 Calle Major is the little church of Santa Maria. As he drew almost level with this church the royal coachman noticed the carriages in front slowing up. He was forced to rein in his own eight horses. Such an occurrence was very unusual. It was customary for the royal carriage to keep moving at all times if possible. Miss Cochrane had noticed, looking back every now and then, that while almost all the other coaches had had to draw up for a second or two periodically, the royal carriage had been advancing steadily forward ever since leaving the church. The narrowness of the very crowded Calle Mayor had, however, delayed the front carriages somewhat. The proper distance between them and the King's coach had become difficult to maintain. The King was nevertheless unperturbed by the momentary hesitation. He took the opportunity of pointing out to his bride of an hour the little church on his side of the street. Ena leaned over to her left, across the King, and bent down slightly to get a look at the church. This movement, distancing her slightly from the window on her right, probably saved her from injury or disfigurement. Just as the King was beginning to talk about the church on the left hand side of the street, the man in black made his move from the balcony opposite. He too had flowers to throw. Suddenly there was a deafening explosion. Within seconds the royal carriage was hidden in smoke and from all sides there were shrieks and moans from the many who had been wounded. A bomb, wrapped in a bouquet of flowers, had been hurled from the third-floor balcony of number 88. The man throwing it had had plenty of opportunity, through his experiments with the oranges, of seeing how long such a missile would take to reach the street. Not expecting the royal carriage to stop, however, he had been caught off guard and thrown his bouquet a couple of seconds too soon. The bouquet landed just ahead of the carriage's front wheels between the rear flanks of the last pair of horses.

Ena has recounted[7] the exact conversation she and the King had been having just before their coach reached this point. The King had still not told her anything about the threats against their lives. But up until that moment he had continued to be very worried. Now, however, almost the whole of the homeward route had been safely covered. Within minutes they would be back at the Palace. Suddenly Alfonso had become visibly more relaxed. He had turned and said to Ena in French—which was still their common language—'I had forbidden the throwing of flowers. But now we are out of danger.' The Queen was about to ask 'What danger?' But it was just at that moment that the coachman unexpectedly began to rein in his team of horses. Moments later all was total confusion.

The royal pair could not at first take in exactly what had happened. For a fleeting instant they thought that the loud report might be the first salvo of the royal salute due to be sounded at about this time. But within no time at all their carriage began filling with smoke. They now realized what had happened. The

King took Ena's head in his hands and kissed her saying 'Are you hurt?' 'No, no. I'm not hurt, I swear it,' she replied. The King then said 'It's a bomb,' to which Ena replied with petrified calmness: 'So I thought. But it does not matter; I will show you that I know how to be a Queen.'[8]

A splinter from the bomb had struck the King on the breast and Ena noticed that her dress, whose long train she had piled up on the seat in front of them, was covered with blood. But the blood was not Alfonso's as the splinter had struck a medal pinned to his tunic and had done no harm. Nor was it her own blood. It was that of a guardsman riding along on the right side of the carriage, shoulder high to the window. He had been decapitated by the explosion and his blood had splashed through the shattered window. Seconds earlier Ena's face had been but a few inches from this window. She had avoided almost certain injury by leaning over to her left to look at the church of Santa Maria.

By now there was panic on all sides. Heart-rending were the moans and shrieks of the wounded. The King tore open the left-hand door of the carriage and, shouting from the footboard, tried to calm the crowd. 'It's nothing,' he cried. 'There's nothing to be frightened about. We are unhurt.' But he did not yet know the extent of the carnage. The royal carriage suddenly shot forward again as the terrified horses reared in the air completely out of control. Just then a figure appeared through the stench and swirl of the smoke. It was the King's Master of Horse, the Count of Fuenteblanca. He told his royal master that at least one of the horses had been killed by the blast and that it was impossible for them to proceed in that coach. The King thereupon ordered the carriage of respect to be made ready and that Princess Beatrice and the Queen Mother be informed that they were unhurt. The King then climbed down from the coach and helped his wife to descend. It was then that she noticed not only that her wedding gown was stained with blood but also that her white satin slippers had turned an ugly purple. There was blood everywhere and some of the sights that met Ena's eyes as the smoke began to clear weᴿe imprinted on her mind all her life. But she could still only see a few feet ahead of her and had to grope her way round like a blind person. Though the King did his best to help her and whisper soothing words of comfort, she kept tripping over bodies. She felt nauseated and faint but was determined not to collapse. The roadway near the carriage was strewn with disembowelled men and horses. As she made her way to the other coach she had to step aside to avoid the headless body of a bugler. Not far away lay a civil guard, his legs severed and bleeding freely.

They stumbled toward the carriage of respect which was still hidden by smoke from all but the nearest onlookers. These did their best to raise a cheer and the King waved to announce that neither he nor his bride was hurt. But those further away could be heard crying 'Murder, murder! The King has been killed! The Queen is dead!' Officers shouted orders amidst mounting confusion. Severely wounded but still managing to smile, the Marquis of Sotomayor helped the royal pair into the other carriage. He then mounted guard as the King gave the order: 'Slowly, very slowly, to the Palace.' The Duke of Horrachuelos meanwhile flanked the carriage of respect on the other side. He kept his sword drawn and did not realize that his own face was covered with blood. Contradictory orders were still being issued as a detachment of infantry, with fixed bayonets, surrounded the slowly moving substitute royal carriage. Those in the next coach further up were asked to hurry on to the Palace to procure help and to spread word *en route* that the King and Queen were unhurt.

Inside the carriage of respect the King turned once more to his wife to make sure she was quite all right. Only now did they notice that her veil was badly singed. He lowered the blinds to shield her eyes from more scenes of devastation and then held both of her hands in his. He then said to her: 'My dear, my dear. Nothing has happened.' The remark was patently untrue. But Alfonso made it with a smile 'that went up to his eyes', and which Ena remembered vividly even in her old age.[9] Twenty minutes later they reached the Royal Palace. Many of the waiting courtiers were still in ignorance of exactly what had happened. Expecting to see the resplendent bridal carriage they were amazed to see the newly-weds stepping from a plain brown coach drawn not by the eight magnificent royal horses but by six very ordinary chestnuts. It was at this moment that Ena made her most supreme effort to behave as normally as possible. The strain of so doing somehow made onlookers more ill at ease than if, in true Spanish style, she had had to be carried screaming hysterically from the carriage of respect. This would have enabled steam to be let off on every side to the intense relief of all. The Queen's petrified agony of self-restraint, on the other hand, only served to increase the general tension. In her own mind, however, she felt that this was the only way she could prove herself 'worthy of my husband'.

Ena could not, meanwhile, get certain memories out of her head, particularly the sight of the man with no legs. She and the King retired briefly from public view after their initial return to the Palace. 'Both Alfonso and Ena broke down,' according to the Prince of Wales.[10] 'Of course the bomb was thrown by an anarchist,' the Prince added. 'The man is supposed to be a Spaniard and of course they let him escape. I believe the Spanish police and detectives are about the worst in the world. No precautions whatever had been taken. They are most happy-go-lucky here.' A few days later, moreover, the British Ambassador, Sir Maurice de Bunsen, wrote a letter to *The Times* saying 'How glad I am that it so happened that I and my staff were, by a fluke, at hand. In two minutes we got up to the royal carriage—being the first to reach it from outside.' He nevertheless paid handsome tribute to the 'Spanish troops who lined the street at the point where the bomb exploded and to the presence of mind of the officials who brought round the spare State carriage and reorganized the procession . . . I was struck by the admirable manner in which all concerned did their duty.'[11] At the same time, great harm was done abroad to Spanish prestige and the whole lamentable episode confirmed Edward VII's worst fears about the backwardness and hopelessness of Spain at the time.

Alfonso and Ena meanwhile had no choice but to recover their inner self-possession as best they could. The King made anxious enquiries about the amount of dead and wounded. He was told that the number of those killed and the full extent of the injuries could not yet be ascertained for certain. In fact over 100 had been wounded, 24 mortally. Those killed included the Marchioness of Torlosa and her niece who had been standing on the balcony immediately under that from which the bomb had been thrown. Ena's calmness during the elaborate but subdued 'wedding breakfast' that followed was due largely to her instinctively having set up a shutter in her mind against the reality of all that had just happened. 'It has been said that so much was she in control of herself that, during tea afterwards at the Palace, she was able to show dismay that her husband dipped his bread and butter into his cup. "Mon ami," she exclaimed, "tu tremps ta tartine dans ton thé!" '[12]

Stories of this kind, when passed around by courtiers and their gossiping wives, did little to help the Queen in her early efforts to establish a home and a place for herself in her adopted country. Ironically, however, as Ena herself was to confess years later, amidst the tragedy and horror of that afternoon and evening, she did not forget something which might not have occurred to others. It seemed a trivial matter indeed and something unlikely to take up much thought on a day highlighted by so near a brush with death. But Ena was thinking not only of the dead and wounded but also of something quite different. She was pondering on the fact that she was probably the only bride in the world to have no wedding photograph.[13] Later on, for similar reasons, the Spaniards came to look upon their new Queen as being, in certain respects, rather superficial. A similar judgement was arrived at by those who knew the Queen in her declining years and had opportunities to see and meet her in many different circumstances. Tragedy went off her like water off a duck's back as one

The wedding reception

close acquaintance said of the Queen. Had it not been for this facility—this 'incredible resilience' Princess Alice called it—she would surely have gone under in the sea of sadnesses through which much of her life had to pass.

In her own way—distinctly detached though it admittedly was—she was as sympathetic as was her husband toward the sufferings of the innocent on the day of her wedding. But there was a sense in which her reactions to the events were almost akin to those of a child. In this respect she responded to the natural

consequences of her closeted upbringing and to the new atmosphere now prevalent around her. She was not for example the
only one who seemingly recovered high spirits when the time
came for the evening festivities at the end of the wedding day.
Scores of special representatives sat down to the magnificent
banquet that had been prepared at the Palace. The Press was not
privy to this private gathering and had to be content with a
description of the externals of the evening. The chief object of
their attention was the spectacular fireworks display put on
outside the Palace. But all its brightness, according to one
newspaper report, 'failed to lift the gloom that had fallen on
the community as a result of the terrible events of the wedding
day.'[14]

Inside the Palace, however, it was clear that 'everyone was only
too glad to fasten on any incident that would relieve a tension that
was to some extent unavoidable.'[15] This was the description of the
fifteen-year-old Princess Pilar who was to sit between an Arab
and a Chinaman neither of whom spoke a word of any language
she knew. The antics of this trio broke the ice for everyone else
present. The Chinese envoy, clad in gorgeous robes, was very
short-sighted and was wandering round the long table peering at
name cards. Princess Pilar, already at her place, got up and ran
after him. Tapping him on the shoulder with his name card and
making him read it she led him to his proper seat. The King, who
missed nothing on such occasions and loved to play the fool
himself, laughed heartily. The young Princess thereafter kept up
an animated conversation with her two neighbours by means of
sign language. This made them laugh so much that a diamond
bow in the Princess's hair fell into the soup. Her gallant Arab
neighbour immediately fished it out and, after sucking it clean,
dipped it into his glass, wiped it with his napkin and handed it
back to the Princess with a profound obeisance. 'After this all
pretence of ceremonial behaviour was frankly abandoned.'[16] At a
later stage during the banquet one of the guests asked the King if
he had remembered that this 'happy and triumphant day' was the

first anniversary of an attempt made on his life in Paris. The King replied with much good humour, 'Yes, I remember. But the bomb has grown!' Such, by now, was the atmosphere at Court despite the horrendous happenings of a few hours earlier.

The Madrid crowds in the meantime were intent on 'personalizing' the whole affair round the King and Queen. It presented an opportunity for exercising their lungs at a romantic but dramatic moment and also to see more closely what their new Queen was really like. Early next morning a large concourse of people were outside the Palace clamorously demanding to get a glimpse of the royal couple. Ena, still resting after her traumatic seventeen-hour day, eventually appeared beside her husband on the balcony. But she did so without changing out of her night attire. According to one interpretation 'Queen Ena's spontaneous girlish action in coming out to the people just as she was, introduced that touch of humanness and informality so dear to Spanish hearts.'[17] Not all Spanish hearts, however, were touched by such behaviour. Those of the courtiers and their censorious aristocratic wives were in no way melted by the young Queen's action. Could one imagine the ever dignified Queen Mother acting in such a way? Perish the thought! But these ladies and gentlemen had worse shocks in store for them later on. For the time being their displeasure was compounded by envy that the beautiful young English Queen had, at least for the moment, made a favourable impression on so many of Madrid's ordinary citizens.

Later in the day she and the King drove out in an open carriage through the city's streets with no attendants or escort of any kind. Such action aroused frantic enthusiasm with the populace not only in Madrid but everywhere that the story about them was spread. And this meant to all parts of Spain. The students cheered loudest of all for it was they who had most to hope from the rumoured intention of Queen Ena to 'liberalize' many things in their woefully backward country. This would be a distinct setback for those, at Court and elsewhere, who had a vested interest in backwardness. Such people thus noted with satisfaction that the Queen's drives through Madrid on the morrow of the bomb attempt were not an unqualified success. For there was something artificial in Ena's wave; something tortuously forced about her smile; something akin to fear in her eyes. Who, it may be said, could blame her after such an experience? Had she been Spanish, however, she might, without necessarily deserving it, have received more sympathy. She might, for example, have languished in shock for several days after the wedding and then made a series of spectacular and exuberant appearances, flashing a radiant smile in every direction, blowing kisses and hugging those who pressed close to the car. When the crowds pressed close to Ena, on the other hand, she visibly shrank back. She thus failed to gain, then or ever, a deep rapport with the Spanish masses. Had it not been for the bomb all might well have been different. But the bomb produced a cloud over her life in Spain which was never to disperse, a shock to her inner being from which she never fully recovered.

Ena, moreover, unlike Spanish women, was no good at plumbing the depths of melancholy one minute and then, at the next, rising to dizzy heights of exuberance and joy. She was a victim of her self and her upbringing. Before going to sleep at the end of her long, seemingly interminable wedding day, she looked back on its events as having posed, within an hour or so of her becoming a Queen, a supreme test for one of those maxims her grandmother had never ceased to instil into her: 'Young woman, when one is born a Princess, one cannot behave like others.' As her thoughts went back to Queen Victoria, however, she suddenly thought of something else as well. She thought of the jewellery which she had always so wistfully coveted. It was yet another strange thought to have on that night of all nights in her life. But think it she did. The thought was tempered by the realization that beautiful jewellery—always, as she had supposed, the rightful prize of monarchy—had sometimes to be won through blood and tears. That night she remembered thinking[18] that she had indeed earned a diadem: 'But it was not enough to rid me of my headache.'

All in all 'such a day was unlikely to inaugurate a peaceful reign or a happy marriage. For Queen Ena, it inaugurated neither.'[19]

[6]

Queen and People

COUNT ROMANONES, probably the greatest politician of the Alfonsist era, was to write that at the time of the King's marriage 'the organization of the police was very deficient.'[1] But the confusion surrounding the so-called 'security' arrangements before the wedding was as nothing compared to the chaos that followed the bomb outrage. Foreign papers carried more detailed reports than did Spanish ones of the sequence of events but their datelines were often qualified by the phrase 'delayed by the Censor'. 'Awe pervades Madrid' was a characteristic sort of headline under which would appear descriptions of behaviour untypical of Spaniards. They were subdued, irritable and nervous in the aftermath of the bomb attack. And with the dying down of the cheers and rejoicing which greeted the royal couple the day after the wedding a different sort of emotion became discernible among the general public. They were naturally looking for a scapegoat. There was widespread outrage that anyone should have dared to try to kill their King. Why should anyone wish to do such a thing? Why, asked some—forgetting all about long-standing political troubles—if not because he had taken a British wife who, despite the cheers for her prettiness, clearly still had a long way to go before winning Spanish hearts?

In the flurry of premature arrests during the first wave of police panic an Englishman was taken into custody. He was Robert Hamilton, a Bank of England clerk who was holidaying in Spain and had come to Madrid to see the wedding. After an exchange of telegrams with London the British Embassy in Madrid was convinced that suspicions against Hamilton were baseless. The insistence of the Spanish authorities on continuing to hold him on the flimsiest of pretexts awoke strong British resentment. But it had another ironical result. As one paper at the time put it[2] 'It has also reawakened the animosity of the ignorant Spanish rabble against the British' on the grounds that Queen Ena's coming to Madrid 'was the cause of the attempt on the King's life.' Actually it was not only the 'ignorant rabble' who believed this. Others higher up in the social scale held similar beliefs even if they did not express themselves on the subject so openly or crudely. Much was made—in a manner as unfavourable as possible to the Queen—of Ena's reaction to the moment of danger and its immediate aftermath. This, as already mentioned, was something unfamiliar to Spaniards. Her extreme calm seemed unnatural to the point almost of repugnance to onlookers and those who, within minutes, certainly within hours, were given a graphic description of how the royal couple reacted to the attempt on their lives. The King, not unnaturally, received high praise for his unhesitating resourcefulness and ready courage. The Queen of one hour, because her courage took a more stolid form, began from that moment to gain a reputation for frigidity. She was suspected of being all the things most Spaniards least admired: cold, aloof, insensitive, Anglo-Saxon, Protestant at heart and (in upper-class eyes) 'liberal'. Even the buoyant and optimistic King sensed, within hours of the bomb attack, that somehow everything had been changed in the twinkling of an eye.

This fact was particularly evident to one of the distinguished guests at the wedding reception. He was Mr Frederick W. Whitridge, the special American Ambassador for the occasion. He and his suite 'had the opportunity for a brief conversation with King Alfonso during the reception.'[3] When the topic of the bomb attack came up the King shrugged his shoulders and said 'Yes, fortunately it was unsuccessful, but it will come again. It may be any time, perhaps tomorrow, perhaps within a month, perhaps within a year, but it will come.' The face of the King, according to the same report, wore a look of resignation as he gave this forecast of the future. Although he had borne himself with signal courage throughout the terrible experience, the courtiers had witnessed 'a trying scene as King Alfonso and Queen Victoria* hurried within the castle after the attempt was made to assassinate them. For the moment Alfonso's nerves were completely unstrung and, turning to Queen Victoria, her dress spattered with blood, he exclaimed, "Why did I bring you to this country? It was wrong. You never should have come here."' Within a cruelly short time, in other words, the Queen had undergone a fundamental change deep inside herself. She was never quite the same again and her subjects were aware of the fact. As one author put it, 'The shock went deep into her soul and she naturally fears a repetition of the horror when she is in the city.'[4]

These words were written not long after the events in question, the author adding, 'The people, therefore, are a little disappointed at their greetings not meeting with the quick response of the first days in her new land.' As Spaniards would do anything for a smile, and love to see happiness, this inborn terror, begotten of the tragedy of her wedding-morn, would form a barrier between the English Queen and her people, were they not reminded of the source of the set expression on her face.'[5] Even that reminder, however, was not to be enough as time went on. It did not take much for discerning Spaniards to see that the English consort of their quintessentially Spanish King would probably never become 'one of them'. Even her most enthusiastic, not to say sycophantic, of biographers[6] is hard put to find anything very stirring to say about his heroine's appearance among her people on the morning after the wedding. The Queen was unlikely ever again to have such a golden opportunity of establishing herself firmly in Spanish hearts. Unfortunately she failed her first test

* After her marriage, Ena was referred to by many Spaniards as Queen Victoria or Queen Victoria Eugenia.

rather badly. The enthusiasm of the crowd as the royal car edged its way through the density of its ranks made even the demonstrativeness of the day before seem restrained by comparison. For by now the temperature of the public had reached fever pitch. There was a wild, almost hysterical, desire to express intimacy and solidarity with the young and romantic royal couple who had escaped death on their nuptial day by a hairbreadth.

The car in which they were touring the city was an open one. Men, women and children fell over each other to get near it and, if possible, to touch or shake hands with the royal pair. The King eagerly lent forward to accept their rapturous gestures; the Queen shrank back in dismay. For him it was a moment of supreme triumph and delight; for her, one of profound distress and terror. In the Puerta del Sol the crowd was so dense that the driver had to come to a complete stop. The car was surrounded and practically submerged. The King held out his hand which was avidly seized and shaken over and over again. 'The Queen', as Graham so lamely comments, 'looked on, evidently moved by the scene.' But her natural terror in a crowd which, as in this case, seemed to her to be completely out of control, made her sit in the back of the car like a statue, the stricken look in her eyes belying her unavailing efforts to respond to the rapturous greeting of the uninhibited populace. No one at that moment could have foreseen that twenty-five years later the Queen would be a more popular figure than the King.

Despite her initial defeat, Ena managed, by very slow stages, to improve her position and regain her popularity. There were, after all, numerous opportunities for this decorative young woman, with whom the still popular King was so obviously in love, to capture the hearts of those around her. On her first appearance in the great ballroom at Madrid's Royal Palace a few days before the wedding a positive gasp had escaped from the glittering, sophisticated and usually rather cynical collection of distinguished guests. 'Qué guapa!' 'How handsome!'—was the expression that rippled through their midst with a genuinely admiring intake of breath. The Princess's translucent skin and corn-coloured hair presented a spectacle of royal beauty so different from that which was typically Spanish that all were lost in unfeigned admiration. Her height, bearing and obviously radiant health all added to the favourable impression. All she had to do was to prove herself as time went on to be a truly 'Spanish Queen'.

On the day after the wedding the Court was once more assembled at the Palace for Alfonso and Ena to hold their first General Reception as King and Queen. Such occasions were meat and drink to Spain's courtiers whose whole, otherwise empty, lives centred and depended on events at the Palace. It mattered to them not in the least that it was a Palace totally cut off from the daily life of ordinary Spaniards as the King's aunt, the Infanta Eulalia, never ceased to point out. And so, on the morrow of the wedding, Queen Victoria Eugenia, as she was henceforth to be officially known in Spain, was officially 'introduced' by Alfonso to the notabilities of his kingdom. She had rested after the drive through the excited capital that morning and had tried to conceal from her husband the extent to which this had proved a terrifying and exhausting ordeal. Now, in the apartment of the Palace known as the Camera al Gobierno, their Majesties received the Spanish grandees, the Ladies of Honour, the Knights of the Golden Fleece, the Cardinals and other high ranking church-men, and the Captains-General. The latter were the local military commanders and were men of considerable power and influence. When this brief reception was over, the King and Queen moved into the vast and imposing throne room dominated by a ceiling ablaze with the frescoes of Tintoretto. Alfonso was himself wearing the uniform of a Captain-General, while Ena wore white satin trimmed with Alençon lace. Their respective suites stood behind the raised dais which bore the two thrones while the members of the Government were on the right. This was the first time that Ena had sat on the throne as Queen. Her love of jewellery was evident in the pride with which she wore her brilliant diamond-set crown. The lions of Castile were embroidered in gold in her red mantle which was bordered with the royal ermine.

In the course of his reply to the President of the Senate, General Lopez Dominguez, the King said that 'On this the first day when the Queen accompanies me in presenting myself to you, we both wish to offer you a testimony of the profound gratitude with which we receive your felicitations, and of the very high esteem in which we hold your assistance in raising this noble and beloved Spanish nation to the high position which it deserves.' These were brave words but unfortunately it soon became clear that 'Don Alfonso had greatly underestimated the harm which Morral's attempt upon his life had inflicted upon Spanish prestige abroad; because he dismissed such incidents as an occupational hazard there was no reason why foreigners should adopt the same attitude, and he was soon involved in a misunderstanding with his wife's formidable uncle, the King of England.'[7] The latter refused to return Alfonso's state visit and let it be known through Sir Maurice de Bunsen that a visit to Madrid was out of the question since the British Government was 'decidedly of the opinion that in taking this course His Majesty would be incurring considerable risks.'

This view was formed after Edward VII had heard his son's views of the scene in Madrid at the time of the wedding and was influenced by the fact that the murderer was still at large while his niece was driving about the Spanish capital in an open car totally unprotected from any possible repetition of a murder attempt. The suspected Englishman, Hamilton, turned out of course to be completely innocent. Despite British protests he was nevertheless held for questioning along with the dozen or so others rounded up by a dazed and panic-stricken police force. One of those held was a harmless fourteen-year-old boy. Hamilton was brought before a judge called Valle and interrogated for an hour before being released. Morral had meanwhile escaped quite easily from Madrid. After throwing the bomb he had calmly left 88 Calle Mayor by the back door and was soon on his way back to his native

Barcelona. A description of the wanted man, however, had meanwhile been circulated, though one policeman, stationed opposite, had asserted that there were two men on the balcony and not just one. The description of Morral's alleged but non-existent companion was one of the reasons for the confusion and the mistaken arrests. Finally, two days after the attempt, Morral, disguised as a workman was, by chance, recognized in the little town of Torrejon de Ardos, midway between Madrid and Alcalá. He has handed over to a guard but Morral drew a revolver and shot the man dead. Being immediately chased by a group of the town's inhabitants, Morral then shot himself through the heart. The body, having been identified by Señor Cuesta, the proprietor of the boarding house from which the bomb had been thrown, was returned to Madrid for burial. The corpse was vilified and cursed by as many of the public as could get near it, their fury being aroused by the fact, unusual even in the case of the worst of such outrages, that 24 people had been killed and over 80 wounded. Such murders had no place in the hearts of those ordinary Spaniards who did not know and had not seen their new Queen but had a strong instinctive feeling that her presence in their country would bring a welcome difference to their lives.

One of Ena's first really gruelling tasks was to attend the tremendously elaborate royal bullfight planned as the climax of the spectacles marking the post-nuptial festivities. Matters were not helped by the refusal of the official British delegation to attend owing to the repugnance among the British public for Spain's national sport. Thus the Prince and Princess of Wales and their suite, as well as Sir Maurice de Bunsen and his staff, were all conspicuous by their absence. The Queen, however, had no choice but to be present and she, at first, delighted the crowds with her beauty, enhanced by a dress gleaming with white lace and the roses entwined in her white mantilla. In those days bull-fighting was a far gorier pastime than it was to become later. Subsequent reforms, and mitigation of the sufferings inflicted on the unprotected horses, were largely due to the Queen's influence. This, her first 'corrida', was ironically a great disappointment to the regular spectators as many of the more blood-curdling features were omitted as a concession to the young English Queen. Brought up on horseback with an intense love of ponies she was horrified by what she saw. 'One maddened bull literally tore a horse to pieces under the railing of the royal box from which Queen Victoria looked down.'[8] The crowd roared their approval as eight bulls were dispatched, four of them by cavaliers on horseback chosen from among the first families of Spain with the Duke of Medinaceli, the Duke of Alba and the Marquis of Tovar as their patrons. The Queen was meant to echo the wild cheers of the onlookers. Her forced smile, betraying her dreadful feeling of inner sickness, was almost worse than nothing. It was the best she could do to witness the holocaust 'without emotion'. By not actually showing her disgust she felt she was doing her duty. Once again it was not enough. At the many bullfights the Queen was forced to witness in years to come she always brought special field glasses which, unknown to the other spectators, prevented her seeing what was actually happening.

Despite everything there were still two ways whereby the new Queen could win the hearts of her adopted subjects. One was to live up to the promise of her radiantly healthy looks by bearing her husband a succession of fine children, including several male heirs who were sound in mind and body. The other was, in gradual and subtle ways, to find a place in the hearts of those millions of ordinary Spaniards who, though largely illiterate, were intelligent and much more aware of what was going on around them than most of their 'superiors' suspected. The trauma of the childbearing side of Ena's life was a saga of its own.* The prior question of how far Ena in the early years managed to win over—or win back—ordinary Spanish hearts involves asking

---

* See below, Chapter 7.

'what kind of Spain' it was to which she had come. It was, first of all, a Spain where, as already seen, the same elitist oligarchy was enabled to remain in perpetual ascendancy behind the camouflage of counterfeit 'parliamentary' government. The intellectuals of the 'Generation of '98' gradually exposed such government as corrupt and unstable, and efficient only as a means of running the country in the interests of the privileged few. One of the greatest names among the intellectuals was that of Giner de los Rios, champion of an educational system which would be independent of Church and State. His establishment of the Independent Institution of Education 'marked Giner out as one of the great educators of all time.'[9]

Another giant—or rather giant-killer—was Joaquin Costa who, in the early years of the century, managed so to expose the evils of 'caciquismo' that the sham form of government which it made possible could not be expected to last much longer. Costa called for a 'surgeon of iron' who could cut out the cancerous growth and remake the country in the interest of those ordinary people who represented the real Spain. Unfortunately, however, no such surgeons came forward. In their stead came the anarchists, men imbued with the desperate logic that a form of government they conceived as totally corrupt was, by definition, irreformable. 'It was not a parliamentary regime with abuses—the abuses were the system itself.'[10] The only thing to do with such a system was to destroy it. The anarchists, whose aim this was, had been active in Spain ever since the restoration of the monarchy. They became famous for the spectacular acts of violence aimed at terrorizing political leaders and arousing the general public from its apathetic acceptance of a corrupt status quo. Such apathy was largely the result of the inhibiting, not to say numbing, effect of religion. For the people of Spain had always been very religious.

They were religious, however, in their own, peculiarly Spanish, way. Their instinctive piety by no means meant that they loved the Church as an institution. Indeed they had every reason to hate it as such. As Don José Castillejo put it, 'The Anarchists have destroyed many churches, but the clergy had first destroyed the Church.' The reason for this was the serious degeneration of the Church through the nineteenth century. Once the champion of the poor it had greatly changed in character as a result, ironically, of losing so much of its property in the anti clerical days following the French Revolution. The clergy and monks, cut off from the land, became alienated from the people and were forced to seek other methods of enrichment. From this arose their alliance with the wealthier classes. Only such an alliance, surviving into modern times, could account for the many cases of Europe's most naturally religious people being associated at various times, long before the Civil War, with the burning of churches and convents and other attacks against nuns and religious Orders.

Many Spaniards, especially working-class women, hoped that the new English Queen could rescue them from the various forms of injustice under which they staggered as a result of the clerical-upper class alliance. When Ena came to Spain, moreover, most Spaniards were still monarchist-minded. Conscription, before it came to be abused, had tended to consolidate the working classes behind a King who was still popular as head of the Army.[11] It was still remembered that in the 1870s it was the Army which had stood for liberty and the Republic against the hated alliance of Carlists and Ultramontanes. The latter were those who believed in a powerfully centralized Roman Catholic Church having, in each of its 'subject' countries a special mandate for the preservation of Christian 'law and order'. Such order was incompatible with 'liberalism', even of the milk-and-water, early twentieth-century, Spanish variety. According to the principal catechism in use in Spanish schools[12], liberalism taught that the State was independent of the Church and that it was therefore 'a most grievous sin against faith'. The Spanish Church in other words needed the State to do its work for it and to impose by the force of law an outward substitute for that inner loyalty which it had failed to evoke by persuasion and example. The answer to the question 'Is it a sin for a Catholic to read a liberal newspaper?' was 'He may read the Stock Exchange News.' The sin 'committed by him who votes for a Liberal candidate' was 'generally a mortal sin.' The Church, in alliance with its upper-class patrons, taught working people to conform to their 'proper place' in society. In practice this almost always meant domestic service. And yet it was the people rather than the clergy and the numerous, very wealthy, religious orders who were the true heirs of a sturdily independent, national Spanish Church, once proudly free of excessive outside influences, including those of Rome itself.

Naturally Ena could not be expected, overnight if ever, to take in such features about the world's most paradoxical and individualistic national region of Roman Catholicism. But it was in that very independence of Spain's humble believers, coupled with their deep distrust of most nuns and monks, that lay their strongest hopes of reaching the heart of their new Queen. And it was religion—not 'the Church' but religion in its true sense— which very nearly succeeded in forming a strong lasting bridge between Queen and people. Unfortunately there were too many with a vested interest in keeping Queen and people apart. The first three years of Ena's marriage were vital ones in this respect, climaxed as they were by the tragedies of 1909 which made that particular year an important turning point. Indirectly if not directly it is surprising to see how often Church and 'clericalist' influences are operative as between throne and people at this period. In 1909 the strongly authoritarian Antonio Maura was Prime Minister and he had decided to call up reservists in Catalonia to replace troops lost in Morocco while attempting to take possession of some newly acquired iron mines. By Socialists and Republicans 'the monarchy was denounced as a monster full of pus, sending the poor of Spain to defend Moroccan mining concessions; gatherings of mothers at railway stations, and counter demonstrations of Catholic ladies distributing crosses to the troops, inflamed tempers.'[13]

Subsequent rioting in Barcelona's 'tragic week' (1909) was brutally repressed with a 175 workmen being shot in the streets.

Executions followed including that of Francisco Ferrer, founder of the 'modern school' where anti-religious instruction was given. There was no evidence to show Ferrer's connection with the Barcelona rising and he was not living in the city at the time. But he had long been considered by many to have been the instigator of the attempt on the King's life on the wedding day since Morral had allegedly been his pupil and friend. An opportunity to get rid of him had long been sought. But the taking of it in 1909 turned out to be a major political blunder. The King realized that his Government had gone too far and perceived the need for some quick backtracking. Maura fell but his followers claimed that it was the events of 1909 which—by inducing the King to turn away from repression toward the safety valve of Romanones and the liberals—which 'marked the first step in a process of concession to the revolution from below which would end, in April 1931, with the overthrow of the monarchy.'[14] Alfonso, however, who revelled in the dangerous game of playing factions and parties off against one another, believed that he could, by such means, extricate himself and his country from any crisis which either might have to face.

Political events, however, are not everything. Spain's largely emotional desire to make up for the loss of Cuba and the Phillipines in the 1898 war with the United States had been responsible for the new colonial adventure in Morocco. It was to continue, punctuated with periodical disasters costing tens of thousands of Spanish lives, from 1906 until 1927. The suffering undergone by Spanish troops in North Africa was monumental. Queen Ena's initiatives in mitigating such suffering were, it seems, deliberately played down at the time—for political reasons. And in subsequent accounts her work in starting and organizing a proper Spanish Red Cross is often glossed over for fear of revealing too much of the undercurrents of jealousy, intrigue and even corruption that went on behind the scenes. One particular author[15], however, who was travelling through Spain in the early days of Ena's married life was making it his chief aim to find out what ordinary Spaniards thought about such people as churchmen, politicians, royalty and aristocrats who were naturally much closer to the levers of power than they were themselves. The result of his investigations was an important book whose object was 'to show what the people of Spain believe to be the truth about those who exercise authority over them, gathered from conversations with Spaniards of all classes, but principally working people in town and country.'

'The crucial question in Spain', as this author put it at the time[16], 'is the religious question . . . Not the belief or disbelief of the people in their religion, but the relations of the Church—i.e., that of the priests and, far more, of the Religious Orders—to the nation.' Hatred of the 'good fathers', he concluded, had become so widespread by 1909 that 'unless measures are taken to restrain the interference of the Church in public and private life, an explosion will occur.'[17] Such findings tallied with those of another author visiting Spain at about the same time. He wrote that 'the poor people who greeted the Queen with such loud acclamations on her arrival in Spain wonder if she knows that the liberal gifts bestowed on such festivals as the King's Saint's Day (23 January) to the Orphans of the Sacred Heart of Jesus, the Real Asocación de Beneficia Comiciliaria, etc., are devoted to the maintenance of the friars and nuns of these associations rather than to the benefit of the needy.'[18] What may seem, here, like a comparatively trivial example was in fact symptomatic of a long-standing abuse productive at that time of widespread grievance. While the Queen, moreover, was deliberately kept in ignorance of such things, the poor, for their part, were prevented from knowing what their new Queen was really like and what she was doing, particularly with regard to her highly successful War Fund. The clericalist party supporting Maura (in power from early 1907 to the end of 1909) preferred such ignorance to exist on both sides. It helped to direct unpopularity away from the government and on to the royal family which was considered by the clericalists (ever the principal allies of the ultra-conservative Carlists) to be dangerously 'liberal'. Ena was the principal victim of this campaign. But the truth could not be suppressed either wholly or for ever. When grateful Spaniards began to find out what the Queen was trying to do for them they took her to their hearts. Such people were mostly from the distinctly poorer classes. Her very success with them brought her further enmity from the ranks of the rich and well-connected.

The whispering campaign which meanwhile clouded the early part of Ena's reign had several fronts on which to operate. It was, on the one hand, put about 'by various Ultramontanes that "Queen Victoria (Ena) was on the worst terms with the Queen Mother who had never forgiven her for having been brought up a Protestant," and that "Maura had refused to let her go to England after the Barcelona affair because she was so miserable in Madrid that she declared she would never return to Spain if once she got back to her own country."'[19] Such stories were particularly insidious because of the grain of truth which made them all the more plausible. At the same time the Press was carefully censored during the last months of Maura's administration and 'everything that could tend to recall the King and Queen to the minds of the people and increase their popularity was suppressed.'[20] Most conspicuous of all, by their absence, were pictures and news items about the Queen in connection with her setting up of the War Fund. The Fund was taken up with enthusiasm all over the country but almost all the publicity went to the Marchioness of Squilache who was the Fund's honorary secretary. Pictures of the Queen in connection with the Fund were very scarce. Greatly encouraged, on the other hand, was the repeated publication of postcards of Don Jaime de Borbon, the Carlist Pretender. This was according to the wishes of the Church which, during this formative period, was maliciously unfavourable toward the former Protestant Princess who was now Spain's 'Catholic' Queen.

The attitude of the Church was, then, a paramount—if hitherto underestimated—element in bringing about Queen Ena's initial unpopularity in Spain. There were factors at work in bringing this about whose potency would seem incredible today. Churchmen were then so hidebound and jealous of their own preserves that they took strong exception to the very way in which the War Fund was launched by the Queen. For it was the first charitable appeal ever issued direct from the Court to the nation without the intervention of the Church. While ecclesiastics were offended by the principle involved in this there was soon a practical clash as well. At this time in Spain it cost as much as twenty-five pesetas, or about double a week's average wage, for people to get married in church. Many poor people therefore went through a civil ceremony only. The cost of this was one peseta. For this offence they were made to suffer, particularly when it came to elegibility for charity or other benefits. In the case of the War Fund it was at first stated that applicants for relief must bring certificates of birth, baptism, marriage, etc., from their parish priests. The Queen and her committee, however, decided to give this condition the widest possible interpretation. From an early stage in the war, relief was in practice given to any child whose father was at the front even if the mother did not bear his name. Abuses there may have been but the large amount of genuinely deserving cases could not otherwise have been dealt with. The Queen gained the lasting gratitude of many thousands of ordinary Spaniards. But she incurred the lasting enmity of a large part of the clergy.

Her chief immediate consolation lay in the immense success of the War Fund appeal. Even the poorest of the poor contributed to the Queen's War Fund, heavily pressed as they were by other financial strains. They were being crippled, for example, as the Queen eventually found out, by the 'consumo' or tax on food. This was a crushing burden on the really poor and drove many out of Spain altogether in despair. The religious orders meanwhile collected 'spare' bread from tradespeople threatening to tell their clients they were 'bad men' if they did not part with it. Many believed that such bread was distributed to the poor. In many cases, however, it was used by the priests' housekeepers* to be turned into 'pasteles' and 'dulces' for sale to the well-to-do. At the same time, and by ever increasing stages, the trading classes in general found it more and more difficult to compete with the cheaper goods and services, such as printing, chocolate-making, boot-making, needlework, and so forth, being carried out in the convents, which were immune from all taxes. Such traders, and they were very numerous, came to be among the most virulent opponents of the Church later on. Herein lay the ultimate cause for those atrocities committed against certain sections of the Church, especially during the Civil War, which were ascribed to 'reds' infiltrated or influenced from outside the country. No such infiltration or influence was necessary. The majority of the religious orders, male and female, had earned the deep hatred of the otherwise god-fearing masses many years earlier. The final outlet for such hatred was the advent of the Second Republic. But it is important to remember that such anti clericalism on the part of the Spanish populace was primarily economic in its origin. It would indeed have been surprising if a whole section of the people, whose livelihood had for years been systematically undermined, had not wished one day to exact revenge on those by whom they had been ruined. It was Ena's misfortune that she was unable to do more to mitigate the sufferings of those millions of ordinary Spaniards whom she never came truly to know and who never came truly to know her. Both she and they were the victims of a system.

'When I looked at the young Queen,' wrote one author soon after Ena's marriage, 'so tall, so elegant, and so alone in a foreign land, I felt how difficult it must be to fulfil her role to the satisfaction of all parties.'[21] This same author, noting the excitement caused by the announcement that the expected royal heir's layette was to be made entirely in Spain, called in at Madrid's best shop for babies' clothes. But she noticed that the garments were

---

* Known as *barraganas*.

not of as fine quality as she would have expected. The proprietor explained the reason: 'All the best things are made in the convents, and we have the second and third best. The Queen, I believe, meant to benefit the trade of Madrid, for she was so sweet and gracious when she called here, but the priests gave most of the work to the societies in which they were interested.' Such 'societies' or 'associations' were the religious orders most of which, technically speaking, were illegal. They stayed in being through a loophole in the law. By the 1851 Concordat with the Vatican only three orders were to be allowed in Spain, two of which were specified and one of which was to be left to the Pope to choose. As he never exercised his choice, every order that wished to establish itself did so with impunity. The King himself recognized the abuse and said, 'Yes, there are indeed far too many anti-clerical associations in Spain.'[22]

Education was the other big bone of contention and some feared that a liberal-minded young Queen from an 'advanced' Protestant country would put strange ideas into the heads of Spain's womenfolk in this regard. In a mountain village one day a Franciscan friar met someone he took to be a Frenchman.*[23] He thus felt he could talk freely on the evils that the King's marriage might bring to the country. The new Queen, he said, 'will do untold harm by trying to introduce her English ideas about the education of women. The women of Spain have quite as much education as is good for them. More would only do them harm.' Even had she wanted to, however, Ena would never have been able to make any appreciable difference to the educational system then in operation. Such criticism as she incurred within this context arose not from what she did but from what she was: a foreigner. This, and the fact that she had had to change her religion to become Queen of Spain, were the two biggest factors which she had to live down. That she never quite succeeded was

* In fact he was the Englishman, Rafael Shaw, by whom the incident is related.

something which she minded much less in later years and found her own way of dealing with.

The earliest years, however, were full of discouragements. For a year or more, for example, before the fall of the Maura administration in 1909, accounts of the charity and generosity displayed by the King, the Queen and even the royal family in general were growing rarer and rarer in the papers 'which had formerly supplied these little pieces of information to the many people who like thus to be brought into contact with the home life of their rulers.'[24] The omission was introduced gradually enough for people not to notice it at first. It was only when soldiers returning from the war began talking of the gifts sent out to them by the Queen that it became more generally realized that such actions on her part were being kept from the people. One of her principal achievements was to supply thousands of vests to be worn under uniforms. These were never mentioned at all in the Press. Yet a returning soldier said they must have numbered thousands for 'there seemed to be enough for all of us; at any rate, all I knew had them.'[25] It was thanks to such vests, he explained, that there were not many more fever patients when the torrential October rains fell on an army totally lacking proper winter clothing and adequate sleeping accommodation. For nights on a stretch 'men lay on soaked mattresses or blankets only, sunk in a bed of mud ... (but) the Queen's vests kept us warm in the middle, and that helped us to bear the wet and cold.'

Non-publication of such details was not due to lack of space in the papers nor to any ill will on the part of editors. The relevant facts were being withheld on orders from higher up, i.e. government and Church circles, even though full particulars were allowed of the generous gifts by commercial houses and private individuals. And there were long daily lists of the many subscribers to the War Fund. In the liberal papers this was referred to as 'The Patriotic Fund presided over by H.M. The Queen.' But the Conservative papers called it 'The Patriotic Fund under the Committee of Ladies.'

It may seem that too much is being made over a matter of a few vests. But the principle involved mattered deeply in a Spain which, socially, religiously and politically, was as unlike Ena's native England as almost anything could possibly have been. In England it would have seemed natural for the Queen to take an active part in work for the benefit and betterment of her subjects. In Spain Ena came up against a very different sort of attitude and found herself facing the implacable opposition not so much of the official Church as of that veritable army of women of a certain kind whose militancy was formidable. These were, for the most part, outwardly religiously, well-to-do and upper-class women who worked closely with the clergy. The arrangement was mutually advantageous. They were bountiful benefactors of the Church, particularly of their own pet religious orders, and, invariably dressed entirely in black, were the staple hard core of all weekday congregations for Mass, Benediction and other church services. They went regularly to confession, always to the same confessor, with whom they exchanged confidences and compared notes. They were powerful figures in their local parishes where they enjoyed such jobs as being 'wardrobe-keepers' for the 'santos'. The latter were statues of the saints, usually Our Lady, which they would dress and undress before and after the numerous feast days while keeping in their houses the jewellery and other treasures belonging to such statues.

From orphanages (supervised by the priests or religious orders) they could count on a regular supply of servants who could be relied on to work hard for practically nothing and would never dare to steal or misbehave since what they said in confession, to which they were obliged to go frequently, would normally be relayed back to their mistresses. Many priests, as was even admitted at the time, thought little of breaking the 'seal of confession' in such comparatively 'trivial' cases. They felt that the end justified the means in cases where 'Christian order', as established within 'la familia', was a desirable and praiseworthy objective. There were, of course, many households where this system operated with happy and beneficial results for all concerned. It was a form of paternalism taken to its logical conclusion and its relative absence in the Spain of today is cited by some as a cause of social unrest and dissatisfaction among the 'lower classes'. There are consequently groups at work in contemporary Spain which are trying, under the guise of religion and 'Christian order', to bring back the spirit of the old system in a new form. As for the 'church-crawling' women who indirectly played an important part in Ena's life, they were known, as a species, as 'beatas'. As opposed to 'religiosa', a word used to describe a woman of genuinely spiritual and generous-minded impulses, the expression 'beata' connotes a woman of canting and sanctimonious mentality. The type is easily identifiable, not only in Spain, though such women happened to be particularly numerous there in Ena's day. Many were socially very ambitious. Some managed to become ladies-in-waiting at court and, as such, were a painful thorn in the Queen's side. Their snide criticisms and uncharitable gossip, hypocritically dressed up with righteous indignation, were a constant source of friction. Apart from anything else, they disapproved of such work of the Queen's as was likely to bring her approval from ordinary people. The 'beatas', accustomed for so long to obey their confessors implicitly, would have no part in any activity disapproved of by the Church. The army of 'beatas' thus looked with haughty disdain on Ena's 'meddling' in matters which were not, in their view, her proper concern.

The 'beatas', nevertheless, became a familiar part, however trying, of Ena's life. She spoke with feeling about them on many occasions later on. In an interview she once gave an example of their influence on events. One Easter the Queen received from England the present of a new afternoon dress. This was soon after the First World War. When she sat down in the dress the Queen's knees became visible. 'The "beatas" of that period,' she recalled, 'were scandalized.' They arranged for the Jesuit who was due to preach a few days later at the Palace to bring the matter up in his sermon and, if only indirectly, to reprimand the Queen for her disgraceful immodesty. The King got to hear of their plan and cancelled the visit by the Jesuit in question.[26]

A final note on the Queen's initial rapport with her people can be supplied within the context of Carlism. This was thought by many to be virtually dead at the beginning of the century. For 'that prearranged swing of the political pendulum between Conservatives and Liberals that had eased the tasks of King Alfonso XII and Queen Maria Christina slowed down to a dead stop during the early years of Alfonso XIII's reign.'[27]. This abrupt ending of a false calm produced renewed hopes among the Carlists that they might be able to exploit the young King's difficulties to further the claims of their own new champion, Don Jaime. This, in turn, caused the popular revival, in a new form, of a song much favoured among the people forty years before. The song had shown how much ordinary Spaniards had loved their then Queen Isabel II, around whom the anti-Carlist forces, however heterogeneous, were rallied.

That Queen, for all her faults, had never lost her place in the hearts of the people. In 1909 there still seemed every hope that Queen Ena—or Queen Victoria as most Spaniards called her—could find a similar place in those same hearts. It was in that year that the former Carlist pretender, Don Carlos, had died, his place having been taken by his son Don Jaime. Hence the importance of the song which, in its original form had contained the words:

Si la Reina de España moriera
Y Don Carlos quisiera reinar;
Los arroyos de sangre correrían
Por el campo de la libertad.
('If the Queen of Spain were to die and Don Carlos wanted to reign, the field of liberty would run with streams of blood.')

Once more, in 1909, the people sang these lines, but they substituted the word 'Victoria' for 'de España' and 'Don Jaime' for 'Don Carlos'. In this way, the song was brought up to date. And it was, in its own way, a remarkable tribute to a 'foreign' Queen on the part of so intensely nationalistic a people. For these same people knew the horrors of dynastic strife. The vendettas of their 'superiors' had brought untold suffering to them. But now, the beautiful young 'Queen Victoria' brought hopes of peace and dynastic harmony, especially as, by 1909, she had produced two male heirs.

There were other factors at work as well. Memories, especially in chronically 'separatist' Catalonia, were still fresh in 1909 of the visit by the King and Queen the year before. The visit had been deemed advisable by the Maura government in order to conciliate the population of a traditionally rebellious city. While they were there the inevitable bomb went off—or at least was reported to have gone off—by the sea shore. Rumours of further planned bombings began to circulate. The Queen received great praise for her courage in face of such a danger within three years of the Madrid tragedy. But, once again, no word of such praise was permitted to appear in the Press. 'It was only the common talk of the ordinary people.'[28] One paragraph slipped through in a popular paper when it was stated that 'the alteration of their Majesties' itinerary, by which they would spend two days in Madrid, was dictated by the Queen's wish to embrace her children before going to Barcelona.' The next day the paragraph was carefully corrected to explain that the Queen's only reason for going to see her children was that they were suffering from some 'childish ailments'. 'But the people were not deceived by the second notice. They said that Doña Victoria's conduct was worthy of a Queen of Spain.'[29]

Most ironically, that expression 'childish ailments' was used with no knowledge of the children's real state of health. Behind the closed doors of the Palace, however, a handful of people knew of something that was known to few outside. The first scenes were already being played out of a drama in which Queen Victoria Eugenia was to take the principal role. It was a role which was destined to change the course of her marriage, her husband's reign, and the history of her adopted country. It belongs to that part of Ena's story which sees her as a mother.

[7]

The Shattering of Dreams

THE excited interest shown by the people of Spain in their new Queen during the course of 1905 and 1906 was very much like that shown in Britain in 1981 over the new Princess of Wales, the former Lady Diana Spencer. Both girls were under twenty when they got married and Princess Ena was strikingly like the Princess of Wales at the same age. Ena, though slightly fuller in the face, had the same tall and commanding presence and very much the same colouring of skin and hair. She seemed to be a typical beauty of the English rose type and few have doubted that the King of Spain was, for the time being very much in love with her. Ena had not, at first, been in love with him in any real sense of the word. But she had been dazzled by his position and charm, as well as being influenced by the strong pressures all around her. Alfonso too had been pushed hard if not, by any means, by his mother then certainly by the politicians then advising him. The result was a marriage that was desirable for both countries for reasons of state that had managed to look less like an 'arranged match' than most of its kind at the time. But it was blown up on all sides into a romantic love affair even though cynics at the Spanish Court could not resist remarking how different the two were from each other. Ena was striking-looking, gracious and correct but she very obviously lacked her husband's demonstrativeness, vivacity and restless energy.

Alfonso did his best to cajole her out of her shyness and the delayed shock of the bomb in the weeks and months that followed the wedding. The honeymoon was spent at one of the royal

La Granja

residences, La Granja at San Idelfonso. 'And here it was, in the beauty and silence of Castile, that Their Majesties found an ideal spot for what was at once a honeymoon and a rest from the tragic excitements of the past week.'[1] Most royal residences in Spain at this time, however, seemed more suitable for art collections than for human beings. The effort to make an exception of La Granja had been only partially successful since, apart from anything else, the entire Spanish Court took up residence there during the summer months. La Granja was thus not the cosy hideaway its name—meaning The Grange—might have suggested. Ena, on arrival there, found herself in the midst of a Spanish replica of Versailles. It was the creation of the first Spanish Bourbon king, Philip V, who had been hunting in the neighbourhood in the year 1720 and become captivated by the surrounding countryside. On a precarious mountain ledge, 4,000 feet above sea level, he discovered a house belonging to a small group of the monks of El Parral. Philip decided that just such a spot would accommodate his periodical longing for solitude. Paradoxically, however, he also loved grandeur and thus decided to transform this remote and improbable spot into a royal residence comparable to anything possessed by his native France. A modest mountain retreat overlooking Segovia was thus to become a splendid house and garden that would rival Versailles. It was a daunting, seemingly impossible, undertaking for which a veritable army of workmen was called into being. General Franco was to accomplish something similar two centuries later at the Valley of the Fallen, if only at the cost of many lives among the ex-prisoners-of-war who were killed in the erection of his massive war memorial and its vast, eerie church carved into the side of a solid mountain.

Philip V had been no less ambitious. Thousands of tons of rock were blasted away to be replaced by hundreds of tons of rich soil brought up from the fertile valley below. A breath taking garden of 360 acres was planted where once there was only forbidding rock. At enormous cost a complicated maze of pipes carried up the necessary water. The result was the most beautiful and expensive garden in Spain. The fountains were even more spectacular than those of Versailles. There were 26 in all, almost each unique and some sending multiple jets up to a height of over 80 feet. The most exciting was the Baños de Diana with a jet of 130 feet high. It was a miracle of engineering which amused its royal creator for exactly three minutes. The impatient Philip was fortunately not so ambitious over the Palace itself. Instead of anything as massive as Versailles he remained content with a more restrained and cheerful looking two-storey château which came to be called the Palace of San Idelfonso, or La Granja. The young Queen, if somewhat overawed, had to admit that she was fascinated by the fairy-tale surroundings of her honeymoon home.

She also confessed to the King, for the first time, that she was very nervous of the responsibilities suddenly thrust upon her. The reaction of her husband was that of the King at his best. His

Alfonso and Ena on honeymoon at La Granja

buoyant and optimistic nature provided, at this moment, a crucial counterpoise to Ena's new-found sense of uncertainty. Such rapidly changed circumstances had made her secretly frightened of most people but she usually managed not to show it except in the form of what often looked to others like aloofness. At La Granja she was gradually able to relax and it was while they were there that she came to realize that her husband was deeply in love with her. Together they explored the wild Castilian countryside

[129]

of which La Granja itself commanded such magnificent views. It reminded Ena of Scotland and there is no doubt that she was supremely happy.

They stayed for about six weeks. The Court arrived in early July to get away from the sweltering heat of Madrid and to stay for the rest of the month. Alfonso and Ena now had fewer opportunities to go off and play golf and tennis and Ena began to be left more and more on her own. She presumed this was inevitable and that Alfonso had duties which inevitably kept him away from her. But little was explained to her at this stage. She had to feel her own way along. She could fall back on books being a voracious, if never profound, reader. She was amazed at how little Alfonso seemed to know of the classics of his own or any other country. His almost exclusively military style of education had left him cheerfully ignorant of literature, languages and even history. It had always been necessary to give priority to his physical well-being and the King, as a young adult, became used to defying tiredness by aggressively competitive bouts of energy whether on the polo field, the golf course (where Ena was his teacher) or when out shooting. Such bouts took a heavy toll later on.

Ena retained her affection for La Granja but was not heart-broken when it was burned down some years later. There were quite enough other royal residences to choose from and to one of these, Miramar at San Sebastian, the royal couple went off toward the end of July. Here, where Ena had been received into the Roman Catholic Church, the new Queen began in earnest to learn about her new duties. She also began to learn about Spaniards and their ways. 'I feel I know them well,' she already felt able to say, 'and if their impression of me is half so good as my impression of them, then it will indeed be easy to be their Queen.'

It was not, however, going to be as easy as all that. By the time they were back at the Palace in Madrid with the onset of winter, Ena began to get her first real idea of what life was to be like, on a day to day basis, as Queen of Spain. The Palace in the capital was a huge and impersonal place at that time. (Central heating was put in at Ena's insistence in 1910. She never could stand cold houses and preferred them, if possible, to be much hotter than most people liked.) Her daily life was depressingly dissimilar to anything she had known up to then in Britain. She had, it is true, been surrounded in her early years by a certain amount of formality. But it was nothing compared to that which maintained its stranglehold on life at the Palacio de Oriente, as it was called. She could not emerge from her apartments without provoking an immediate and noisy response from the Palace's famous Halberdiers stationed along every passage and on the steps of the great staircases. As she approached they would jump to attention, rapping their halberds on the marble floor, and shout 'Viva la Reina!' Life lost all its former cosiness. She had no English friends with whom to share her thoughts or on whom to offload her loneliness. But she was grimly determined to do her duty and was realistic and in no way self-pitying about the situation. She was reluctant to write anything to her mother that might upset her. But she embarked, at this time, on what turned out over the years to be a long correspondence with her beloved cousin and confidante 'May', then Princess of Wales and afterwards Queen Mary, wife of George V. 'We are staying in Madrid the whole winter and precious cold it is going to be, as we are already freezing.' This she wrote to the Princess on 7 November 1906, adding 'Perhaps you know from Mama that I am expecting and in consequence life is not quite so enjoyable as before.'[2]

When early the following month, the news that the Queen was pregnant was officially released there was widespread rejoicing. The Queen's disappointing behaviour in the aftermath of the bomb attack was quickly forgotten. People remembered instead the excitement with which they had originally picked her out as the King's most likely bride and the favourable impression that she had made at the very moment of arrival on Spanish soil when, in response to a happy inspiration, she had dropped low in curtsy to the Spanish flag. Throughout the winter of 1906 and spring of 1907 the 'reina hermosa'—the 'beautiful queen' as Ena was now called—was sustained by a wave of unstinted popular support. Such popularity would burst its bounds if the radiant young Queen should now present the King and the nation with a healthy male heir. The need for this was acute and deeply felt. Such a birth would deal a heavy blow to the Carlist cause which, represented at this time by Don Carlos, an effete and affected bon viveur living in luxury in Venice, had become widely discredited. The brutality of its troops and its other excesses were of too recent memory. But one thing had ruefully to be admitted. The Carlist line was more prodigally favoured with male heirs than that of Alfonso XIII. This main Bourbon line had always produced too few sons. Ferdinand VII had had none. His daughter Isabel only one, Alfonso XII, and he had died without a male heir. Conceived in the nick of time, however, Alfonso XIII, born posthumously, had survived a sickly childhood to be the sole link on which the Bourbon reigning house depended for its survival. If he should now be blessed with several sound male heirs the whole future of Spain and its precarious dynasty would be put on a completely different footing. Such was the heavy responsibility of Queen Ena—a responsibility of whose gravity she was fully aware.

King Alfonso, still very much in love with his young bride—she was not yet even twenty—danced attention on her as the period of her pregnancy ran its course. The Queen was in an agony of nervousness. The perpetual presence, day and night, of her austere and not overfriendly mother-in-law under the same roof was an inhibiting factor. Ena's knowledge of Spanish was still almost non-existent. This did not stop all those around her gabbling in their native tongue on practically every occasion. The attitude of the Queen's senior ladies-in-waiting was distinctly cool. That of the 'damas chicas', the junior ladies charged with the more menial day to day tasks, was well meaning but generally irksome to the fun-loving Ena. She soon had reason to look upon them as the 'frumps' that they undoubtedly were. And here again the language barrier isolated and unnerved the Queen. Despite being surrounded by a noisy Court in an ever-active Palace where any kind of privacy was impossible, Ena had never felt more alone.

Despite all the handicaps, however, she had youth, beauty and vivacity on her side. Princess Alice, Countess of Athlone, recalled that as a girl Ena was undoubtedly 'spoiled', in a technical sense, by her grandmother. But she had never, in her youth, allowed this to make her selfish or unduly demanding. (Her tendency toward self-indulgence came much later in life.) As a young married woman, therefore, she combined self-discipline with a natural zest for life. In this way, her arrival at the Royal Palace in Madrid during that first winter of her reign precipitated something of a crisis in Court life. Her very youth and vitality were resented. Some of the ladies-in-waiting looked as if they had been there for a century. Some had been there for more than half that time. The Dowager Marchioness of Ayerbe had been appointed as far back as 1850 while the Duchess of Fernan-Nuñez had come not long afterwards. Such persons, to say nothing of the Queen Mother, took delight in casting a gloom over the Palace. They seemed to think that nothing less was appropriate for the solemn dignity of royal life. The Queen Mother, moreover, was still in mourning for her late husband, though he had died twenty years earlier. She was to keep up such mourning, and the deeply depressing black clothes that went with it, for the rest of her life.

Such ladies were made uncomfortable by the presence in their midst of an attractive young Queen who refused to reflect that gloom in the 'harem' as observed by the Sultan of Morocco's Ambassador. The Queen Mother tried to preserve, virtually intact, the tremendous formality of a Court ceremonial ('el ceremonial borgoñon') originally laid down by Charles V. Maria Christina, with her own Habsburg background, was determined to preserve the utmost stiffness and austerity at Court. Ena's increasingly lively presence seemed to be a living rebuke to such a funereal atmosphere. And though she was too tactful to show it, the perpetual proximity of her mother-in-law was a terrible trial to her. The latter was an 'old maid' by nature. Marriage to Alfonso

XII had not changed her. It had come about, as already seen, through the need to provide the King with a wife after the tragic death of his one and only true love, the short-lived Queen Mercedes. Maria Christina, as already mentioned, had been an Abbess in a very grand Austro-Hungarian convent before being allowed out to marry the King of Spain. When her beloved only son married Ena, the Queen Mother was willing to take second place at the Palace in theory only. She never took it in practice. She tried to dominate every conversation at meal times and to make her presence felt at all times during the day. Ena was lucky if she could have tea alone with Alfonso, which, most days, she tried to do. This they had in the Queen's private sitting-room, or boudoir. It was a room which became particularly precious to her as time went by.

The Queen Mother, despite being a heavy cross for Ena to bear, was never anything else but a thoroughly virtuous woman. For this very reason she was, ironically, never really popular. She earned respect rather than affection. She was restlessly inquisitive about everything Ena was doing and continually making well-meant suggestions as to how she should comport herself. She became greatly concerned when it was known that Ena was pregnant and immediately arranged for special prayers and Masses to be said in the royal chapel. Ena's doctors advised her not to go out in a car because of the nausea it was likely to bring on. Instead they suggested 'carriage exercise' in a Victoria. So the Queen, with one of her ladies, would ride out in the afternoons. On one excursion she spoke loudly and clearly in Spanish direct to the coachman. 'Find me a place that's not windy,' she directed. It was one of her first Spanish phrases. It stuck in her mind ever afterwards because of the great effort that had gone into learning it. Most surprisingly Ena never had anyone assigned to her to teach her Spanish. She had to teach herself and it was a year and a half before she could speak the language with complete fluency. This achievement increased her confidence in other directions and she was able, by slow stages, to introduce small but significant changes into the household routine. Her principal aim in the early days was to mitigate the unremittingly Spanish, and rather heavy, character of the meals, taken, of course, very late according to the custom in Spain. At Ena's prompting the cooking became more French in style and was put under the care of a brilliant chef who had been trained by the famous Paul Marechal. Informal luncheon parties and other entertainments were later to become a feature of life at the Palace as far as it was directed by Ena. Rival 'parties' of a much more stiff and boring nature were arranged by the Queen Mother. It was thus that life at Court ultimately came to be split into two bitterly competitive camps.

At length the Queen's gynaecologist, Dr Eugenio Gutierrez, later created Count of San Diego, announced that the baby would be born in the second week of May 1907. On 10 May, at two o'clock in the morning, Ena's period of labour began. It was to last twelve hours and was excruciatingly painful. Ena thought she would die of the pain which she was obliged to undergo without any anaesthetic. The arrival of her mother from England had been a great comfort but could not wholly make up for the more ominous and brooding presence of her mother-in-law who insisted on being involved with every step of the drama. 'We Spaniards,' she said imperiously to a cruelly suffering Ena, 'do not cry out when we bring a King into the world.' Ena made no reply but instead gritted her teeth as the pain mounted in intensity. To herself she said, 'And now they will see what an Englishwoman is like!'[3] The additional presence of an English doctor, Bryden Glendinning, was a comfort to the Queen at this moment. Gathering meanwhile in the council hall near to the Queen's room was a vast concourse of notabilities. It consisted of ministers, courtiers, diplomats and churchmen, all dressed in full ceremonial costume. At exactly twenty to one in the afternoon the door of the council hall burst open to admit the Prime Minister, Antonio Maura. He was scarcely able to contain his emotion and excitement.

'Gentlemen!' he exclaimed. 'Her Majesty the Queen has just

given birth to a Prince. Long live the King! Long live the Queen!'
Exactly a quarter of an hour later Alfonso himself entered the
crowded chamber. He looked pale but was obviously deeply
moved.[4] In fact it was the proudest and happiest moment of his
life, a moment of unique preciousness and solemnity. To honour
the occasion he had dressed himself in the uniform of a Captain-
General and was wearing the Charles III Medal on his breast. In
accordance with an ancient tradition he bore in his son and heir
naked on a silver salver for the assembled Court to see. The
precious boy weighed nine pounds. He was blond and seemed
healthy and robust. A mighty cheer went up from the normally
staid 'audience'. The future of Spain now seemed more assured.
Everyone's dream seemed to have come true. The usually
phlegmatic Prime Minister was beside himself with glee. 'We
have an heir!' he cried. 'About as small amount of one as can be
imagined. But we have him!' The Pope agreed to be the child's
godfather 'and Spain went mad with excitement.'[5] Plans for an
elaborate christening ceremony—to be held exactly a week
later—were immediately given their finishing touches. The
baby—styled, as was traditional for the heir, Prince of Asturias—
would be receiving twelve names, the first being Alfonso after his
father. In family circles, he was to become known as 'Alfonsito'.

It was just under a year since Alfonso and Ena had got married.
All the thrills, excitements, dangers and difficulties of that period
seemed now to melt away into a moment of undiluted rapture.
Alfonso, who did nothing by halves, had been in love with Ena
from almost their first meeting. Ena's sentiments were very
different. Her love for Alfonso was much slower to grow but was
to outlast his by very many years. The birth of the Prince of
Asturias was to prove the turning point in their love affair, their
marriage and the whole history of modern Spain, though no one
could have suspected this at the time. But for thousands, if not
millions of Spaniards, at the time, a dream seemed to have come
true, for no one more than for the King himself. He was baptized
according to plan on 18 May but the general reception 'to

solemnize the birth' in the presence of the full Senate was not held until 12 June. The next day the royal couple and the heir to the throne left Madrid for La Granja. It was not a moment too soon for the exhausted Queen. After an unusually cold winter there had now been a violent change in the weather. 'We left Madrid yesterday,' wrote Ena to the Princess of Wales,[6] 'and no words can describe how delighted I was to get away with Alfonso and the Baby into the country as the heat was getting quite unbearable.' Ena also related how happy she had been made by the comforting presence in Spain of a certain Mrs Green. The latter was the monthly nurse who had attended the Princess of Wales at the births of her children. Ena reported that Mrs Green 'has been so kind to me all this time and was the greatest comfort during those awful 12 hours before Baby was born.'

The Queen added, in the same letter, that the baby was 'really rather sweet'. She was still nursing him herself. When it had been announced that she would be doing this there was great rejoicing among Spain's working people. For her decision to do so was a distinct break with tradition but it was not greeted with any such satisfaction by the upper classes. When soon afterwards, it was stated that '"owing to the Queen's state of health and having regard to the duties of her position" the infant Prince had been handed over to a wet nurse like any other rich man's child, a sigh of disappointment went up.'[7] It was immediately realized that the Queen's health, which was excellent, had nothing to do with the decision. What lay behind it was the reluctance of the royal doctors to forgo the substantial commission they demanded for procuring 'suitable' wet nurses for the royal baby. The Queen was thus deprived of intimate daily contact with her infant son whose progress and development seemed to her to be sluggish. She could not bring herself to accept the worst implications of what the doctors had been fearing for some time. The Queen's only previous English biographer stated that 'in looks he favoured his mother rather than his father, and as he grew older the resemblance became more marked'.[8] The remark was as true as

[137]

another was completely false, namely that 'Alfonsito proved as bonny and healthy a boy as could be desired.' The attempt to preserve the myth that the Prince of Asturias was physically normal went on, in other words for fully fifteen years. The truth, when it was discovered for certain, accounts for the dire verdict that 'with the birth of the Prince of Asturias there began a drama which was to darken for ever the matrimonial life of the couple who had married for love, and only for love, disregarding whatever the considerations of state.'[9] This is to exaggerate the romantic side of the affair. But it is true in the sense that Alfonso disregarded the ample warnings he received that Princess Ena could be the possible transmitter of a hereditary disease peculiar to the British royal family.

The true state of affairs had been suspected after the Prince of Asturias was circumcised. According to an authoritative source[10] the custom of circumcising the royal children a few days after being born had long existed in the Spanish Court. It was thought to have originated with the Castilian monarchs who had had Jewish advisers, many of them doctors. The custom had been continued because it was said to hold out no dangers. 'In 1907 there came the turn of the Prince of Asturias . . .'[11]. The doctors and nurses, in white robes, gathered in the palace nursery. The little body about to be operated on was stripped, the scalpel made a careful ring-shaped incision and there was left hanging a portion of skin. The wound was disinfected when, having proceeded to suture it with great care, they were surprised to find that the bleeding did not stop. It seemed that they had stumbled on an almost certain case of haemophilia. The royal family, on being informed of this development, were plunged into a state of consternation.

When it became certain that the Prince was indeed a sufferer from this deadly disease the effect on King Alfonso was particularly devastating. The great dream was shattered. On more than one occasion[12] he expressed his thoughts on the subject by the words 'I cannot resign myself to the fact that my heir has contracted an infirmity which was carried by my wife's family and not mine. I know that I am unjust. I recognize it; but I cannot think in any other way . . .' Nor did he ever do so. His bitterness increased with the passing of the years and was never forsaken even on his deathbed. It did not, however, reach bursting point at the beginning. Every hope, however irrational, of a false alarm, faulty diagnosis or miraculous reprieve was clung to for as long as possible. At the same time, a desire for more children, in the supposition that they might be born in perfect health, became a fierce one on Alfonso's part. Ena was no less desirous to make some amends for the terrible act of which, though herself entirely innocent, she knew her husband believed her to be guilty.

On 23 June 1908, she gave birth to a second son at La Granja. His principal baptismal name was Jaime and his birth delighted both parents. For the time being Alfonso was mollified and it looked as if his love for Ena might not, after all, turn into the hatred which Alfonsito's illness had seemed to be bringing on. For little Jaime, contrary to what has often been said and written, was born perfectly healthy. He possessed all his faculties and senses and was obviously intelligent. As a result, the mercurial Alfonso rallied in spirit. He began, in fact, to be his former cheerful self again. He had almost managed to persuade himself that Alfonsito might be all right after all. True to his own, eternally boyish, addiction to military symbolism, he arranged for the Prince of Asturias, when only a little over a year old, to be enrolled as a member of the first Royal Regiment. The boy was therefore solemnly entered on the regimental roll of officers and described as residing in Madrid and as being a bachelor. The King lived out his daydream to the full. In the barracks of the regiment in question a regulation bed was prepared for the heir to the throne and a special spoon was kept in readiness for the first occasion when he would dine in the mess. Official papers were even drawn up to catalogue the Prince's regimental career. As they had to bear the signature of the officer involved, they were subscribed with the words 'Prince of Asturias, his mark'. The

Alfonsito, Prince of Asturias,
dressed in soldier's uniform,
with King Alfonso

[140]

Queen entered into her husband's wishful thinking and made for Alfonsito a miniature soldier's uniform complete with shoulder straps, belt and sword. This so pleased the King that he at once arranged to be photographed with his little son, in military dress, sitting on his knee. The resulting portrait was touchingly treasured by the King all his life which, comparatively young though he was when he died, lasted longer than that of his ill-fated eldest son.

Alfonso was further heartened by the alertness and precocity of the Prince of Asturias. When they were out driving one day Alfonsito, still only two, asked his father for a cigar. Upon being given one, the boy solemnly presented it to the coachman with an authentically royal gesture. Alfonso's heart ached at the thought that this beautiful child might not live to succeed to his throne. But he willed himself to believe that, despite everything, the boy would one day do so.

At this same time, the royal couple were rewarded by the safe birth of a baby girl on 22 June 1909. She was called Beatrice after her English grandmother. The strain on Ena, however, was beginning to tell. Within six months she was pregnant again. She accepted with grim stoicism that her prime duty was to produce heirs for the Spanish royal line. But it was less easy to accept the fact that the King now went to bed with her not to make love but only so that she should bear him children. Her next baby was due in June 1910. June, it seemed, was now the month, during which she was to produce, each year, a new baby. At the beginning of May, however, it became clear that all was not going well with the pregnancy. Ena was conscious that the life inside her body was ebbing away. The obvious and humane course would have been delivery, with no further delay, by Caesarean section. This however was not allowed. Such a step, it was thought, would impair Ena's ability to produce further children. The decision turned out to be a particularly cruel one as far as the long suffering young Queen was concerned. For she suddenly became aware that the baby inside her was already dead. Even so she had to wait for a 'natural birth'. No cutting was to be permitted. The stillborn baby was a boy, the 'birth' occurring prematurely on 20 May 1910. He was to have been called Fernando. Alfonso was in London at the time to attend the funeral of Edward VII. When he got back to Madrid he received a number of letters from all over the world. On this occasion they contained commiserations rather than congratulations. One particular letter, which has been preserved in the Royal Archives in Madrid though it was deemed unworthy of an answer, left the impressionable Alfonso with an uneasy feeling. It was written from England on 25 May 1910 by a certain Elizabeth Newton, an obvious crank but one who showed herself to be surprisingly well informed.[13]

She upbraided the Spanish monarch for coming to England at a time when he should have been at home supporting his wife. 'Your place at this time,' she wrote, 'was beside your wife, your allegiance was due to her and to none other. Heaven has punished you by causing your son to be stillborn.' What startled Alfonso almost more was the writer's objection to his presence in Britain now that 'Albert Edward' had succeeded to the throne as George V. For Miss Newton claimed that the new King's 'true wife is the one whom he married first in Malta before he even thought he would become heir apparent to the throne'. 'Albert Edward,' she went on, 'lied to the nation when he denied that marriage and the greater part of the nation knows that he lied.' The rumour about King George's prior marriage, unfounded but often repeated, was new to Alfonso and he was shocked by it. The unpleasant letter came at a bad time for him. He was inclined to see such things as evil omens. He was soon sliding into one of his periodical troughs of deep depression.

Matters were not helped by the fact that the illness of his eldest son was beginning to be talked about in many places despite the most strenuous efforts to keep it as secret as possible. News, both good and bad, always, in the end, got leaked from the Royal Palace. Unfortunately it was invariably consumed with relish by the general public, often in the form of misleading half-truths.

For this the fault lay principally with the palace authorities. They were at all times blissfully unaware that the goings on within the palace were almost immediately discussed and broadcast beyond the palace walls. This was because they themselves remained in ignorance of what was being thought and said by ordinary Spaniards. As the King's outspoken aunt, the Infanta Eulalia put it, 'The voice of the street is not heard inside the Palace.' This was a tragedy which turned out to have far-reaching consequences. A refusal to take the public into their full confidence was a grave miscalculation on the part of successive governments as well as of the Court itself. This was true in no case more disastrously than in that of the Prince of Asturias. In the world outside Spain there was, sadly, a thriving market for rumours of the most ugly kind. One of the most sensational reports to appear in a foreign paper was that which was published in the *American Examiner* on 17 May 1910.[14] It stated baldly that the heir to the Spanish throne was defective. This report was unfortunately only too true. But the non-release from official sources of any actual details as to the little Prince's illness gave rise to suppositions of the wildest kind. The *American Examiner*, not in the best of times inclined to favour the Spanish monarchy, made up for lack of hard news with all kinds of mischievous speculation and irresponsible comment. The article, in fact, was a scurrilous attack on Alfonso whose family history was held to be responsible for the illness of his eldest son. It showed that the true nature of the little Prince's disease, and its origin, were still not understood. The Spanish Court, however, remained stubbornly unwilling to release the true story. The readers of the *American Examiner* were thus pesuaded to believe that Alfonsito's illness was linked with 'centuries of madness' in the Spanish royal family and that the 'sins of the father' had now been visited on the innocent little boy of three. The piece went on to say, rather patronizingly, that 'few persons believe that King Alfonso XIII is particularly bad but after three operations on his throat there is a strong possibility that ailments of this character will shorten his life.' This prophecy,

[143]

which turned out to be substantially true, was followed by an accurate but unflattering physical description of the Spanish King. 'His head is asymmetrical, his upper jaw is too small, his lower jaw is displaced, his palate is too narrow and he has obstructions of various kinds in his throat.' The supreme irony was that 'knowing the burden of ancestral sins under which he laboured, Alfonso and his advisers chose for him a wife of unusual health and vigour, in the hope that she would put new strength into the Spanish royal family.' But the experiment, it was stated, had failed. This much was only too sadly true.

To read such wounding words, however, was gall and wormwood for Alfonso on whom, at just about this time, another heavy blow now fell. His second son Don Jaime had been showing promise of providing great satisfaction and happiness. The boy took very much after his father both in looks and in disposition. From his earliest days he tried to imitate the King in everything. Alfonso was delighted with him. Then the blow struck. Jaime has often been described as having been born deaf and dumb. But such was not the case.[15] He could hear and speak quite normally until he entered his fourth year. It was then that he suffered a double mastoiditis. The required operation broke his auditory bones and he could never hear or speak properly again as long as he lived.

Alfonso at this point went into one of those periodical declines which very few people, even his mother who thought she knew him so well, ever suspected. Ena, in fact, was the only person who had any full knowledge and understanding of the morbid and dark side of Alfonso's nature. For behind his deceptively carefree exterior were hidden certain tendencies that fell little short of manic depression. Paradoxically, at the very time when he was turning so much against the wife whom he held responsible for his misfortunes, he also turned toward her for help. Trying so hard to play a rugged, virile role as far as the outside world was concerned, there were times in private when he turned into a bewildered boy ashamed to go to anyone except his wife for help and consolation. Irrational and illogical such behaviour certainly was. But it was also very human, and as such it found a responsive chord in Ena. Thus, in the 1910–11 period, when relations between Alfonso and his wife had become intolerably strained, a new element entered into the Queen's feelings toward her husband. It was grimly clear to her that he had fallen out of love with her. Her role from now on was to be limited to that of figurehead Queen and provider of children. Alfonso, when his normal fun-loving self, had already embarked on that career of indifference toward her, soon degenerating into flagrant infidelity, which was to characterize the rest of their life together. Another dream was shattered. Yet Ena, who had not at first been truly in love with her husband, could not now help conceiving for him a sense of tenderness, even of pity, which was born of a unique understanding of his complex character and was to outlive all the vicissitudes and vagaries of the years ahead.

As already mentioned, the Palace in Madrid had eyes and ears of its own. Life within it was lived on the regal equivalent of an 'open plan'. Alfonso and his mother were alarmingly indiscreet in front of the servants who were, quite wrongly, presumed not to hear or be concerned with what went on. In fact, it was their chief, if only, interest in life. Many of them lived locally and came in daily. Their houses were mostly near each other in a small area of Madrid near the Palace. They were a ready prey to the blandishments and bribes of the rumour-hungry foreign journalists. It was mostly in this way that reports found their way into foreign journals and newspapers which, though often inaccurate in detail, were in most cases uncomfortably true in substance. So it was that certain aspects of the secret life of Alfonso XIII came to be known outside Palace and Court circles.

Ena got her first inkling into the dark and hidden side of her husband's nature in the course of the year 1910. One particular incident was reported in the 28 May 1911 edition of an American periodical, the *World Magazine*. It started off with a fact which was already fairly well known, namely that Alfonso was inclined to be neurotic about his health. This led on to his having a virtual obsession about a 'nemesis' which hung over him and was associated, on the one hand, with a certain Dr Moure and, on the other, with a particular month of the year. 'My nemesis,' he said, 'is written in the month of May.' This expressed his view of life in general which was well known to be fatalistic. Ever since the first of his several visits to Dr Moure, the Bordeaux tuberculosis specialist, the Spanish King had lived in fear of the ultimate effects of the malady from which he suffered. The disease in question was then very much more serious than it is today and Dr Moure had reported that the King's condition was 'not respond-ing readily to treatment.' This had been said at a consultation the King had had with Dr Moure on 14 May 1905. It had stuck in Alfonso's mind ever since and he had often broodingly linked the date with certain other incidents occurring in the same month though in different years.

One day, all of this suddenly became too much for Alfonso and Ena was surprised to see him coming into her room one afternoon looking horribly pale and troubled. Ena was playing with their eldest son who, on the arrival of Alfonso, was taken away to his nursery. Alfonso then dropped to his knees and spent an hour praying. After this he remained, for an even longer period, weeping uncontrollably. Ena did her best to comfort the pathetic monarch who looked so young, so wretched and so defenceless. She was deeply affected by this total breakdown the like of which she never previously experienced. At length she asked the King to tell her what was wrong. Alfonso made no immediate answer but, after a short time, went over to a writing table and wrote the following lines on a piece of paper.

```
May 7   —  1886   born
May 14  —  1905   Dr Moure
May 31  —  1906   married
May 10  —  1907   first son born
May  ?      ?        ?
```

The question marks in the last line were added with painful slowness while, as if in an agonized trance, the King tried in vain to penetrate the forbidding mists of an unchartered but terrifying future. After a while Alfonso, with as much help as Ena could give him, began to recover something of his normal composure. Within a few days he was acting as if the incident had never occurred. Indeed, in later years, he seemed completely to have forgotten this and similar breakdowns. Such was his nature. One of Ena's closest Spanish friends, who saw much of her in Switzerland in the 1960s, said of her that it was part of her tragedy that she could never forget anything that had ever happened in connection with her life with Alfonso. He, on the other hand, could forget everything that he did not wish to remember. After their estrangement in 1931, Alfonso never wanted, if possible, to see Ena again. To see her was to be reminded of his guilt. Ena, on the contrary, always harboured the desire to see and be with him. To do so was to be reminded of a tenderness that had, paradoxically, arisen at just the very moment when Alfonso's original love for her was beginning to turn toward an indifference which was to end in something akin to hatred. By such conflicting elements are human emotions conditioned. In such strange and different ways do males and females react to the forces of adversity.

Alfonso naturally brooded on the possibility that his stillborn son, who was to have been christened Fernando, might have been healthy. Medical opinion was inclined to think that he too was a haemophilia sufferer.

A year and a half later, on 12 December 1911, a second daughter, Maria Christina, was born, and then, on 20 June 1913 a boy, Don Juan. With this birth, Alfonso's natural optimism flooded back, for this latest son was without any trace of haemophilia and seemed completely sound and healthy. The King's hopes rose further when yet another son was born on 13 October 1914, and christened Gonzalo. Such hopes were, however, soon dashed. This son too was a haemophiliac. For Alfonso it was the final blow. His bitter words about the 'infirmity

Ena with her three eldest children. *Left to right*: Beatrice, Jaime, Alfonsito

[148]

which was carried by my wife's family' now expressed his feelings
more than ever. Such feeling he was never to lose. His and Ena's
marriage now became a marriage in name only. In a certain,
rather awful way, this was a relief to Ena who was worn out from
childbearing. She had had seven children in seven years. For her
pains and unhappiness she had earned little gratitude from her
husband or from Spaniards in general. Her childbearing years
had produced a ribald piece of doggerel about which even the
'dignified' ladies at Court sniggered behind their fans. It went as
follows:

One month's pleasure
Eight months pain;
Three months leisure
At it again;
Oh, what a life
For the Queen of Spain.

At this stage, however, Ena became determined to make a new life
for herself. She found one world among the poor and needy. Here
she was popular and well received. She found another world
among the rich and well-connected. Here she met polite but firm
resistance amounting, in some cases, to cynical hostility. But she
was not put off. She would find her own friends where she may
and ignore or outmanoeuvre those who had, in various ways and
for various reasons, showed themselves to be her enemies. From
now on, in fact, she would fight back, even if it meant engaging in
a lonely struggle.

[8]

Going it Alone

DURING the first eight years of her marriage Ena had little choice but to conform to the etiquette, customs and sometimes onerous demands of her new life as Queen of Spain. She forced herself to get used to the disagreeable necessity of never being able to eat a meal with her immediate family only, but always with the entire royal retinue. This consisted of the King's military staff—in practice his handpicked cronies, fellow playboys and womanizers; the Queen Mother's secretaries; her own lady-in-waiting; and the King's secretary whom Ena described as 'A disgusting little man who always spat on the floor.'[1] In the very first months of her life in Madrid she had the services of a Mistress of the Robes 'inherited with the Palace'. She was a formidable but capable woman who had palace etiquette and protocol at her finger tips. Ena decided to be guided in everything by her thus saving herself from unnecessary criticism from her austere mother-in-law and the other hawk-eyed ladies whose stifling presence was an in-escapable element of Court life.

In those days the announcement of each new royal birth to the people of Spain came from the Court Chamberlain. After such announcements the Queen was required to visit nine churches in the city. Such journeys took her to parts of Madrid to which she would not normally venture. She was often appalled by the sights that met her eyes. Some of the streets were pitted with such enormous holes that carriage wheels were in danger of being broken by them. 'People', she reminisced, 'still lived in caves not very far from our Palace.' After one particular visit to the poorer quarters she decided, as soon as possible, to set up three welfare organizations. One was to be a proper Spanish branch of the Red Cross. The others would be two 'Leagues', one against cancer and the other against tuberculosis.

She initially encountered many difficulties. The years of child-bearing naturally limited her activities and many of the major schemes had to be put off until a later date. There was resentment and opposition to her plans to reform the medical and nursing worlds owing to the implication that considerable improvements were required. But improvements there certainly had to be. Spain's standard of doctoring at this time was appallingly low. But even worse was that of nursing due, in most part, to an archaic and wholly unrealistic approach. There were not, at this time, any properly trained nurses in Spain and no nurses who were not members of religious orders. There was a general belief that if a lay woman went near to a man in bed she would not leave the bedside unsoiled. Florence Nightingale had encountered a similar mentality more than half a century before. There was a general saying in Spain that 'A woman without a nun's veil is a lost woman if she goes near a man in bed.' The Queen was determined to demonstrate the fallacy behind such thinking. But she had to go slowly.

Ena was not a clever or particularly imaginative woman. But she had quite a lot of common sense and often surprised people with her shrewdness. She was faced with the problem of how, if her schemes to start new hospitals and to train nurses were to succeed, such schemes could be financed. She was told that she could not rely on Government funds as such. But she realized that Spaniards in general loved to gamble. She thus launched a lottery which the Government agreed to back and organize. Tickets at various prices were widely sold. Many people at Court were persuaded to invest in the more expensive ones. The result of these lotteries, declared annually on her 'name day', 23 December, were immensely successful. This largely overcame the financial chaos which had, for so many years past, bedevilled all efforts

Ena in Red Cross uniform

to build new hospitals and generally to improve the medical service. The chief defect of the system had lain in its inadequacy. Spanish doctoring at its very best was as good as any in the world. But 'the big doctors were those of the Royal Palace, specialists who charged enormous fees and confined their activities to the important Madrid hospitals.'² In such hospitals much laboratory work was carried out to the benefit of science in an abstract sense. But little of it was of any value to 'the man in the street, the victim of heredity or of a train collision.'

The formation of the Red Cross Society in 1916 under the Queen's personal direction marked a turning point and as from this date the whole medical system began to improve out of all recognition. Many people still had gruesome memories of what had happened in 1885 when 40 out of every 53 persons affected by the cholera epidemic had died. A new challenge had come with the onset of 'Spanish flu' in 1918. The Queen's reforms had not yet become well enough established to combat this new epidemic with anything like total adequacy. Thereafter, however, the country was at last convinced that a centralized hospital system for the whole nation was an absolute necessity.

Within ten years the national system had been revolutionized. The Queen worked really hard at the detailed arrangements needed to keep the new system moving forward. She was also an active President of the Anti-Tuberculosis League whose first main achievement was the establishment of a new dispensary in Madrid called 'The Victoria Eugenia'. Many new centres sprang up later in other towns and there was continuous work in enlarging and improving existing premises. Within a few years the practice of having fully trained lay nurses working round the clock in Spain's hospitals had become firmly established. The Queen, particularly in the twenties, was a frequent visitor to the hospitals in which she had taken a special interest. One of her greatest allies in the immense work that was accomplished was the Duchess de la Victoria. She naturally became very friendly with the Queen who, as time went on, became more and more in need of friends.

[153]

The First World War was a particularly testing period for her. The war split the Spanish royal family in two. The country was officially neutral but the sympathies of the upper and professional classes were openly on the side of the Central Powers. There was widespread fear that, if the Allies won, the cause of traditional monarchy in Europe would suffer an irreparable blow. A Carlist type of reaction to the war thus became prevalent, though it was equally evident that the working classes, along with the Liberals and Socialists, were in favour of an Allied victory. The King, who managed to keep his own feelings strictly secret, once said that 'There is no one who wants to fight but the *canaille* and myself.' The remark was patronizing and cryptic but was taken by some to mean that, in his heart of hearts, largely because of his pro-French sentiments, he wished for an Allied victory.

The greatest test for Ena's tact and patience lay in the fact that her mother-in-law was wholly pro-German in her outlook. Both Queens, moreover, had close relatives fighting on opposite sides. Queen Maria Christina's brother, the Archduke Frederick, was fighting for Germany and Austria-Hungary. Ena's two brothers were fighting for Britain and France. Neither Queen knew for certain where Alfonso's real preferences lay. Blasco-Ibañez claimed that Ena 'resigned herself to living in isolation in a court where everyone, her husband included, was a German sympathiser.'[3] A terrible moment came for Ena when her younger brother, Prince Maurice of Battenberg, was killed in action. Spain's principal Carlist leader, Vasquez de Mella, undiplomatically chose this moment to address a pro-German meeting. A strong contingent of Court ladies was prominent among the aristocratic audience. The Carlist leader shouted his hatred of Britain and his praise of Germany. The applause was thunderous and layers of flowers buried the speaker's feet when he came to the end of his speech.

The Queen Mother would watch each day's news with intense interest. Her satisfaction at each Austrian or German success was never concealed. Occasionally she would unbend so far as to say

Queen Ena laying the foundation stone
of the New Sanitorium for Tuberculosis in Madrid

to Ena, when news favoured the Allies, 'Your side had a good day today'. But there were many occasions when the tension between the two women was all too visible. At such times it was invariably Ena who suffered most for, while she took pains to conceal her feelings, the Queen Mother made no attempt to do the same. On one particular day, Count Romanones, the great Liberal politician, was lunching at the Palace. While he was there, news was brought to the royal family of the death at sea of Lord Kitchener as a result of German action. The Queen Mother made no effort

[155]

to conceal her delight. Ena, on the other hand, was visibly shaken. Kitchener had dandled her on his knee as a child. She had conceived a lifelong love and affection for him. While Queen Maria Christina was digesting the news with obvious satisfaction, Romanones noticed that Ena was digging her fingernails into the upholstered sides of her armchair.

Alfonso meanwhile adroitly kept on friendly terms with both sides. He found a diplomatic way of identifying himself with the struggle without appearing to compromise his neutrality. He got the idea after receiving a letter from a humble French woman asking if he could use his good offices to trace her son, missing since the battle of Carleroi. The King made personal enquiries and the man was eventually traced. Alfonso quickly spotted the advantages for all concerned, including himself, in extending such activity. His astuteness was matched by his resourcefulness, and he set up a very successful network, with headquarters at the Palace itself, for tracing and, in special cases, repatriating missing prisoners of war. The King deservedly earned praise from all sides for his devotion to the cause of the 'Wounded and Missing' regardless of nationality. His grief was genuine and considerable when his strenuous efforts to prevent the execution of Nurse Edith Cavell came to nothing. The failure upset Ena even more.

Ena became involved in her husband's work as far as time permitted. Primarily, however, 'The Great War turned the Queen's attention more than ever in the direction of working for hospitals; she had already done much for the hospitals in Morocco, and she was now ready to work for the wounded Allies.'[4] Her newly created Red Cross became a vital link in the international relief chain and she expanded her work in another direction with the setting up of the Needlework Guild—the 'Ropero de Santa Victoria'—whose activities became more extensive and important as time went on.

Ena's war work was a blessing to her in one vital respect. It helped her to forget her loneliness and sense of isolation and to forget somewhat her worries about her family and friends in

England and elsewhere. But she could not forget altogether. 'It is very hard', she wrote to Queen Mary,[5] 'to be away from my old home at such a time as this and especially so since Maurice's death when I know that Mama is so sad and needs me so much. I would give anything to be able to go to her but that I fear will not be possible for a long time to come.' Ena went on to lament that no one was spared from the suffering brought about by such a war. She and her old friend, the former Daisy Cornwallis-West, now Princess of Pless, consoled each other by corresponding as frequently as wartime conditions permitted. Both were in the same uncomfortable position of living in neutral countries with mothers-in-law who wanted Great Britain to lose the war.

All this time Ena was painfully aware that Alfonso's attitude toward her had radically changed. The total period during which he had remained in love with her had probably not been more than two years. Three at the most. But for a long time after this Ena clung desperately to the hope that his love for her was not totally dead. It was just at about the time the War started that this hope began to fade. Many years later she related to a friend of long standing that in the early part of her life she was happy 'for seventeen years'. By this she meant roughly the period from her childhood until about 1914. Alfonso's love had not turned to hate; merely, at this stage, to indifference. The sexual side of their marriage, which had never amounted to very much, had now broken down completely. Alfonso had not taken long to realize that his wife was not at all sexy by nature. By his standards, in fact, she was positively frigid. Her awareness that he thought this made it even more difficult for her to respond to him in the way that he would have wished. Inevitably the King, in view of his passionate nature and complete unwillingness to curb it, was soon seeking his pleasures elsewhere. Ena's very beauty even began to become something of a mockery to Alfonso. The presence of such demure good looks combined with the complete absence of allure or sex appeal was a combination which was little short of hateful to the King.

Within, at the most, three years of their marriage Alfonso began to enjoy the thrills and perils of extra-marital bliss. It amused him to pretend that his affairs were conducted with anonymity. When an American showed him the manuscript of an intended biography of himself, Alfonso had no comment to make except about the chapter provisionally entitled 'The Loves of the King'. Alfonso archly suggested that the title should instead refer to the loves of the 'Duke of Toledo'. This was a subsidiary title and one which the King liked to assume when playing the make-believe game of moving about 'incognito'. It was an illusion that pleased him and it played a central part in an adventure which lasted for about two years between 1908 and 1910.

The story of it went the rounds of Madrid and was eventually published by a newspaper in supposedly definitive form.[6] During the summer of 1908 the activities of a certain young gentleman known as Monsieur Lamy began to attract attention. He was to be seen living a brilliant life in Paris. He did not act or dress like anyone famous, let alone royal. And yet there was something intriguingly familiar about him. For a long period of time he would be seen in the constant company of a charming brunette. And then, for an equally prolonged period, he would keep appearing without her. Then, suddenly, the brunette in the case began to be seen in Madrid and was eventually observed, more than once, entering the Royal Palace. It soon became obvious that 'M. Lamy' was really King Alfonso indulging in the illusion of living the 'secret life' of a Paris boulevardier. All he had really done, however, was to take advantage of the fact that there was a real M. Lamy who lived quite respectably in the Avenue Henri Martin and who happened to look strikingly like the Spanish king. Men-about-town in Paris and Madrid became fond of boasting that you could tell M. Lamy and the King apart if you knew the King. This was their way of implying that *they* knew the King. This particular little game went on until July 1910 'when Alfonso grew prudent and gave it up.'

It is not certain whether the full story came to the ears of Ena at the time. Quite soon, however, Alfonso became involved in the first of his more than merely casual love affairs. This was with a lady called Genevieve Vix. She was not, however, the great love of Alfonso's life. That person was to appear later. There were numerous passing affairs in between and Ena found herself powerless to halt the process. She lacked the personal attributes that would be needed and was bereft of allies who might help her. The Queen Mother knew exactly what was going on but was unwilling to do anything to alleviate Ena's suffering as this would involve her in a direct confrontation with her son. Members of the Court were equally well aware of what was happening and revelled in each new twist and turn of events. In their eyes the King could do no wrong.

Her misery was tinged with desperation as she began to find herself increasingly out of her depth. Two women added immeasurably to Ena's difficulties and discomfiture in these years. One was the Duke of Alba's sister, Doña Sol. The other was Princess Beatrice of Saxe-Coburg who was her cousin and contemporary and had been, theoretically, one of the candidates for Alfonso's hand when he had visited London in 1905. Beatrice had, in 1909, married King Alfonso's cousin and namesake, the Infante Alfonso, and had come to live in Madrid. She was a frequent visitor at Court and immediately spotted a golden opportunity for mischief-making and harmful intrigue. While feigning continued friendship with Ena she had never really forgiven her for being the royal Princess to be singled out and chosen as a bride by the dashing Spanish monarch. When, in due course, Alfonso again set eyes on the lively and flirtatious Beatrice, so different in every way from his wife, he made little secret of the fact that he himself felt that he had made the wrong choice.

Beatrice quickly became the King's confidante and ally, but not, it is generally agreed, his lover. According to one story she was the first person to be certain, apart from Alfonso himself, that young Alfonso had haemophilia. It was then she who, playing the game of being Ena's 'best friend', broke the news to the young Queen. Ena is said to have received the information with a soul-searing wail so utterly despairing that it seemed to come from some inaccessible hell beyond the grave. Owing, however, to the attempts to hush up the infant's illness, and the many denials and counter-denials that accompanied this, there have survived so many theories as to when the malady was definitely discovered that some of the more colourful versions have to be treated with caution.

Ena was lucky that Beatrice was not continually in Madrid. She also profited by occasional respites in Alfonso's indifference. In times of acute distress, as already recounted, the King seemed to forget all else and all others and to lay his soul bare to his wife. On such occasions he became like a bewildered son needing comfort and protection: a far cry from the swashbuckling worldly monarch which he liked to appear.

Ena also gained support and sympathy when, at the end of 1916, she became dangerously ill. Attempts to improve medical standards had not gone nearly far enough to be of any help to her, even among the supposedly best doctors who looked after the royal family. Her illness was wrongly diagnosed, an acute case of appendicitis not being noticed. She nearly died of peritonitis. Outwardly at least, Alfonso showed concern. When writing, while recovering, to the Queen of England she said that 'Alfonso joins me in sending you both our love and all good wishes.'[7] This was something she practically never said in her letters home and it seems possible that Ena's new brush with death brought her husband and herself closer together, if only momentarily.

Unfortunately such reprieves were short-lived. Beatrice had time on her side and ample opportunities to satisfy her incurable taste for intrigue. With the ending of all sexual aspects of Alfonso's and Ena's marriage the King's life style became radically different. He fell increasingly under the influence of his 'amigotes', or cronies, that is those grandees and others who shared his taste for womanizing and had a vested interest in providing it with outlets. Particularly influential were such companions from his earliest days as the Marquis of Someruelos and the Duke of Almodovar, also the Marquis of Viana. They realized that if Alfonso could be drawn far enough along the paths of promiscuity a point of no return would fairly quickly be reached. With the King, their lord and master, thus setting the pace, their own proclivities could be indulged in with all the frequency and ease which they desired.

At first, however, they hesitated, as mere men often do. It took a woman to propel them firmly round the first corner, after which there was to be no looking back. This woman was none other than Ena's cousin Beatrice. Though many suspected her of herself being the King's lover, she knew that her ends could be better served by quite different methods. She derived, it is true, great satisfaction from flirting outrageously with Alfonso, particularly when she knew Ena could not help noticing. But her main activity was more subtle and more sinister. Behind the scenes she egged on such of the King's cronies as Almodovar, Someruelos and the Marquis of Viana for all she was worth. She became a principal agent, with the help of these men, in procuring for Alfonso a series of delectable girl friends and mistresses. The King was quite unable to resist the temptations which flesh and Bourbon blood were heir to. But the Rubicon was not crossed by Alfonso without certain inner agonies and conflicts. Not for nothing was he the grandson of Isabel II. Nymphomaniac though she was, she possessed a brand of piety, based mainly on superstition and fear, which continually pricked her conscience. She was, in this respect, much helped by her own kind of cronies, a bogusly stigmatic nun called Sister Patrocinia and an extremely 'understanding' confessor called Father Claret. Alfonso's guilty conscience had more complex manifestations. It was partly responsible for his periodical flights to the Queen when he wanted to pour out his troubled soul. He went to her, of course, not to confess his sins but, perhaps as a substitute, to lay his other troubles, mostly worries about health, at her feet. On such occasions he seemed to forget everything else that had happened. But when the fits of remorse were over he equally quickly forgot these occasions as well and returned with renewed gusto to his life of dissipation.

Ena, meanwhile, unlike the irrepressible Beatrice, was not what the Spaniards called 'lista' or quick-witted. She was, by comparison, slow on the uptake. But she was by no means unaware of Alfonso's inner conflict. The King, through the very fact of being his own master, was in a particularly invidious position. In the absence of restraint from any strong-willed person whom he respected—his mother as already seen hesitated to step in—he was a dangerously 'free agent'. In such situations, as human nature regrettably demonstrates, there is no more repugnant tie than that which theoretically binds you to someone whom you no longer love and who holds no vestige of sexual appeal for you. The fact that you owe your loyalty to that person only makes the whole position somehow even more intolerable. If you are a saint and something of a natural celibate, it might be possible to be 'faithful' to that person. But poor Alfonso was neither of these things. As his infidelities became more and more frequent and increasingly flagrant his remorse increased to a point where it almost maddened him. His tangled emotions produced a vicious circle of frustration. This he tried to eliminate by taking it out not on himself but on his wife. Her crime—in producing a defective heir to the throne—became unnaturally enormous and monstrous in his eyes. *She* was the cause of his misery. *She* had introduced into his family this hideous disease from which his handsome and adored eldest son was wasting away—too incapacitated to be trained for his normal duties, too ill, most of the time, even to be seen in public.

This reasoning provided the cause, the excuse, the occasion—according to interpretation—for the new pattern of Alfonso's life. The cronies played their full part and invariably joined Alfonso on his nocturnal adventures into certain private houses and better class brothels around Madrid. Their conspiracy with the young

Princess Beatrice went smoothly. At Court, the King's conduct was an open secret. Many stories circulated and were retailed with gleeful approbation. One night, for example, a young nobleman was in a Madrid house of assignation. As it was known that he was a friend of His Majesty's he was entrusted by the proprietress with the King's signet ring which had been left there the night before. The man arranged to hand it back discreetly to Alfonso who, upon receiving it, asked the young gentleman to kneel down. He thereupon playfully dubbed him Duque de Lealdad—Duke of Loyalty.

In the eyes of practically everyone at Court the King had every excuse. The Court ladies were no exception. Even the most outwardly stiff-necked of them followed the game with avidity. They included some of Ena's 'damas de grandeza', that is senior ladies-in-waiting, several of whom were themselves competing for the King's favours. Neither their exalted rank nor long lineage debarred them from having the same desires as ladies of humbler station and even professional status. To sleep with the King became a widespread and almost respectable ambition. In more sober circles, however, worries were beginning to emerge as to the ultimate harm that might redound on the King and his throne. It eventually became clear that Beatrice's insidious activities had become a liability to Alfonso himself, to say nothing of the deepening distress being caused to Queen Ena. But rescue was at hand. Its source was, in some ways, a surprising one, namely the Queen Mother. She had still not got on to any more intimate terms with her daughter-in-law. But she was a just woman. Such is the inequity of life that, for this very reason, as already mentioned she was not generally popular. The Spanish people, who loved fixing nicknames to people, had been inspired, in her case, by her possession of what they deemed to be all the 'deadly virtues'. They dubbed her 'Señora Virtudes'—the Virtuous Lady. It was a sobriquet conceived in contempt but which ultimately backfired on its inventors.

In the case of the mischievous Beatrice, the Queen Mother,

concerned primarily for her son and the overall proprieties of the situation, finally decided to act. Things had gone far enough. The spectacle, now obvious to so many, was seen by her as undignified and degrading. It was on an occasion when Beatrice and her husband were staying with the royal family at Miramar in San Sebastian that Queen Maria Christina decided to make her move. She requested Beatrice to quit the country. Beatrice refused. Orders were then given, nominally by the King himself, that the Princess should leave. With great reluctance and resentment she now had no option but to obey. Her departure was, in a sense, a relief to Alfonso. But it came too late to make any substantial difference to Ena's life. Her fortunes, by the early twenties, had become guided in a certain direction from which there was no going back. As the Queen Mother's niece, the Archduchess Christina, Princess of Salm-Salm, put it, 'I think my aunt Christina is beginning to regret her lack of loyalty to Ena.' But by now, as the Archduchess also pointed out to one of the grandees on duty at the Court, Alfonso and Ena no longer had any sort of shared life which they could try to pick up again. The cronies had won.

A person who had contributed greatly to this state of affairs was the woman who, apart from Beatrice, was the other painful thorn in Ena's side. This was Doña Maria de Soledad—always known as 'Doña Sol'—who was the sister of Alfonso's life long friend 'Jimmy', the Duke of Berwick and Alba. Theirs was one of the oldest and most illustrious families in Spain. They have houses in various places, notably the fabulous Palacio de Liria in Madrid which resembles a private museum. The family had always been Anglophile, the first Duke of Berwick having been the illegitimate son of King James II. The seventh Duke of Berwick succeeded to the Dukedom of Alba, as four-teenth Duke, in the year 1801. Thereafter the titles were held together.

Ena had met Doña Sol when they were both quite young as the latter spent much of her childhood with the Empress Eugenie at

Farnborough where Ena was an occasional visitor. Sol married the somewhat older Duke of Santoña who died a few years after their marriage. It was thus that Dõna Sol, who never remarried, came to play a central role from then on in the life of Alfonso. Like Beatrice she was fond of intrigue and pretended to be a great friend of Ena's. While she was still married she made a great point of asking the Queen to come and visit them at their beautiful house at Ventosilla. Doña Sol, in fact, did actually help to break the ice for Ena with the stiff upper crust of Spanish society in those difficult early years of her marriage. But when Ena and Alfonso started to drift apart—from 1909 onwards—the whole situation began to change. Still professing to be Ena's friend, Doña Sol in fact moved over entirely to the King's side. After her husband died she became a familiar and seemingly ever-present figure in Court circles. It was not long before people leapt to the conclusion that she was the King's mistress. Many people believe to this day that she was. Alfonso's descendants look very embarrassed if her name is mentioned and they invariably refuse to discuss her. Almost certainly, however, she was never a royal mistress. Things might have worked out better for Ena if she had been. For as a lover her influence over the King might have been only short-lived. As a 'friend' her influence could go on indefinitely. In fact it did.

Doña Sol, moreover, was extremely plain. She was not the sort of person with whom Alfonso was likely to fall in love. She herself knew this. But she also knew that she could gain a hold of a different kind over him. She was intelligent, witty and well informed. She and the King could relax completely in each other's company. They enjoyed talking together and Alfonso respected Doña Sol's opinions on social and even political matters. Alfonso was, furthermore, flattered to know, as he did, that Doña Sol was in love with him. It was really more of dog-like devotion than love in the ordinary sense: the kind of love a pet has for her master. Alfonso enjoyed the implications of this relationship. They complemented those of his relationship with

Beatrice who usually tried to dominate the situation and force things along at her own pace. Doña Sol was willing to play a waiting game. Unlike Beatrice, she did not overplay her hand. She wanted to be around and in favour for as long as possible. The fact that she achieved this was a bitter pill for Ena to swallow. Alfonso made no secret of his preference for Doña Sol's company over that of his own wife. As the rift between King and Queen widened, Doña Sol went more and more over to the King's side. Suspicions that she was the King's lover turned to certainty in the minds of most of the courtiers. Apart from anything else it suited most of them to think this. Also, Doña Sol was 'one of them'. She ingratiated herself with the ladies and gentlemen-in-waiting, but one of the latter was shrewd enough to sum her up with probable accuracy. 'She was an arch intriguer, and a mischief-maker,' he asserts. 'But almost certainly she never went to bed with the King. Of his close woman friends, in fact, she was probably the only one who didn't.'

When the Court became thoroughly split between those respectively favouring the King or the Queen, Doña Sol, along with such stalwarts as the Duchess of San Carlos, were solidly for the King. An indication of how Ena felt about it all emerged in her reaction to a step taken by the only English servant she had ever been allowed to keep, on a permanent basis, at the Spanish Court. This was the tall blond manservant Searle one of whose principal duties was to stand behind the Queen's chair at all meals. This duty he performed with ramrod-like solemnity. For many years it seemed that nothing could disturb his unswerving loyalty to Ena. His very presence was a comfort to her in dark moments. Eventually, however, he married Doña Sol's maid. Ena felt bitterly let down and described his action as a 'desertion to the enemy camp'. These were strong words but they exactly expressed Ena's feelings as to how far things had gone against her by the middle twenties. But she would never have accused Doña Sol of being an evil person. On the other hand, there were others on the scene, one in particular, whom she very much felt came into this category. This was the Marquis of Viana, the King's principal favourite. Compared to his evil influence on the King, even the machinations of such as Almodovar and Someruelos were becoming as nothing. He was a thoroughly unpleasant man whose obsequious manner toward the Queen only increased her distaste for him. She had no illusions as to the fact that he was, in the final analysis, her principal enemy at Court. In procuring women for her husband, if necessary of any type, he did not neglect to cater for his own amusements. Worse still was his poisoning of so many minds against the Queen. For this he had little motive other than the fact that he had contempt for Ena as a foreigner who, above all, lacked glamour and sex appeal.

Throughout all this Ena's resilience was astonishing. Her critics said, and still say, that she was not astute enough to realize exactly what was happening. Her admirers, on the other hand, insist that though she had many faults she possessed one overriding quality. And this was loyalty. It was a characteristic that was as strongly present in her make-up as it was lacking in that of Alfonso. She also understood her husband better than most other people. Somewhat in the same way as Maria Christina had come to love Alfonso XII despite his multiple infidelities, Ena's affection for Alfonso never disappeared. It even mellowed into a wistful but hopeless sort of love as the years went by. Alfonso, for his part, was in love, if at all, only with the image of what Ena might have become for him but never did. His many affairs, on the other hand, had, so far, never stirred any real love in his heart. The passing satisfaction which they provided never cured a fundamental loneliness from which Ena knew he was suffering. Thus when, suddenly, in the early twenties, Alfonso fell deeply in love with a certain woman, it might have been thought that Ena's disappointment would now turn to despair.

This did not happen. Was it because the woman in question looked strikingly like Ena herself? No one can tell. What is certain is that many things were thrown into the melting pot during the twenties in Spain. It was a period of dramatic change for the country as a whole and for the royal family in particular. The political situation deteriorated seriously and the monarchy was saved from itself only by a resort to dictatorship. Alfonso also needed to restore his personal confidence and psychological balance. This he seemed to be doing in the company of his new love. For her part, Ena, after the war, had begun to carve out for herself a new and more exciting life. Her own circle of friends came to challenge and rival the representatives of the more traditional section of high society. The Queen was thus able to balance her former isolation with a new spirit of independence. This even made possible something in the nature of a peaceful co-existence between Alfonso and Ena. The former's position insulated him from any but the most subdued form of criticism. The latter's dignity and loyalty were now bolstered by a new found sense of security and liberation. In the end, indeed, as will be seen, her efforts to establish a full life for herself in her own right were almost too successful.

Alfonso's new love was called Carmen Ruiz-Moragas. His feelings for her were very different from that awoken by any of his previous mistresses. She was an actress of great beauty but not considerable talent. Had it not been for her training with Maria Guerrero she might never have become prominent enough to attract the King's attention. He fell in love with her almost at first sight. She soon realized that this was not one of the King's, by now notorious, passing affairs. She instinctively realized, almost straight away, what were the emotional needs of this man who inwardly was so tortured and lacking in self-confidence despite his energetic outward display. Something similar had happened in the case of Alfonso's father. He had found solace in the arms of an opera singer called Elena Sanz. She too was a beauty of only second-rate artistic ability. But she had become for the King just what he needed at the time and had borne him two children. Carmen Moragas was to do the same for Alfonso XIII. By him she had a boy and a girl. The fact that both were healthy acted as a sort of private revenge against Ena on Alfonso's part. *He* could produce sound children; *she* could not. Alfonso's pride as a lover and father was restored. 'The Moragas', as people called her, was faithful to Alfonso through the twenties without expecting him to have no other lovers particularly, as had been happening for some years, during his trips to Paris. These were of no consequence to Moragas who was never in love with the King.

They called their son Leandro. He was strikingly like Alfonso and was sent to school at the Augustinian College which was housed in part of the vast Escorial Palace a little out of Madrid to the north. While there Leandro pondered on the strange and sometimes unfair vagaries of history. For in another part of that strange, monastically austere Palace, built by Philip II as mausoleum as well as a home, there lay buried Don John of Austria. He too had been the son of a Spanish king and he too had been illegitimate. He had nevertheless been accorded full honours by the State which he had gallantly served. Leandro knew that, whatever happened, he would always have to live in a half-world. He saw little of his father in later years but they once met by chance on a railway station. They embraced silently, these two men so physically alike. They exchanged few words. There seemed little to say. The meeting was brief.

Their other child was a daughter called Maria Teresa after the King's sister. She was amazingly like Ena in looks since her mother, as mentioned, strongly resembled the Queen. She too knew that a life of pretended anonymity lay in front of her. She made the best of it and married an Italian but died young. Alfonso's liaison with Moragas was brought to an end by his departure from Spain. It was a relationship which had helped to soothe the King's nerves during the increasingly hard battle he waged to save his throne. But he and his mistress seldom spoke of politics. This was due largely to tact on the part of the actress who had very much a mind of her own. It was only after the fall of the monarchy that her true opinions came out into the open. She then declared herself for the Republic and published her closely reasoned views in some detail. The King was hurt by what he considered to be a betrayal. But by that time he had lost very much more than just Carmen Moragas.

Alfonso's children by this, his favourite, mistress were not his only illegitimate offspring. Estimates vary as to what was the total number. One of the saddest cases was that of a daughter born to an Irish nanny-*cum*-governess who was employed for a short time at the royal household in Madrid. Alfonso took a fancy to her and she became pregnant by him. She was brutally dismissed from the royal service and sent away in disgrace. She only set eyes on her daughter once and was never allowed to see her again. The daughter had a nomadic and lonely existence eventually losing all desire to go on living at all. She died young with little money and few friends.

Alfonso's special interests often took him to Paris where the Spanish Embassy was diligent in catering for his needs. Alfonso's taste for this *mise-en-scène* had remained sharp ever since the M. Lamy interlude. His visits there were a regular feature of his life from about 1913 onwards. One of his favourite French mistresses was Melanie, Madame de Vilmorin. She bore him a son, Roger, in about 1915. The de Vilmorins were a well-known French family and one of their number, Genevieve, came to interview Ena many years later in Lausanne. One of Roger's half-sisters married Admiral Toulouse-Lautrec. On his trips abroad Alfonso always took with him several pairs of black satin sheets. These, he felt, showed up to better advantage the extreme whiteness of his skin, a characteristic of which he was always very vain. Some of the King's lady friends laughed privately about this little quirk of Alfonso's. But in his eyes the black sheets greatly enhanced the pleasure of the many hours of amorous relaxation spent between them.

As already mentioned, Alfonso's exotic private life style became well known in Court circles, many of whose grand ladies naturally did not want to be left out of the action. They were willing, at the very least, to play with the dangerous but alluring fire that was on offer, even though most hoped to stop short of compromising themselves irrevocably. But while it lasted it was too good to miss. The lives of such ladies at home were usually insufferably dull. They knew, in most cases, that their husbands were unfaithful to them though they themselves were expected to honour the tradition, then still strong in Spain, that there was one law for men and another for women. They would rarely have risked having affairs with any old lover. But if it were to be with the King, that would be different. He, for one thing, was above the law in the eyes of Court and society. And this extended a sort of vicarious protection to his aristocratic bed mates. Doña Sol, not being a rival as such in the mistress stakes, was, in a certain sense, an arbiter and pacemaker of Court morals. For her, unswerving loyalty to the King was the paramount criterion. 'Alfonso right or wrong' was her motto and this was the view of the majority. Ena had so far failed to charm enough of the courtiers, either male or female, to bring about any modification of this principle. So the King achieved virtual immunity from criticism for any of his actions, least of all on the grounds that he was being cruel or unfair to his wife. He was, in Doña Sol's word, the 'acreedor'—or rightful recipient—of the love and loyalty of all his subjects.

Another view held at Court was that Alfonso was after all a Bourbon. He would have had, in any case, to be allowed considerable latitude in the sexual sphere. But Alfonso was reckoned to have a special grievance and therefore an adequate excuse for what he did. He received the lion's share of what sympathy was going for the misfortunes in the royal family. There was little left over for Ena. The well-known 'accessibility' of the Bourbon monarchs thus came to have a new meaning in the days of Alfonso XIII. One or two ladies of high rank were surprisingly earthy and candid in their choice of words to describe the situation. One Court lady said that the Bourbon 'accessibility' had come, in Alfonso's case, to mean 'anywhere, any time'. Another verdict was that of a Duchess who is still alive and had better remain nameless. 'Most people', she said, pointedly generalizing, found going to bed with Alfonso 'very good but only once'. According to her, the experience, if repeated, was not to everyone's taste. For the King was reputed to be a selfish lover. He had a voracious appetite that needed to be satisfied. It was somewhat the same with food which he gobbled up hungrily as soon as it was put on his plate. In matters of love he had little time for finesse except in certain special cases. The most notable of these was Carmen Moragas.

Without knowing all this, unpleasant though it may be, it is impossible to gain any idea of what Ena's life was like and of what her sufferings were. The very fact that Alfonso possessed tremendous charm for all around him, was not, in itself, an irksome factor for the Queen. She was surprisingly free of jealousy over this. She herself was a victim of this fatal charm whenever he turned it in her direction, even if this happened to be at some otherwise hateful or dark moment in her emotional life. The most intense part of Ena's suffering, at its height just before the First World War, arose from the humiliation of realizing how popular would have been a Spanish royal marriage that had produced sound and healthy children. Her manner of combating the agony in this was not, however, felicitous. It was misunderstood and made her more unpopular still. For she met this supreme moment of adversity with an exterior so calm and controlled that she was accused, particularly in relation to the illness of the Prince of Asturias, of being hard and cold. As one of her few very close friends, the Duchess of Lecera, told one of the grandees serving at Court, 'They don't know the truth which is captured by what the Queen has said to me: "I can't face it".'

This was true. Queen Ena, quite literally, could not face up to the reality of her eldest child's illness and the resultant aberrant behaviour of her self-willed and impetuous husband. She was able, in an extraordinary way, to turn her back on the situation and, after the first shock was over, to plunge into a different life at other levels in order to escape the harrowing consequences of living constantly with reality. It was the beginning of a long process which those who knew her years later, after the Second

World War, were to find very pronounced. Tragedies, as one of them said, slid from her as water from a duck's back. Such a facility made her seem superficial in the eyes of some, indifferent in the eyes of others and positively cold and uncaring in the judgment of still more. It was not in her nature, however, to make scenes. She would never have dreamed of publicly or openly defying Alfonso. And she was not in any way inclined to get her revenge by taking a chain of lovers of her own. At no time in her life, in fact, did she have a lover. This can be asserted with confidence. This was due not necessarily to any great sense of virtue, except in so far as she always remained remarkably loyal to Alfonso despite everything. The less creditable fact was that she was not at all sexy by nature. She flirted mildly with many handsome men in the course of the twenties when this new phase in her life opened. But that was all.

Was she likely, during this period, to regain any of her lost happiness? Or would she have to be content with seeking mere distraction instead? She naturally had no idea of what lay in store for her. But, just as on the day of the brush with death within hours of her wedding she could find consolation in the possession of jewellery, so now she found consolation in the very fact of being Queen of Spain. It was a role which, despite everything, she thoroughly enjoyed. And when the First World War was over she became determined to find happiness of sorts, if necessary in a world of her own, where her husband could not go on hurting her for ever.

[9]

A Court Divided

ENA'S quest for happiness from new sources after the First World War came to depend on three factors in particular. One was the new and more soothing rhythm and routine of life which, with the end of childbearing and war worries, now became possible. Within this new routine, even at the darkest moments, there was always something, particularly the annual visit to England, to which Ena could look forward. Secondly, the success and widening of her work for medicine, nursing and other causes proved to be a powerful antidote to personal frustrations and disappointments from other quarters. Thirdly, and probably most importantly, Ena, in a social sense, became virtually a different woman in these years, gathering round her a new and brilliant set of friends who were to shake the Spanish society of its day to its foundations.

The usual practice was to spend the winter months—October to the end of May—in Madrid. In the past such winters had been depressing and cold. But Ena's domestic initiatives had at long last resulted in a considerably improved and more cosmopolitan cuisine as well as more adequate heating for the Palace. Though the winters were long, her work and new social outlets made a vast difference to her daily life. And always to be looked forward to during these months was the visit to England in June and/or July. The autumn months would normally be spent at the seaside Palace of Miramar in San Sebastian, the King's favourite residence. This was often tedious for Ena as Alfonso insisted that they should be there to join up with the Queen Mother in time for her birthday on 20 July. Ena would have preferred to have

[174]

extended the time spent in England with something like a visit to Cowes; but it was rarely possible. At least, at San Sebastian, there was ample opportunity for tennis, golf and riding, in all of which Ena still engaged with enthusiasm. Alfonso would sometimes ride or play with her and there were occasions, on some relaxed afternoons, when Ena would almost persuade herself for a moment that all was well with her marriage, with her husband and with Spain. Before returning to Madrid Ena, with, or more often without, Alfonso would go to pay her yearly visit to the Empress Zita, the widow of the last Emperor of Austria-Hungary who had come to live in Spain. This routine was varied by shorter visits to one of the other royal residences outside the capital as well as to Barcelona and quite often, as dictated by political exigencies, Paris, Rome, and other foreign capitals.

In spring, for example, the royal household would often transfer itself to the beautiful Moorish Palace of the Alcazar in Seville in order to be in that fascinating city during the Easter feria. Ena was particularly popular in Andalusia and people would greet her uninhibitedly as she and the King drove through the picturesque narrow streets. In no other part of Spain was her beauty so openly admired. While waving to the crowds she would overhear, among the chorus of 'Vivas' such remarks as 'Por Dios, what colouring!' or 'Santa Maria, gold is poor beside her hair!' One day a woman in the crowd shouted out, 'You are not only Queen of Spain; you are Queen of all beautiful women!'

Such incidents did much to restore Ena's self-confidence and at such moments she felt proud to be riding along in an open carriage beside the handsome King. She would often steal him a sidelong glance to see his reaction to the praises she was receiving from the people. If she was rewarded by one of his flashing smiles her heart was quick to melt toward him. She was invariably more yielding than vindictive and there was a lingering sense in which both she and Alfonso always retained something of the innocence of their youthful, courting days. The romantic image of the boy King and the girl Queen was thus slow to fade. Alfonso never lost

Ena in peasant dress

his love of fun and games, jokes and jaunts. Ena never lost hers for the 'toys' and trappings, the tributes and treats that went with being a Queen. And there was still much in the Spain of the twenties, more perhaps than in any other country, that lent a fairy-tale touch to life in the various royal palaces. The world of make-believe often seemed more real than that in which problems, personal and political, were piling up. What was a haven for Ena, however, proved to be a trap for Alfonso. Each in different ways, was sucked into it more and more irrevocably as the post-war decade wore on.

Meanwhile, however, another boost for Ena had come by way of her new found flair for clothes. In the early days of her marriage she had been looked upon as distinctly dowdy. In the twenties she was considered one of the best-dressed women in Europe. She went to leading fashion houses in Mayfair and Paris without forgetting the couturiers of Madrid. She set new trends in Spain especially among young people. But she did not let clothes dominate her life. In a curious way Alfonso did. On an average day in Madrid, taken up with parades, ceremonies and official functions, he would rush back to the Palace to change into some other uniform, appropriate or otherwise, sometimes as often as four times in a day. While Ena's self-confidence grew with the years, Alfonso came increasingly to depend on some sort of sartorial 'mask' behind which to operate. He seemed as time went by to be less and less able to face the world as himself.

Ena's average day was often as varied as Alfonso's because of the mounting work load which she took on within the realm of her chosen activities. The efficiency of Ena's Spanish Red Cross became more marked each year. This was evidenced in 1921 when the war in Morocco took a serious turn. Melilla was the scene of the greatest suffering for the beleaguered Spanish troops. The Queen sent representatives to establish greatly needed temporary hospitals. These came into being in Melilla, Tetoan, Larache and Ceuta. A voluntary squad of highly trained 'Lady Nurses', known as 'Damas Eugameras', became a sort of flying column to spearhead relief action wherever it was wanted. The cleanliness and efficiency brought to Morocco by the Queen's Red Cross was something which that disease-ridden country had never seen before. Her fund-raising activities were meanwhile spectacular, thorough and ingenious. Still more hospitals in Madrid came to be founded or supported by such means, notably the Maria Christina, the Principe Alfonso, Victoria Eugenia and, perhaps above all, the Santa Adela. The Queen was a frequent visitor at the new centres, hospitals, nurseries, dispensaries and other institutions that had come into being, directly or indirectly, through her efforts. By the end of the twenties it could truthfully be said that 'The Queen of Spain and her representatives have accomplished in Spain a work that can never be destroyed and that will never be forgotten.'[1]

Ena's popularity among ordinary people naturally soared. The same thing did not happen among the more traditional ranks of the aristocracy. Staid and solid representatives of the old school, and there was a depressingly large quantity of these about, did not take kindly to the Queen's new successes on the social scene. For Ena was boldly launching out in fresh directions. Her desire to do so was partly a reaction to the general attitude and demeanour of Alfonso of whom she had long ago said, 'He tires of everything. Some day he will even tire of me.' That this prophecy had become sadly true was, by the early twenties, not only apparent to Ena herself but, which made it all so much more humiliating, to the whole of society as well. For it was now apparent that the royal couple's appearances together on social and artistic occasions were largely a matter of form. It was invariably apparent that Alfonso could not wait to escape into more congenial company. Even at the theatre or the opera he was restless and fidgety. While, on such occasions, Ena admired the art on offer, Alfonso had eyes only for the artistes. The prettier ones among the latter came to expect a visit backstage from one of the King's equerries to arrange a rendezvous. The King would subsequently be seen hurrying off with his playboy companions. The Queen would return to the Palace—alone except for her obsequious but often inwardly smirking ladies-in-waiting. The worst feature about Alfonso's multiple infidelities was the fact that they were carried out with a maximum of inconsiderateness and insensitivity toward his wife. 'He made a fool of her,' in the words of one lady who knew—and still does know – Madrid Society well.

In general, however, within the upper echelons of Madrid Society, even today, there is a virtual conspiracy of silence about the domestic behaviour of King Alfonso. This results in a reluctance to speak in anything but generalities about the Queen who is frequently damned with faint praise. But there are just enough people from those circles, not all of them still living in Spain, who are willing to be frank, though reluctant to be quoted directly, about what happened sixty years ago.

As already described, the Spain of that time was still, in many respects, about a hundred years behind the times—and many were proud of it. Those, at least, were proud who had most say in the country's destinies, namely the aristocracy (including, of course, the Court) and the Church. These powerful factions worked together with the Army as their traditional, though not invariably reliable, ally. The key to the situation was provided by the Church in ways already mentioned. The Queen, often feeling compelled to side with the Church, forfeited popular esteem by so doing. The profound unpopularity of the Church, however, did not undermine its immense power. It was unrivalled in its pretensions to be the guardian of the nation's conscience and was ruthlessly uncompromising about moral lapses among ordinary people. But it was tolerant of immorality on the part of the King. The setting of such double standards troubled few. It was recognized as being necessary for the preservation of the system as a whole. The vast majority of (otherwise unemployable) court-iers depended entirely on the King's favour for their status and prestige. Loyalty to the point of sycophancy was therefore necess-ary. When courtly eyes turned toward Ena they were correspond-ingly critical. The nobility were, almost from the first, out to fault the Queen. Stories of the two great 'mistakes' made by Ena after she became Queen of Spain are still solemnly retailed to this day in certain over-stuffy Spanish and royalist circles. One's initial reaction to being told how 'disgracefully' Ena behaved is to prepare oneself for a shock. The actual revelations come as an almost comic anti-climax. The first accusation against Ena is that she dared, when she began to acquire the necessary confidence, to act as Queen of Spain rather than meekly to play second fiddle to her formidable mother-in-law. The second charge was that she scandalized the society of the day by wearing indecent clothes.

The latter criticism arose because Ena was occasionally seen in evening dresses whose level of décolletage, though quite normal in London or Paris, scandalized the moral susceptibilities of the Spanish upper classes. (Such susceptibilities, as has been seen, were left unruffled by the King's stream of love affairs.) But the Queen had only to appear in the royal box at the opera in a slightly off-the-shoulder evening dress—as often as not bringing murmurs of admiration from the audience at large—for some bossy lady-in-waiting to rush forward with shawls to cover up the Queen's 'nakedness'. Ena usually gave in gracefully to such restrictions, however petty. On one occasion an evening dress was delivered from the house of a French designer. The skirt was slit to just above the knee, according, but not quite to the fullest extent, to what was then the fashion in Paris. But the dress brought blushes to the faces of the 'frumps' at the Spanish Court and the offending split had to be filled in with cascades of lace.

Among the younger and more cosmopolitan set, however, there was a strong undercurrent of support for the Queen and her style of living. They observed wistfully how relaxed Ena seemed, especially when away from Madrid, as during the summer months at the seaside Palace of Miramar at San Sebastian. It was obvious—if irksome to the old guard—that Ena's natural, liberated and enlightened approach to life was ripe for taking root in Spain. She showed that royal dignity was compatible with unaffected friendliness when, particularly at San Sebastian, she went into the waterfront teashops and joined the other ladies in taking refreshment. When she became one of the first women in Spain to wear a tight-fitting bathing suit, her action was applauded by healthy-minded young people. By the same token, however, the Queen's 'boldness scandalized a great many of her subjects.'[2] Officialdom made sure that the Queen's modern ideas would be hedged around with as many precautions as possible however ridiculous these might be in some cases. The Duke of Sutherland once saw her bathing at San Sebastian. Two soldiers, fully armed and uniformed, stood guard on each side of her. They kept abreast with her until, still staring impassively ahead, the waves had reached up to their necks. All in all, as Marie, Grand Duchess of Russia wrote[3], Ena 'was by far the most human representative of her kind in spite of the long period of years spent in the stiffest court in Europe. She achieved perfect balance between ease and simplicity on one side and the obligations of her rank on the other.'

The other charge against Ena arose from her unwillingness to take lying down the slights of the Queen Mother, to say nothing of those of the majority of people serving their time at Court. For the first few years Queen Maria Christina managed fairly easily to outmanoeuvre her well-brought-up and inexperienced daughter-in-law. After the First World War, however, Ena got fed up with being upstaged and quietly but very firmly asserted her rightful place. Her show of independence was resented by the frumps and the cronies. But Ena, as Princess Alice (Countess of Athlone), was to tell the author many years later, was 'irrepressible'. 'You could squash her here,' as the Princess put it, illustrating her words by pressing her thumb down on the table in front of her. 'But', she would add with another appropriate gesture, 'she would only pop up over there.' (The Princess was over ninety at the time of this conversation. But, when giving this particular description of her cousin Ena, her almost unlined face lit up with a smile so dazzling that it made her look for a moment like a young woman again.)

Had Queen Ena willingly submitted herself to effectively taking second place to her virtuous but tactless mother-in-law, she would probably have gained little in popularity with people who had been determined from the start to belittle her and make her position difficult. But her sudden show of spirit from the early twenties onwards turned latent resentment into open animosity. The mature Queen Victoria Eugenia of the 1920s was very unlike the shy and bewildered girl who had first come to Spain at the age of eighteen. The old guard now had reason to fear for the means whereby Spain, at Court and society level, had contrived for so long to conceal its decadence beneath a veneer of elaborate religious practices and Jansenistic moral attitudes. The social counterpart of such an outlook had contributed during the Regency of Queen Maria Christina to make her Court the most boring and uninteresting in Europe. Ena's attempt a generation later, to change this state of affairs was about to meet with fierce rearguard opposition.

The trouble was that, while Ena's critics were, for the most part, suffocatingly dull, she herself was only happy in the company of those who were witty and amusing. She thus creamed off from the society of her time a group who came to be known as the 'elegantes'. This meant, literally, the elegant ones, but the image they created was more like that of the 'bright young things' in the England of the twenties. One section of society thus took on a distinctly 'new look', a look which the morbid, perpetually 'mourning' frumps, including, essentially, the Queen Mother, distinctly did not like. And yet Ena was not the true innovator of this new look. Ever since the death of Isabel II, there had been a rising inclination among the more intelligent sections of society to be less crudely insular and to become more sophisticated and cosmopolitan. Ena's arrival on the scene gave fresh impetus to this tendency which was welcomed by many as a healthy reaction to the introspective and stifling 'insimismo', as it was called, of a former age. They were ready and eager to let Ena try to preside over a breakaway social group where a traditionally-hated 'for-

eign' (mostly French) influence should be allowed to have more
sway. Ena's first big obstacle was the constant presence of her
mother-in-law under the same roof. Though the latter occupied
self-contained apartments in a corner of the Palace, her presence
was a permanent, indeed dominating feature of daily palace life.
In England, it would have been normal for the Queen Mother to
move out altogether and to live in a home of her own in a different
part of the city. But in Spain the concept of 'la familia' rules
supreme. This dictates that mothers-in-law and daughters-in-
law are expected to live together. In view of the intimacy between
Alfonso and Maria Christina this had caused difficulties from the
very beginning, as already described. But after the First World
War it was the Queen who increasingly took the lead. She now
had perfect command of Spanish, she also had her own firm, if
very small, circle of friends. On these she came to depend heavily,
too heavily as it was later to turn out. Alfonso meanwhile, kept to a
small circle entirely of his own, while a growing friction rose up
between the two factions, on either side. Language was one of the
symptoms of the split in society. The 'elegantes' spoke mostly in
English. Their rivals adhered more pointedly than ever to Spanish (not being much good at English anyway). English, moreover,
seemed the natural language for conversation to those used to
cosmopolitan gatherings. Such people were not necessarily 'elegantes' in the full sense of the word. They included such as the
Montellanes, the de Leceras, the Santa Cruzes, the Albas and the
Santoñas. The Duchess of Santoña, Doña Sol, claimed, as
already mentioned, to be a faithful friend of both the King and
Queen, though Ena would not have agreed. To others, tending
obviously toward the 'elegante' camp, French came most naturally as a social language. This group, headed by the Duke and
Duchess of Plascencia and the Medinacelis, were considered to
belong to the 'witty' Parisian set. In practice it was not always clear
who was clearly in which set, if any. People began to size each
other up with considerable mutual suspicion. One person might
say to another, perhaps even his own cousin, something like: 'So

you're an "elegante" then.' It was said in a reproving, almost accusing tone of voice as if to imply 'I've found you out!'

The cleavages in Spanish society which had first appeared during the First World War, deepened decisively in the decade that followed. Cleavages begat jealousies. The Queen herself was partly to blame. She loved parties and entertainment. She found it well nigh impossible to refuse invitations, and she naturally received many from those who were not thought fully acceptable in the strictest social circles. Thus a new name grew up, this time invented by the Queen's growing band of enemies. Those who entertained the Queen and gained her favour were labelled 'aisladores'. The description, really an epithet, implied that these new friends of the Queen were insulating her and cutting her off from the mainstream of society. It was partly true and, later on, Ena's 'base' was to become dangerously narrow. For the time being, however, while one set of society, that headed by the Queen, enjoyed itself, the other tended to remain overshadowed by frumpery. The latter had to combine the difficult task of turning a blind eye to the King's infidelities and social crudities with preserving an air of respectability. In their heart of hearts, many would have liked to be included in the Queen's guest list, but from this particular 'royal enclosure' they were excluded. Jealousy and backbiting were natural consequences of this situation.

The Duke and Duchess of Lecera were among Ena's best friends. But they gained excessive and finally fatal influence on her. It was thus that the 'aisladores' were ultimately harmful to Ena by being too possessive. Their elitism became the inevitable excuse for a charge of frivolity within the Queen's set, some of whom did not disguise their contempt for the dullness of the Court establishment. They openly commented on the boringness and lack of imagination that characterized the world of Maria Christina and of the King's aunt, the Infanta Isabel, and dismissed them as 'latas' (bores). This they were, though it was extremely impolitic to say so. Such impetuosity is a characteristic of the 'bright young thing' mentality which holds little to be sacred. The Infanta Isabel, moreover, was in fact widely popular. A fat and homely figure, long since widowed, she represented 'old royal Spain' at its best—thoroughly unenlightened but basically just and well-meaning. She had no sympathy for any brand of republicanism, understanding neither its causes nor its ideals. But she feared that republicanism would one day be made inevitable if only because of the outlook of the royal family itself as personified by her nephew Alfonso. Her loyalties were torn and it would have been merciful had she died before Alfonso was forced to leave Spain. As it was she lived just long enough to see the declaration of the Second Republic. Her main emotion was remorse that the blindness of her own family had once again, as it seemed to her, brought the country she loved to such an accursed pass. Her last words were 'tengo verguenza' (I am ashamed). She was a good woman and it was a mistake and a solecism on the part of the 'elegantes' to dismiss her as a mere bore.

Alfonso had little time for either set and invariably showed his impatience with official entertainments and formal social occasions. He would seek out his 'amigotes' and they would slip away from parties as quickly as possible to play cards, drink and talk, and then, in all probability, disappear for the rest of the night.

As time went on Ena started entertaining her special friends with music and dancing. The Queen Mother, though invited, seldom attended such parties. Instead she invited the courtiers to her own 'bailecitos', intimate but stiffly formal affairs attended by some 150 persons taken from the 'palatine list'. Such functions filled the gap to some extent for those who were not among the 'elegantes.' Ena usually went to them but found few congenial dancing partners among the mostly inimical courtiers who habitually attended. Gradually, however, some friends did emerge from such ranks and she even had mild flirtations with them. Such 'flirtations', if they even deserve the name, were a welcome distraction from the necessity of conversations with women of the 'fat old frump' variety. Ena had her daily fill of these and found

Ena dressed for a party

painfully boring the interminable stories such ladies had to tell about the illnesses of their numerous relations.

By contrast to the prevailing morbid preference for heavy formality, Ena longed for ceremonies and parties with gaiety and glamour. Her Lord Chamberlain, the Duke of Santo Mauro, tried to provide a background for this by giving occasional Sunday dances. They were hardly the last word in hilarious abandon but were considerably more entertaining than Maria Christina's dreary 'bailecitos'.

If Alfonso was as bored as his wife was with official Court life, this was of little help to Ena. He had a different way of showing his boredom, which resulted in his ignoring Ena almost completely during his hectic day-to-day existence. He lived in his own world of 'amigotes', polo and love affairs.

The King and Queen met together, of course, for meals at the Palace. But these followed a curious pattern. They were preceded by a rather elaborate procedure with those involved meeting first in a small drawing-room. The grandees took it in turn to be 'in-waiting' and these would always be there and there would always be one grandee present at each meal. It was his job to jump ahead opening the heavy doors of the ante-rooms leading from the small drawing-room into the dining-room. This took some time but the meal itself, once started, did not take very long. There was little real conversation but the King, a messy eater, would talk a lot while gulping down his food. His remarks were almost all addressed to his own ADC's who would sit near him. They naturally spoke in Spanish. The two Queens were left to carry on a conversation with such guests as might be present. Ena spoke English whenever possible while the Queen Mother invariably favoured French. Both would use Spanish when occasion demanded.

An observant guest at such meals in the first years of the King's married life would have been aware that Ena, though always correct and polite, was seldom fully at ease. Unwittingly, she made conversation all the more difficult. She was often being up staged by the Queen Mother who, despite a tendency to be tactless, kept the conversational ball rolling with a barrage of questions even if she did not always listen to the answers. Having lived in the Palace so much longer than Ena she never felt anything but thoroughly at home in it. This gave Maria Christina a distinct edge over Ena in palace circles in general, at least until after the First World War. The Queen Mother and the King, moreover, were recklessly unguarded in what they said and as to the subjects they chose to discuss in front of the servants. Such stories would have had no chance of appearing in anything but foreign papers at the time, though the Spanish Press was permitted, within limits, to engage in political controversy and criticism.

Ena's main efforts were to combat the stifling 'insimismo' of her immediate surroundings. She had been condemned during the first seven years of marriage to be an annual bearer of children. Then, during the First World War, she had been treated as an outsider by a pro-German Court. Her role as a child-bearer had been productive of grief. Her status as a foreigner had brought her humiliation. 'From now on', she said, 'I am determined to live as a woman'. In the greater world beyond the Palace there was no lack of people with admiration for her beauty and character, who wanted to be friends with her for her own sake. This greater world was international in outlook and Ena presided over it with charm and grace. Friends and relations from England fitted into this world as did notable visitors from Rome, Paris and Madrid. They found a readier welcome in the Queen's set than in any other. One reason was brutally simple. The conventional courtiers, men and women, were very bad linguists. They were ashamed of their inadequate English and French and so, with a show of disdainful superiority, shunned the company of guests from these countries whenever possible. When Ena tried to introduce them to figures in the international set she found them graceless and unbending. They could not refuse the Queen to her face but they deferred to her wishes with a minimum of goodwill. 'It all became a rather unpleasant game', said one of the Queen's staunch allies who himself tried to bridge various gaps and break a lot of ice by his own parties on such neutral ground as the luxurious and exclusive Royal Club at Puerto de Hierro, on the northern outskirts of Madrid. This was the 'club madrileño' *par excellence*, with sumptuous premises set amidst the stunning Velázquez countryside. It was something like London's Hurlingham but considerably grander. Glittering parties would be given as the climax to an afternoon of polo. The 'elegantes' invariably outshone the other Spaniards present and would be fully at ease chatting with such guests from abroad as the Wellingtons, Pembrokes and Londesboroughs, the latter being the parents of Ena's sister-in-law the Marchioness of Carisbrooke—formerly Princess Alexander of Battenberg.

There were many other visitors to Spain from England in the twenties. Quite a lot of them were difficult to 'place' socially in traditionalist Spanish eyes. Intellectual attainments cut little ice in circles such as that of the King, where philistinism prevailed. One visitor was the colourful novelist Elinor Glyn who came in 1923. She had a cutting tongue but a brilliant pen. Ena made strenuous efforts to ensure that her reactions to Madrid life would be favourable. The novelist lunched with the British Ambassador, Sir Esmé Howard, but the occasion was not considered socially important enough for the King and Queen to attend. Ena worked behind the scenes and the Albas, the Duke of Alianza and the Duchess of Parcent were among those who threw themselves into the task of entertaining this 'difficult and dangerous' English-woman. Miss Glyn recorded her impressions in a book called *Letters from Spain.* Ena, she wrote, 'looked like a fairy queen, so young and fresh and lovely'. In her silver turquoise and aqua-marine lamé dress she looked 'a dream of beauty all the time'. At a fiesta of Spanish dancing she noticed the crowd pressing round Queen Ena 'murmuring ecstatically: "La Reina"! "La Reina"!'

Another visitor to Madrid in the twenties was Mrs Ronnie Greville, a formidable figure on the English social scene of the day and a close friend of Ena's. A rather silly myth, however, had grown up about her, turning her into a 'terror of Ambassadors, Viceroys and Governors-General'. There was a tendency to treat her almost as royalty, putting horse and carriage at her disposal and having to invite the most illustrious people 'to meet Mrs Greville'. Alfonso and Ena went to the luncheon given in Mrs Greville's honour by the British Ambassador. Primo de Rivera, by that time dictator of Spain, was present. But he spoke no English and Mrs Greville spoke no Spanish. The luncheon was not a great success and Ena was, rather understandably, blamed for this in official Spanish circles.

Was the Queen, by now, going too far? Her special efforts on behalf of English visitors could not, in Spanish eyes, be entirely excused on the grounds of cosmopolitanism. She herself claimed she was trying to provide a bridge for traditional Spain with the outside world. But such efforts did not endear her to the aristocracy. She failed to win them over and took refuge more and more among her own friends and visitors from abroad. After the King's affair with Carmen Moragas had started opinion polarized still further. Some felt that he had at last gone too far, not so much in what he was doing but in the way in which he was doing it. They sympathized with his agony over the defective heir but could see the misery brought to the Queen by his crude callousness. Others felt that the Queen had driven her husband into the arms of a more understanding and sensitive woman. The divisions at Court thus spread to the whole of Madrid. Even some of the 'elegantes', many of whom were of frivolous bent, deserted the Queen. She had to start scraping around for allies at Court and began to regret that she had not done more to win over the more powerful traditionalists. The truth must be faced that she had, from the beginning, found some of them so intimidating as to make her suffer from a lasting inferiority complex when in their company. But neither she nor they would give way. It was a sad and apparently incurable impasse.

Some of those who claimed to be Ena's closest friends were not in all cases her strongest assets. Their motives in befriending her were not always wholly selfless. The Queen came to be something of a pawn between factions who had long nursed rivalries and jealousies. And the Queen's 'camp' was extremely small compared to that of the people whom she began to call, with an exaggeration born of disappointment, her 'enemies'. From 1926 onwards the Queen felt increasingly hemmed in by a persecuting atmosphere around her. One of her more unselfish allies was the Duchess of Montellano who received the Queen at all hours and was ever a sympathetic confidante. Another great friend was the prestigious Duchess of Medinaceli whose friendship was invaluable. Someone of rather different stamp who gained great influence with the Queen was Francesca, daughter of Fernando Lesseps of Suez Canal fame. Her married name was Countess of Mora and though she was loyal to the end to Ena she was disagreeable by nature and not universally popular. She fell out with the influential 'Jimmy' (Duke of) Alba, one of whose functions was to be the ceremonial bearer of certain sacred vessels in religious processions. 'You're nothing to laugh about Jimmy,' she said to him on one occasion, 'You're just a carrier of relics'. It was not a great help to the Queen to have friends who made such tactless remarks to pillars of the establishment, especially in a city where the pettiness of society made mountains out of such molehills.

Another ally of the Queen was the Duchess of Plascencia, as was the Duchess of Ahumada. But as the latter was much disliked in leading circles, her friendship was of doubtful value. Other close friends were the Cuervas's and the Leceras, already mentioned. It has to be admitted that the less beautiful women at Court, being unlikely to catch the roving eye of the King, were more likely to try and find a niche among Ena's circle. Viscountess Fefeñanes was one of these. A pleasant enough woman but rather a fair-weather friend. The King's army of supporters was meanwhile much stronger and numbered such rock-like pillars as the Duchess of San Carlos ('the Dragon'), the Duchess of Durcal and in the final analysis the almost ever-present Doña Sol. Ena became increasingly bitter about those who cold-shouldered or 'deserted' her. By the end of the twenties almost all the members of Spain's Court and high society had turned against the Queen in one degree or another. Their fortunes after all were inseparably linked with that of the King. He was their hero come what may. When he could be seen virtually to have rejected his wife, why should they sacrifice themselves by coming to her help? Besides, they had no reason to suppose that Alfonso would not continue to be their King for many more years to come. The possibility of a Republic had barely impinged on their sheltered and artificial lives. They had failed, utterly and for a long time past, to make an accurate reading of the Spanish national scene as a whole.

As it happened Queen Ena's role within the context of that wider scene was—and had been from the earliest days—a more central and decisive one that has generally been imagined.* The main charges against Ena among the nobility, meanwhile, were that she was too foreign—more specifically too English—as well as being too modern. It is true that she showed an undue preference for English and other 'foreign' friends, feeling that she had been unfairly deprived of such company in the early days. At the same time she was herself so solidly Anglo-Saxon, both physically and psychologically, that her efforts to become 'more Spanish' were awkward and rarely successful. She laboriously acquired a certain expertise in the esoteric art of arranging and wearing her mantilla in the correct fashion. But her loud laugh was unmercifully criticized and someone said that it sounded like 'something from the stable'. This jibe was to stick with her for life. She was totally un-Latin in almost every way and many of her qualities were too 'masculine' for Spanish tastes. At the same time her horror of bullfighting was too pronounced to be kept entirely secret and this was another stick with which she could be beaten even by those,

* See Chapter 10.

and they were growing in number, who were themselves becoming disenchanted with Spain's national sport.

As for her 'modern' tastes, her addiction to smoking was naturally a subject of adverse comment. Few women in Spain at that time smoked and none did so in public. Ena's unwillingness to compromise over this was considered an insult to the genteel wives of the haughty grandees. The fact that smoking, under Ena's influence, was becoming the fashion within the Queen's social set, even among women, was naturally yet another adverse factor. To shock the frumps, in fact, was all too tempting and all too easy for some of the 'bright young things'.

It must be admitted that Ena's lack of rapport with the Spanish aristocracy was partly her fault. Sir John Balfour, however, the distinguished British diplomat who was *en poste* in Spain during much of the period in question, has pointed (in conversation with the author) to factors which might well have frustrated anyone in a similar position. For Ena's life, according to him, was almost entirely overshadowed by the Queen Mother, who, in turn, commanded wide respect at Court. Ena's search for other friends was thus fraught with inevitable peril. Sir John himself first met the young Queen at a *thé dansant* at San Sebastian. These were very much the sort of social occasions, designed primarily for the 'elegantes', which Ena enjoyed but, according to Sir John, 'they were not to the taste of Spain's aristocracy which was strictly "stay-at-home" and stingy.' Their stinginess and frumpery in fact were, as he put it, 'so notorious as to be positively comic'. The British Ambassador, Sir Esmé Howard, once had occasion to call on the late Duke of Medinaceli, the country's leading nobleman, whose wife was an ally of the Queen's. The Ambassador was offered no hospitality and received no more than a curt 'good afternoon'. Such behaviour was typical of what Ena was up against.

Ever lurking in the background was the shadow of the haemophilia. Most of the Spanish nobility believed that Alfonso had never been properly warned of this danger because Ena's mother and Princess Ena herself had been so desirous of the Spanish match. This impression had gained ground when Alfonso, as from the period following the birth of the eldest son, had refused to speak to his mother-in-law unless it was absolutely necessary. Considerable blame thus rubbed off on the Queen who should, in the view of many of Spain's sanctimonious 'beatas', have gone into something like perpetual mourning. The fact that, instead, she revelled in a hectic social life in the company of the 'fast' international set was, in their eyes, the final straw. They found her behavious 'rancio', as if comparing her character to that of a once glorious golden wine which, though full of early promise, had quickly turned to sour vinegar.

[10]

Lengthening Shadows

FEW doubt that the history of modern Spain would have been very different had Alfonso XIII not married Princess Ena of Battenberg. This is not to say that the Queen played an active role in Spanish politics. But neither is it true to assert, as has often been done, that she was in no way involved in this side of the nation's life. Her eldest daughter, the Infanta Beatrice, has put this matter in perspective and the author is most grateful for her valuable comments about her mother. According to the Infanta, Queen Ena never discussed politics with anyone except the King. But with him she did discuss the nation's affairs and he often heeded her advice. For diplomatic reasons this fact was not publicized and Ena was always extremely careful to let Alfonso occupy the centre of the stage as far as the outside world was concerned. As time went on, however, it was she who had the surer grasp of the country's temper. Her hospital and relief work, though distinctly cast on old-fashioned, paternalistic lines, gave her some insight into ordinary people's needs and aspirations. While Alfonso, with deeply depressive occasional lapses—when Ena was able to be of invaluable support to him—remained optimistic until nearly the end, the Queen had, long before that, become well aware of the dangerous factors which might one day bring down the throne.

During the childbearing years the Queen was too inexperienced, and usually too indisposed, to have much influence with the King over national affairs. 1911 seems to have been the first year during which she made an effective intervention. Seven men had been found guilty of the murder in the town of Cullera of a judge and police chief. All but one had had the death sentence commuted to life imprisonment. In the case of the seventh man and reputed leader of the group, it was said at first that Alfonso 'wants a victim' but he later confessed, while trying to come to a decision, that 'these last few days have been the saddest and most difficult of my life'. He was reported to be struggling between the dictates of clemency and the need for toughness during this latest of many moments of crisis. When it was all over he took the unusual step of authorizing a friend to give a newspaper[1] 'my own version' of what happened. It was the Queen, he acknowledged, who had been the most constant advocate of mercy. 'Every time the Queen spoke to me,' he said, 'she encouraged me to show clemency . . . Great was the joy of the Queen when I at last told her that I had decided to grant the commutation. It was one of the happiest moments of my existence.' It was a victory for the Queen but the King managed to spoil the whole effect of his action when, after his Prime Minister, Canalejas, and his Cabinet, had resigned in protest against the commutation, Alfonso accepted the return to office of an identical government within twenty-four hours. It looked too like yet another of those, 'white crises' which the left-wing and foreign papers were so fond of pointing out as 'tragi-comic exercises to rehabilitate the King'. The Queen was not told of the deal whereby the Government, though it had technically resigned—to placate the clerical-military clique who were pressing for the condemned man's execution—had all retained their former portfolios. Such wheeling and dealing was to become a familiar feature of political manoeuvring during subsequent 'Alfonsist' crises.

During the First World War the Queen was an active collaborator with her husband in the work of finding lost prisoners of war. She was particularly concerned with that part of the activity which secured the repatriation of British prisoners via Gibraltar. But Ena never attempted to influence the King as to a preference for one or other set of belligerents and never pressed to know where his real feeling lay. This was a good example of Ena's characteristic exercise of common sense rather than cleverness or guile. Having assured himself of her tact and loyalty Alfonso, thereafter, often sought Ena's opinion on political matters even if he did not always follow her advice. But it was not of course as a political figure in any sense of the word that Ena's main impact on Spanish history came about.

The paramount factor was the haemophilia of the Prince of Asturias. It became clear as time went on that because of this he could never be King. This was made all the sadder, and dynastically more disastrous, by the fact that the second son, Don Jaime, was also debarred by illness from succeeding to the throne. Of Alfonso's and Ena's four sons, the only healthy one was Don Juan (father of the present King of Spain) who was born in 1913. This circumstance came to be looked on as the latest evidence that the Spanish Bourbons had indeed become afflicted with a curse. Foreign sovereigns, it was said, surreptitiously crossed their fingers against misfortune before shaking hands with this unlucky thirteenth Alfonso.

The Prince of Asturias had the deadly blood disease in a virulent form. There were long periods when he was too weak to move. An attempt to prevent the general public from knowing about his infirmity was kept up for as long as possible. But this eventually did more harm than good. To have told the truth would have been better than allowing horrendous rumours to get about. As one Court lady said, 'The lower classes always think the worst. They are convinced the heir to the throne is insane'. What many of them thought was even worse. One rumour which no amount of denials could suppress persisted for years among Spanish peasants. They firmly believed that a young soldier had to be sacrificed every day to provide the warm blood necessary to keep their heir to the throne alive. Alfonso's heart was broken since his dearest wish, as he once said, had been that his sons should 'love nature, exercise their muscles, affront danger and be daring'. Ena's mortification over the whole affair was infinitely painful. It may well be asked, however, if the King and Queen were all that prudent in their handling of their son's illness. His own physical sufferings were, of course, immense since it is an excruciatingly painful disease. But the fact that he was deprived of their company for many months at a time was in some ways harder to bear. It was as if they were ashamed of him and wished him out of their sight. For when, in the early twenties, his infirmity was becoming common knowledge, they decided that it would be better if he did not live with them in the Palace in Madrid. A home was accordingly set up for him, with a retinue of nurses and keepers, in La Quinta, a small house within the precincts of the royal estate of El Pardo, just outside Madrid.

Young Alfonso had no desire to know about state or political affairs. His only real interest was poultry farming. At La Quinta he devoted himself largely to chicken breeding. The doctors could virtually do nothing to help him. He was under the care for most of the time of Dr Elosegui, pupil of Dr Pitaluga. The latter liked to consider himself the royal family's chief consultant over their eldest son's illness. He had achieved a leading reputation in the field of blood diseases, though he was a cause of mischief in this particular case. He was an attractive and worldy Italian with little tact. He was fond of boasting that he had been chosen for the job despite the large amount of Spanish doctors available.

The Prince of Asturias was condemned to an extremely dull life and he felt himself to be more or less imprisoned. Visits from his parents were extremely infrequent. Even if Alfonso could not bring himself to see his stricken son too frequently, it is surprising that Ena did not go more often. In this, as in many other respects, she was too basically frightened of her husband to take any sturdily independent line of her own. It thus appeared as if neither Alfonso nor Ena wished to be reminded of their eldest son's illness and the terrible distress which this had brought them. Meanwhile, at La Quinta, the Prince lived in a simple suite of three whitewashed rooms and a bathroom. He was looked after by a caretaker and his wife and whatever special attendants were needed from time to time. His large desk was littered with plans of property, agricultural journals and his designs for chicken houses. He was also interested in pig breeding. But time lay heavily on his hands. He tried to while it away by walking around the estate in an eternal but hopeless day-dream, listlessly tending his olives and vines. Few at the time realized what his main frustration really was. Behind his blonde, Nordic looks, which he inherited from his mother, there lurked a veritable excess of fiery Bourbon temperament. His blood may have been diseased but it positively boiled with the passions of his sensual forefathers. There were times, especially while he felt temporarily stronger, when he thought he could not bear the strain imposed on him by his surroundings. Then would come another prolonged period of pain and weakness accompanied by inevitable melancholia. He would be left, for some time afterwards, too worn out to feel the need or urge for sexual outlets. Periodically, he would be sent away for treatment at various clinics. But no signs of lasting improvement ever became apparent. This pattern lasted for ten years until, after the royal family had left Spain, the unfortunate Prince was sent to a clinic in Switzerland. There he met the girl whom he would eventually marry. But this, as will be seen, was to lead only to further tragedy for all concerned.

As the twenties wore on and the political crises became more frequent, Alfonso came more and more to identify the preservation of the monarchy with his own personal survival as King. He lived through several attempts to assassinate him and invariably met such attempts with resourcefulness and courage. But he worried increasingly about his health and sought means, physical and psychological, to prove himself a strong man and a strong King. The world was led to believe that he was an indefatigable sportsman. Numerous photographs showed him on the polo field and out shooting. He became, in fact, too associated with the world of 'pichón y polo', something like the English 'hunting and shooting', when his country seemed to need a more serious monarch. Much of his supposed sporting life, however, was a put-up job. He would only play one chukka at polo before becoming too tired to continue. He would then plead some urgent affair of state in order to excuse himself from the rest of the game. When out shooting he would arrange to arrive in time for the finish and to be photographed in smiling triumph beside the day's 'bag'. His friends were willing collaborators in such subterfuges. But his tubercular condition was taking its steady toll, especially on his heart. Ena knew of his secret fears. She never forgot the occasion when he had come weeping into her room. To Ena, Alfonso, until his dying day, presented a very different image than that which was apparent to any other human being. To her, so used to his moods, his mockings and his masquerades, he was always, behind it all, the 'little boy afraid'. The patent presence of such fear was the great leveller in Alfonso's life. But only the Queen appreciated it to the full. Cut down to size, as she alone knew him, Alfonso was someone whom Ena could and would always love.

The counterpart to Alfonso's efforts to 'play the man', was his even more concerted effort to play the King. The greatest personal test of such ambitions came in the year 1921. War had been going on in Morocco since 1908 but it had been conducted with astonishing inefficiency. Alfonso, beginning to get thoroughly disenchanted with parliamentary 'democracy', saw this chance for gaining reflected glory by a stunning military victory followed, perhaps, by some stronger and more stable form of government. In the summer of this fateful year, the King made a rousing speech in Burgos Cathedral at the tomb of El Cid, one of the greatest of Spain's past conquerors of the Moors. 'With what belongs to us on the other side of the Strait,' the King declared, 'we have enough to figure among the first nations of Europe.' But on that very day a terrible military disaster took place in Morocco. It was the worst possible moment for Alfonso to have spoken in such terms and, as he is thought to have done, to have urged General Silvestre to take daringly offensive action against the Moors. Silvestre had no authorization—unless directly from the King—to act on his own. He was only second in command to

General Berenguer who favoured caution. Silvestre, however, plunged forward with 10,000 men, every one of whom was cut down by tribesmen in a narrow ravine at Annual. Silvestre committed suicide. Found among his papers were two telegrams from the King. The first read 'on the 25th I expect good news'; and the other: 'Hola hombres! I'm waiting.' From that moment onwards, rightly or wrongly, Alfonso was deemed guilty in the eyes of most Spaniards for the tragic and unnecessary calamity of Annual. He began thereafter to cast about in some desperation for means to bolster a, by now, thoroughly weakened throne.

A commission of inquiry, in an interim report, found that the advance had been undertaken in the most reckless manner. But certain information could not be published, notably an alleged letter from the King to Silvestre ordering him to 'do as I tell you and pay no attention to the Minister of War, who is an imbecile.'[2] A battle of nerves ensued and it looked as if the King would go under. A second commission of inquiry, after long delays, was due to issue a further and definitive report in September 1923. But a week before the due date, the new Captain-General of Barcelona, Primo de Rivera, knowing that he would have no opposition from the King, proclaimed himself Dictator. The final report on Annual never appeared. Alfonso, at least for the time being, was saved.

Throughout most of this period Ena had been very worried and depressed. In the autumn of 1921, during which year the royal family had been prevented from making their usual visit to England, she expressed relief that what had been a 'horrible summer' was over. The Queen Mother was no less concerned for the new turn of events. She warned her son that the acceptance of a dictatorship, which involved the breaking by the King of his constitutional oath, would be a dangerous hostage to fortune. Alfonso, however, was so relieved by his reprieve that the whole situation seemed to go to his head. He and the Queen paid a visit to Rome two months after Primo de Rivera's climb to power. He introduced the Dictator to the Italian King as 'my Mussolini', and made an exaggerated effort to impress the Pope, Pius XI, of the importance of his own role as the Catholic King of Spain. At a Papal audience he delivered a prepared speech ending with the words 'Spain and its King, faithful to Your holy command, would never desert the post of honour marked out for them on a glorious tradition, to win triumph and glory for the Cross, which is not only the banner of the Faith, but the banner of Peace, Righteousness, Civilization and Advancement.' Spanish liberals were dumb-founded. Previously they had been used to hearing such clap-trap only from the lips of Carlists. Was Alfonso now harbouring the illusion that he bore a charmed life and that by being all things to all men he could bluff his way through to the last? His luck seemed to go on holding. In 1926 the dictatorship was still managing to manufacture economic prosperity, and the hated war in Morocco was brought to an end. But thereafter, the Government's popularity began to decline. The activities of many of its liberal opponents became restricted and some were imprisoned. One was Dr Gregorio Marañon whose family was, during this period, visited by Queen Ena. She let it slip that she was deeply distrustful of Primo de Rivera and what he was doing to Alfonso and the country. She foresaw that her husband could be dragged down by Primo's failure when it came. The King, in the end, got the worst of both worlds by deserting his one time saviour in a manner so opportunistic that it began to seem clear to many that his chief desire now was to save himself. His biggest handicap was that he had alienated almost every important politician in the country by his previous machinations and jugglings at their expense.

These years, around the middle of the decade, saw Ena at perhaps the nadir of her emotional ife. The King's affair with Carmen Moragas had brought out the very worst in one or two of Alfonso's cronies, particularly his principal 'evil genius' Viana. It later occurred to some of them that it might be possible to get rid of the Queen altogether. The King, or so he himself thought, had made a favourable impression with the Pope in 1923. Might there

Ena in the mid-twenties with her mother, Princess Beatrice and her five younger children. *Left to right*: Gonzalo, Jaime, Christina, Juan, Beatrice

not be grounds for an annulment of Alfonso's marriage to Ena if the necessary cards were played with skill? The King's allies circulated what one grandee at Court described as a 'vile paper' about consultations on plans for a royal annulment. Inevitably involved were the Papal Nunciature in Madrid and the Spanish Embassy to the Holy See. Those who got to know about the plan were stunned. They could not imagine the Most Catholic King of all the Spains seeking a Papal annulment in order—if this really *was* his intention—to marry an actress. Pope Pius XI, when he got wind of the project, was said to have indicated immediate disapproval. It was noticed that Alfonso, thereafter, went out of his way to make disparaging remarks about the same Pope to whom he had once pledged fidelity in such expansive and obsequious terms. The whole matter was quickly hushed up and has rarely been spoken of from that day to this.

The principal effect of all this on Ena was to put to the supreme test her renowned reputation for calmness. The authors of one account of the period[3] remark that 'the Spanish are a critical, indeed a censorious people . . . yet no one, however malicious, has ever been able to retail a single unkind or ungenerous remark from the lips of Queen Ena. Perhaps the greatest and most invaluable of all Victorian virtues was self-control and this, to her lasting happiness, Princess Ena thoroughly acquired.' This was true. But it is often the case with highly controlled people that when finally goaded beyond endurance their wrath can be very terrible. So it was with Ena on two or three notable occasions. One of these came about when she felt she could no longer tolerate the treachery of the Marquis of Viana through whom she had, if indirectly, suffered so much. She was convinced that the King would not, purely of his own accord, have acted so callously and cruelly towards her. She believed that Viana had played the part traditionally assigned to the Devil. Alfonso, as was clear, had a guilty conscience. In such a situation he could only do one of two things: either draw back or plunge more heedlessly on. Viana made it his business to see that the King did not waver, on the basis that he might as well be hanged for a sheep as for a lamb. It was not just a question of procuring actresses and other lady friends for Alfonso. The King's whole attitude had to be moulded in a certain direction. Viana was adept at effecting this. But, fundamentally, as Ena felt until the end of her life, Alfonso had been made to act against his real instincts and true nature.

For this she held the Marquis of Viana primarily responsible. She accordingly summoned him to her private apartment and told him that she was thoroughly disgusted with his abominable and base behaviour in having turned the King against her and that she held him principally to blame for most of the suffering she had undergone. Viana, in the obsequious manner which Ena found so contemptible, began to try and excuse himself. Ena cut him short and brought the interview to an abrupt end with the words, 'It is not in my power to punish you as you deserve. Only God can do that. Your punishment will have to wait for the next world.' The Marquis was thereupon dismissed in a state of shock. He had seldom if ever, been talked to in such a manner. He went home that night, suffered a heart attack and died. Ena told this story to several people later in life. The reaction of each of them was somewhat similar and took the form of a question, 'Did you feel in any way responsible for his death?' Ena, by way of answer, shrugged her shoulders non-committally. She never regretted her action and felt that Viana had suffered no more than he deserved.

It was ironical that, as the twenties neared their end and the political situation in Spain was decidedly worsening, Ena's life was showing signs of becoming happier in certain respects. She was learning at last to accommodate herself more to Spaniards of all kinds and the 'elegante' craze had largely worn off. Unfortunately, her own closest friends, notably Jaime and Rosario, Duke and Duchess of Lecera, became selfishly alarmed by the possibility that the Queen would gain the favour of their own rivals. They thus became inordinately possessive towards Ena which greatly alienated a large section of the aristocracy. If the monarch could survive, however, there seemed a good chance that Ena could widen her base of allies as she gained even more confidence. By another irony, it was through a sad event that she was enabled, at long last, to be Spain's undisputed Queen. For in February 1929 the Queen Mother died. Alfonso was crushed but Ena hoped that when his pain wore off they would somehow be brought closer together. Ena was careful to be very slow to make changes in such places as the Miramar Palace which the old

Queen had furnished and decorated so much to her own taste. Ena waited a year before getting rid of the 'endless little Austrian atrocities' with which, as Ena put it, her mother-in-law had furnished the Palace. She hoped that Alfonso would not notice for she respected her husband's innocent and almost childish sentimentality about his mother's possessions.

Ena's new hopes, however, were darkened by the lengthening shadows of political unrest. It seemed as if the grievances of nearly thirty years were all coming to a head simultaneously. Until the arrival of Primo de Rivera there had, since the beginning of Alfonso's reign, been no less than thirty-three Governments in just over twenty years. The age old and ever vexatious 'agrarian problem' had never been solved. Primo de Rivera, author of many enlightened moves, would have liked to break up the large estates, which, because of almost slave labour conditions, had long been the fermenters of rural anarchism. But he left it too late. Where, however, the Dictator had succeeded, he had inevitably done so at the expense of the King's prestige, for, in allowing Primo to take over the absolute government of the country in defiance of the constitution, Alfonso had inadvertently put himself in second place. He had debased the monarchy and could no longer pose as the people's champion and the upholder of parliamentary democracy. The price of originally having permitted the dictatorship in order to cover up his own responsibility of the greatest of all the Moroccan military disasters had now to be paid. With the fall of Primo, forces that had been held at bay for seven years were now unleashed. Alfonso put General Berenguer at the head of his new Government and embarked at the end of 1929 on a desperate effort to save his throne. He was now faced with Republicanism on all sides. But it was moderate Republicanism spearheaded not by violent mobs but by the most respected members of the intelligentsia and academic circles. These were circles which, though attractive to Ena, had never held out any interest for the King. He now regretted his boorish philistinism and long time neglect of the cultural affairs of the nation. He had even had to agree to Primo's closing of Madrid's respected Ateneo where the country's most cultivated men would meet to discuss intellectual and national affairs.

Past efforts to bring Alfonso and the intelligentsia together had never succeeded. It was not his fault that because of bad health and the need for a primarily outdoor upbringing his education had left him almost totally ignorant of cultural and academic subjects. What was more resented was his obvious boredom, which he did nothing to hide, in the company of men and women from academic and similar milieux with whom he had nothing in common. He tried to cover his inferiority complex over this matter by means of attack rather than defence. But it is arguable that he might have saved his throne had he been able to meet and speak the same language as the men of one of Spain's most brilliant generations in modern times. A further disadvantage was the fact that Primo de Rivera's clericalism was one of a series of policies that brought him into positive collision with the country's intellectual forces. This could not have happened at a more unpropitious moment. For, as Richard Herr puts it, 'the cultural rebirth (in Spain) which occurred before the First World War was now coming to fruition. Gathered around the tables of the cafés in Madrid and other cities, politicians, writers, journalists, teachers, artists, and their associates discussed eagerly the latest world developments in all areas.'[4] The Residencia de Estudiantes was a meeting place for such men as the brilliant Andalusian poet Federico García Lorca. Among those with whom he could exchange ideas and inspirations were the famous surrealist painter from Catalonia, Salvador Dali, and the pioneer film-maker Luis Buñuel. As far as censorship would permit new papers and periodicals were coming into existence. Perhaps the most illustrious and courageous of these was the *Revista de Occidente*. This was founded by the great thinker José Ortega y Gasset, in 1923. It upheld the liberal political and intellectual outlook but with moderation and intelligence. The spirit of '98 was very much on the move and it was of course this spirit which animated the first period of the Second Republic until it was tragically undermined from within by opposite forces. Meanwhile, however, new life was coming into the universities and for the most part learning went hand in hand with Catholicism even though it was distinctly a Catholicism that was not of the 'clericalist' variety. The towering Miguel de Unamuno became rector of the University of Salamanca. A full list of the distinguished names among professors, thinkers, writers and similar people would be very long. It would include, in particular, Menendez Pidal, Americo Castro, Claudio Sánchez Albornoz, Père Bosch Gimpera, Gregorio Marañon (a disciple of Ramon y Cajal), Salvador de Madariaga, Perez de Ayala and many others. It was Alfonso's abiding and finally fatal tragedy to have not a single close friend among this illustrious group of his subjects. Efforts were made periodically to bring him and them together but they were singularly unsuccessful. Once, when he was at a gathering with such company, and conversation had become particularly sticky, Professor José Castillejo tried to help things along by remarking to the King, 'I too, Your Majesty, have an English wife.' Alfonso's answer was 'Caramba! Qué bueno te ha caido!' This sarcastic reply meant something like 'How awful for you!' The ensuing embarrassment brought the gathering to a fairly speedy conclusion.

It was the survivors of the Generation of '98 who gave respectability to the cause of moderate republicanism. The country's intellectual aristocrats, as opposed to aristocrats of a different kind, felt that there was by this time no other direction in which the nation could realistically move. Alfonso had so consorted, plotted and counter-plotted with politicians of such diversity, and had in the end let them all down, that he was now bereft of viable support. Ena's prophecy that he tired of everything and everybody had come true with a vengeance. Everybody had now tired of him. Poor Primo de Rivera, a generally benign and well-meaning dictator, had died in Paris a few weeks after his fall from power. His body was brought back to Madrid for a funeral worthy of the man once known as the Saviour of Spain. Whether or not he deserved this title he had certainly, in 1923 and thereafter, been the saviour of the King. But Alfonso, thinking it would be politically inopportune to attend his funeral, pointedly stayed away. His action was greeted with widespread disgust. He began to be compared with his ignoble great-grandfather, Ferdinand VII, who had been noted for his lack of loyalty to friends and supporters. Alfonso, it was felt, had gone one better even than his great-grandfather. From now on he became known as Ferdinand the Sixth-and-a-half. Such, however, is the basically cynical attitude of Spaniards toward statecraft and politics that Alfonso, even at this stage, was not actually hated. In this respect, in fact, he bore something of a charmed life. He got away with actions that in others would never have been forgiven. He was not the man to attract deep opprobrium. His tragedy was of a different order and in the course of 1930 he experienced something almost worse for a King than hatred.

It was now recognized that, try as he may, there was no longer anything he could do for Spain. He had done enough—including great harm—in the past, though as much by misplaced zeal as anything else. He had become not an evil that had to be destroyed but an irrelevance to be dropped as quickly and quietly as possible. Ena, despite all the hurts and humiliations, was desperately sorry for her husband in 1930, particularly after the heart attack he suffered while playing polo at the Puerto de Hierro Club. His doctors said he must henceforth avoid violent exercise and emotional strain. But how he could avoid the latter at this perilous moment in his life defied explanation. Some felt that health worries impaired his political judgement. Certain it is that he made one of the major blunders of his career when, in December 1930, he ordered the execution of two officers, Captains Galan and Garcia Hernandez. They had risen for the republic in northern Aragon, been found guilty by court martial and sentenced to death. The Government was divided as to whether the penalty should be carried out. Alfonso, on being consulted, insisted not only that it should take place but that it should be put into effect that very day, 14 December, which was a Sunday. This event provided the Republic with its martyrs and did more than anything else to turn opinion against the 'Rey Caballero'—the Gentleman King. From this point onwards events moved swiftly.

The year 1931 opened in an atmosphere of mounting drama. One of the best accounts of the period is that given by Alacala Alvaro-Galiano, in a book called *The Fall of a Throne* which appeared soon after the events in question. The author was a staunch, indeed fanatical, monarchist giving the benefit of every possible doubt to Alfonso. And he was justified in so doing to the extent, at least, that the King of Spain was at no time a thoroughly 'bad' man, still less a totally bad King. He was a good man and a good King according to his lights. He was a victim of circumstances which, it is true, he had been partly instrumental in bringing about. His fatal handicap lay in not really knowing his own people. Never was this disability more evident than in the first months of 1931. To these months Alvaro-Galiano brings a wistful verdancy by his almost exactly contemporaneous description of the period. The strangest feature of this period, as his description makes clear, was the King's inability to believe, right up to within hours of leaving the country, that the monarchy might fall at any time. As had already been prophesied about Alfonso he would end up by deceiving himself.

The Queen did not share her husband's illusions. Because of her, however, Alfonso's hopes were boosted in the early part of 1931 by 'an incident which caused a burst of monarchical enthusiasm to break out in the open streets amongst people who had for long appeared to be indifferent.'[5] Could it be that the tide of popular feeling was suddenly turning towards the throne and that the cause for such a turning was the English Queen of Spain? For a short, heady period, this seemed indeed to be the case.

In January 1931, Princess Beatrice had a bad fall, bringing on bronchitis. Ena had hurried to London to be with her mother and for a few days the latter's condition was the cause of disquiet. But the crisis soon passed and Ena left London again on 16 February. She had heard that the Spanish Government had suddenly fallen and that Alfonso was in difficulties. 'My place is at his side,' she said. When on the following day she had arrived at Madrid's North Station, she was amazed by the enormous concourse of people there to greet her.

The country was in a state—yet again—of crisis. This was probably the worst yet faced at least as far as the King himself was concerned. And yet a certain hope hovered in the air: the only hope there could be at that moment was to convoke the Cortes. But of what kind? An ordinary, that is unrepresentative, one; or a constituent, that is representative, Cortes? The former had been suggested and approved by the King, but instant evidence that it would be boycotted by all the monarchical groups led to quick abandonment of the idea by the Prime Minister, Berenguer, and his immediate resignation. It was thus that at the moment of Ena's return Spain was without a Government. How can one account for the incredible exuberance of the welcome that awaited her?

Her arrival, it is true, had been expected and it was not particularly surprising that companies of the 'Monarchist Youth' and groups of aristocrats should have made a point of being at or near the station to greet her. More unusual was the fact that they had been joined by townspeople, trades people and large numbers of working-class men and women. They formed one, undivided crowd, and a huge one at that, and their ovation when the train drew in was deafening. Among those present to greet Queen Ena were her children, the Infantes, the Chief Officers of the Palace, Members of the Retiring Government and certain other officials. (The King was absent.) Because of the vast crowds they had difficulty in getting through to the arrival platform. As the Queen slowly made her way from the train, the enthusiasm of the crowd, whose numbers were swelling, was showing no sign of abatement. 'The Queen, visibly affected, could not conceal her emotion; the tears welled in her eyes causing others to rise in the eyes of those who were present.'[6] The crowds swarmed around the royal car making its progress to the nearby Palace proceed at only walking pace. This had the effect of turning it into a triumphal procession. Nor did the crowds disperse after the royal party had finally found its way into the Palace. They remained outside and continued to cheer wildly. Soon the Queen, accompanied by the King, appeared at the balcony. The crowd went mad. They could not have enough. The cheers went on and on—and on. Not only for the Queen. For Spain too—of course! And for the Queen's children. But also, as it seemed—miracle of miracles surely—yes, for the King as well! Amazed and delighted, the King accompanied his wife several times out onto the balcony even though it was a freezing night. 'The plaza was black with people, handkerchiefs waved, and the joyful acclamations must have sounded in the ears of both sovereigns as a token of fervent loyalty offered by the people of Madrid.'[7]

The King, whether or not duly grateful to his wife for having occasioned such enthusiasm, was greatly encouraged and much moved by the demonstration. He needed all the support he could get at that moment having just failed to pull off a somewhat desperate experiment. He had cast about him for a suitable head for something approximating a genuine coalition. His choice had fallen on Don José Sánchez Guerra who had, however, failed to persuade the necessary but disparate elements to work together. Sánchez Guerra, nevertheless, was a key figure in the final months of Alfonso's reign. For it was he who put a sensational but little known proposition to Queen Ena. The proposition, if accepted, would have enabled the throne to survive. This same statesman, according to Alvaro-Galiano, had 'aimed the first mortal blow at the monarchy'.[8] What that author, however, did not know was what few people know even today about Sánchez Guerra. And this was his proposal to the Queen which, if accepted, would definitely have saved the monarchy and possibly changed the course of modern Spanish history. That Sánchez Guerra, probably alone among leading Spanish statesmen of that period, could have made the suggestion can only be explained by a brief look at his extraordinary career. A former Conservative Prime Minister, he had gained a reputation for energy, if not ruthlessness, in his suppression of the general strike in 1917. He was skilful in debate and something of an intriguer, a left over, in some ways, from the old days of Conservative 'caciquismo'. He became disillusioned with the dictatorship of Primo de Rivera. During those same days, however, he gained the personal acquaintance of the King and Queen. He then left Spain in protest against Primo's setting up, in the King's name, of a bogus, 'National Assembly'. He came back from his voluntary exile to lead, in Valencia, a military rising against the dictatorship. Subsequent Court Martial and prison sentence made him a popular hero. He became the leader of a small but significant group who favoured a constitutional monarchy in order to replace out-of-date royalism without resorting to a Republic. His group was known as the 'Constitutionalists' and they wanted to reactivate the 1876 Constitution which Alfonso had abrogated when consenting to the Primo de Rivera Dictatorship. Their enemies tended to dub them the 'Monarchists without a King'. A more accurate description would have been 'Monarchists without *this* King'. For Sánchez Guerra realized that the main stumbling block to the continuation of the Spanish monarchy was the monarch himself. He was not alone in this realization. The fact was now evident to the most astute of Spain's politicians of whatever political persuasion. But none knew what could be done about it.

The greatest difficulty lay in the absence of any suitable heir to the throne. All would have been different had the legal heir apparent, the Prince of Asturias, been physically fit to assume the responsibilities of kingship. Spaniards as a whole—and possibly even Alfonso himself—would have welcomed the advent of a young and dashing Prince who might bring to the tottering throne the right kind of intellectual and psychological approach so badly needed. As it was, however, neither the Prince of Asturias nor for different reasons, Don Jaime, was fit to become Spain's next

The Prince of Asturias by Laszlo, 1927

King. It was not impossible however, that their surviving son, Don Juan could in due course, be declared legal heir. No one, least of all Sánchez Guerra, could foretell or dictate future events at that delicate stage. But what Sánchez Guerra did realize was the need to play for time.

It thus occurred to him that the dignified and voluntary retirement of Alfonso could be the means of saving the monarchy. But to span the interregnum or transitional period, or whatever it turned out to be, a Regency would be required. Who was to be Regent? Sánchez Guerra felt that no one would be better qualified for such a role than the Queen. And this was the proposition he made to her. The incident has not, as far as this author knows, appeared in any written account of the period but its occurrence was vouched for to the author by someone very close to events at the time and corroborated by others with similar knowledge.

The incident throws considerable light on the feelings of ordinary Spaniards at that time, for, respectively, the King and the Queen. For men like Sánchez Guerra were in a strong position to gauge such feelings and were astute assessors thereof. Nevertheless, his actual proposition to the Queen, was, by any standards, an astonishing one. Ingenious and well meaning though it was, its audacity is incontrovertible. But the strength of the argument behind it could not have been lost on Ena. Her agreement to the plan could be the instrument for preserving the monarchy for the House of Bourbon and of saving Spain from otherwise almost certain Republicanism. It would, moreover, ensure that one of her and Alfonso's own sons would inherit the throne with a good chance, as a constitutional monarch, of seeing his country through the inevitably challenging transitional days that lay ahead with the real hope of establishing permanently democratic government without the price of bitterness and bloodshed. With hindsight it can now be said that—by means of this audacious plan—Don Juan might, in 1931, have become the same sort of King-of-all-Spaniards as his son was to become many years later. In any event, Queen Ena made it immediately clear that she would have no part in any such plan. Though the suggestion took her completely by surprise, she did not hesitate for a single second in giving her answer: it was a firm 'No'. This answer, and the way in which it was given, are cited by the author's principal informant on this particular subject as crowning proof of

Ena's most outstanding characteristic, namely loyalty. It would never have occurred to her to have acted otherwise. She was as loyal to Alfonso—to the end—as he was disloyal to her.

In this respect, however, each acted according to instinct and temperament. Alfonso, as one who knew him intimately all his life put it, was incapable of loyalty even to his own ministers and friends. 'He was unconscious of the defect . . . he couldn't help himself.' This was very much in character with the King. He had, as already seen, confessed his inability to forgive Ena for having brought so deadly a disease into his family. There again he could not help himself. In that particular case, of course, he was conscious of the defect in himself and admitted that, however irrational it was, he could not think or feel in any other way. Alfonso was ever a victim of his own impulses and instincts, whether generous and even quixotic, as they often were, or sensual and selfish as they were more often still. In February 1931, his instincts were those of a desperate gambler in seeking a Ministry led by Sánchez Guerra. The King of course knew nothing of the latter's approach to Ena on the possibility of a Regency, based on his belief that she, at this stage, was more popular with the people at large than was the King. Ena herself did not necessarily believe this. But even Sánchez Guerra himself did not realize how sound his assessment was until resounding proof came with the tumultuous scenes of 17 February 1931.

What were Alfonso's thoughts as he and his wife stood on the balcony of the Royal Palace acknowledging the acclamations of the people of Madrid? Cheers such as this had not rung in his ears for many a worried month. Though they had been occasioned by the return to the capital of the country's English Queen, it was not difficult for the mercurial Alfonso to throw off his despondency as he would hurl aside a cloak—with a gesture of flourishing defiance. Surely this demonstration was a certain sign that the people were still loyal to him! The crowds were cheering for *him*, not just his wife. He was still the King. Despite disappointment at the failure of the Sánchez Guerra experiment, Alfonso with these cheers still ringing in his ears was now gripped with a new optimism.

The failure to form a wide-based coalition did not dispirit him. He at once proceeded to form a new Government under the less than thrilling but unexceptionable Admiral Aznar whose first task, as he knew, was to prepare for the holding of municipal elections. This would test the feeling of the nation and be a guide to the best date for calling a proper general election. The municipal elections were to be held on Sunday, 12 April. So confident did Alfonso now feel that he went off on a holiday to England. This greatly surprised the British Royal family. King George V, who had long disapproved of Alfonso's lightweight attitude to the responsibilities of Kingship, now expressed himself in more positive terms. He severely criticized the Spanish monarch for being abroad enjoying himself at a time when it was his clear duty to be at home. Had the British Sovereign known of the years of unhappiness he had brought to his cousin Ena he would probably have been even angrier. But Ena's sense of honour, and perhaps of pride, had always kept this fact hidden from her family, even her mother. Alfonso meanwhile passed the time pleasantly with his own particular English friends. He had, over the years, cultivated an English set of his own which had little in common with that of his wife. Had he, instead, in the company of that same wife, decided to tour the cities of Spain, getting as close as possible to the ordinary people therein, he might have made a brilliantly favourable impression on them. As it was he returned to his country at the end of March with the municipal elections only just over two weeks away. These elections, as already mentioned, were being looked upon as a preliminary test of the King's popularity. The monarchists assured Alfonso that he had nothing to fear. He awaited the day of judgement with unruffled tranquillity.

[11]

The Voice of the People

VOTING in the municipal elections took place on Sunday, 12 April 1931. The first returns were known that same evening. Every provincial capital except Cadiz voted for a majority of Republicans and Socialists. In Madrid and Barcelona the vote was overwhelming. Almost everyone believed that something sensational and unprecedented had happened. But no one could quite bring himself to accept that one era had gone and another had started. 13 April was a day of rather eerie calm. The Republicans were surprised at the extent of their own success. The monarchists were incredulous. Alfonso was stunned. The news began to trickle in of the results of voting in the country districts. The results in these areas were predominantly royalist. The royalist votes, over the entire country, in fact outnumbered the Republican ones. Many clutched at this straw to argue that the country as a whole was still royalist. But the rural votes were still largely under the control of the 'caciques' and it was recognized that no King or dictator could hope to hold Spain if the towns were against him. Worst of all, for Alfonso, was the attitude of the Military to whom alone he could have turned had he wished to hold his throne despite everything. The Army and the Civil Guard, under the command of General Sanjurjo, withdrew their support. At this humiliating moment for Alfonso, insult was added to injury when even the grandees seemed to be deserting the cause. This was an interesting factor particularly in relation to Ena whose unhesitating loyalty to Alfonso contrasted strongly with the attitude of her husband's fair-weather friends. On the eve of the elections the Duke of Almenara Alta, President of the Nobles' Club, had made an appeal to the upper classes to rally to the monarchist cause. The grandees of Spain, he had declared, had 'the firm intention of serving the King to the point, if need be of sacrifice.' Of the grandees then serving at Court, however, only eight were engaged in any gainful employment. The election results made them afraid that if the King did not go there would be a 'red revolution'. To save their skins they decided to lie low until the dawn of a more favourable era. This, they knew, would come one day, whatever happened meanwhile to Alfonso XIII.

Alfonso's pain was almost unbearable when he realized that he had now lost all viable support and that even his supposed friends had, with few exceptions, deserted him. But one thing did not desert him. And that was his quick-wittedness in moments of crisis. He did not take long to decide, very astutely, to make a virtue of necessity and to announce that he would leave Spain rather than cause bloodshed. As there was so little chance that any blood would be shed on his behalf it was an easy claim to make, however empty. In his heart of hearts, Alfonso did not really believe it himself. But in a strange way, Ena did. Or rather she let herself believe that it was true. Certain it is that from the moment Alfonso made his decision she insisted that he had done so only in order to avoid the shedding of Spanish blood. The fact that she continued to assert this even after it became more generally known that she and the King had already become estranged made her appear to be a completely objective witness. This was a particularly important factor in helping to establish the legend that Alfonso elected to leave Spain in 1931 to avoid Civil War.

Tribute must nevertheless be paid to Alfonso for the dignity with which he faced this traumatic moment. In an interview[1] years later Ena was to say that 'He (Alfonso) was never more calm than in this gravest crisis.' Revealing his own reactions to the election returns Alfonso had said, 'I had the impression of calling on an old friend and finding him dead.' But human nature being what it is, the King hesitated before taking definite steps for his actual and final departure from Spanish soil. In practice the matter was decided for him by others. A key figure emerged in the person of Count Romanones, Foreign Minister in the last royalist Government and a statesmanlike survivor of many years of violent fluctuations in Spanish politics. He was never anything but a staunch royalist and sat in the subsequent Republican Parliament as a Monarchist. For such reasons he was respected on all sides. On the morrow of the 1931 municipal elections he acted swiftly. A provisional Republican Government having been declared on 14 April, Romanones immediately contacted the intended head of the new Government, Alcala Zamora. They met in the house of Dr Gregorio Marañon and agreed that it was essential for the King to leave the country 'before sunset' on that very day. It was Romanones who persuaded the King that this was the only course left open to him. This meant that Alfonso must be out of Madrid within hours. What would happen to the rest of the royal family? 'I will be responsible for the Queen', Romanones assured Alfonso, 'to the point of losing my own life.'

It was thus arranged that Alfonso should leave Spain on the evening of 14 April. He would have to leave with all possible speed without his wife and children. In agreeing to this plan it has sometimes been asserted that Alfonso thereby deserted his family at a moment of danger. Such was not the case. Rather is it true—though the truth is not entirely flattering to Alfonso—that the Queen and her children, when their turn came to leave the country, would be safer if Alfonso were not with them. Some people at the time were very much reminded of Marie Antoinette. They recalled that though she was captured while trying to escape from Paris her life would probably have been spared had she not been found to be in the company of the King.

Throughout the afternoon of that same day (14 April) Ena awaited news in her small sitting-room on the first floor of the Palace. It was a very different sort of room from most of the others in that vast and cold Palace full of great audience chambers, reception halls, antechambers and alike. In this small room apart, at the end of a passage, Ena over the years had read her English papers every day, dealt with her correspondence, and had tea some afternoons—though not as often as she would have liked—with her husband. Here she was surrounded by her needlework, her private treasures and her books. The latter still stand in the same shelves—light reading, for the most part: nineteenth-century and Edwardian novels; popular histories; a few German classics; essays by Belloc, Chesterton, Baring and others, many of them signed by the authors.

For a quarter of a century this room in Madrid's Royal Palace known as the 'Palacio del Oriente' had provided much more for Queen Ena than a mere comforting hideaway. It was a room in which she had spent many long and lonely hours. It was here that she had, in some strange but necessary way detached herself as a woman from her role as a Queen. Thus, by consciously splitting her life and her personality, she had helped herself to cope with burdens otherwise perhaps unbearable. She said as much many years later[2] when using words not otherwise easily explicable. 'It was that room at the Palace' as she put it, 'that witnessed the story of my marriage and of my reign.' In the course of that reign she had, as she went on to say, 'created a second person within me, who laughed and wept at will to enable the Queen to appear passive at all times.' Perhaps—and here lay the supreme irony—this was her crowning mistake. Had she allowed her true personality—that 'second person'—to be seen, if only occasionally, in public, she might have been vastly more popular. As it was, the 'second person' of the woman rather than the 'outward person' of the Queen existed only within the seclusion of her private boudoir. It was into that room, at five o'clock on Tuesday, 14 April 1931, that an ashen-faced Alfonso XIII now walked. He would be leaving the country, he told his wife, the same evening. She asked if they could eat a last meal together—just the two of them—there in that very room. The King said he would make the necessary arrangements and that he would return later.

By the time he came back the provisional Government had

already assumed power. The Second Republic had become a reality with no blood having been shed. Some members of the new cabinet were already taking possession of their ministries. Alcala Zamora was determined that the transitional period should be lawful and regular. The news spread fast to the people of Madrid and crowds were soon pouring out into the streets in an atmosphere of carnival.

The King and the Queen sat down at the small table prepared for them in the boudoir. It was the only main meal they had ever eaten alone together in the whole of their married life. They ate it in almost complete silence[3]. The normal intimacy of marriage had played no part in their lives for many years. Now, at the moment of truth, there seemed nothing to say. Alfonso hurried over his food and prepared to take his leave. He was convinced, according to Ena[4] that the country would want him back. He thus suspended his power only and refused to abdicate. But in his final message to the country he acknowledged that 'I have lost the love of my people.' He told Ena that the Provisional Government had given cast-iron guarantees that she and the children would be allowed to travel safely by train to France on the following day. They were to leave first thing in the morning. His last words to her were 'I leave you in Spanish hands. You can trust them.' Their final farewell was tense and traumatic but devoid of passion or even tenderness. Ena could not penetrate her husband's stiff and awkward demeanour in order to read his true emotions. The only moment in fact at which he was visibly moved before leaving the Palace was when he paused before a portrait of his mother. He stood in front of it for some moments, raised his hand in salute and then moved hurriedly on.

Within a few moments of his leaving her Ena could hear the roar of Alfonso's car, and of the two others escorting it, as he sped from the main door of the Palace. By now it was dark. The main door of the Palace was closed and bolted as soon as the King had left and the palace guards were disbanded. Only a small platoon of Hussars—twenty-five of them—was left to protect the royal family. Had a mob wished to force its way into the Palace intent on murder nothing could have prevented such a massacre. Ena's long and awesome vigil had now begun. She went off in search of the children, five out of the six of whom were with her in the Palace. Don Juan was at the Naval College of San Fernando in Cadiz. It had been arranged that he would travel directly to Paris with his own escort. His safe departure, as that of all the rest of the family, was facilitated behind the scenes by the new Government. Though they wanted the royal family out of Spain as quickly as possible the last thing they wanted was for any of them to be harmed. For some reason Alfonso had not told Ena where he was going. In fact he was at that moment being whisked to Cartagena where a boat flying the Republican flag was waiting to take him to Marseilles. From there he intended to travel to Paris next day by train.

Ena and her five children were thus truly left 'in Spanish hands'. Alfonso had said she could trust them. He proved to be right. Despite the many lurid descriptions that have been given of that last night at the Palace there was no moment at which the lives of the royal family were in any danger. But of course there was no means whereby Ena could know this at the time. Quite soon a vast crowd had gathered on the east side of the building where the Palace abuts straight onto the street. The private royal apartments looked out in this direction. The courtyard to the south was separated from this street by a high thick wall whose main gate was now fastened as securely as possible. This gate acted as an irresistible magnet to the crowd which was beginning to swell to enormous proportions. According to an eyewitness[5] the crowd began pressing so close to the gate that it seemed inevitable that they must eventually burst through and gain admission to the Palace. Their true intentions could not be known by those inside the building who naturally feared the worst. Ena had visions of being hauled out with her children and of their all finally meeting a fate similar to that of her cousins in the Russian Revolution. Such few guards as there were tried to restrain the pressure of the crowd without provoking any open clash. In so doing they succeeded only in becoming sucked into the ranks of the demonstrators, thus leaving the Palace virtually unprotected. Shouting men and women, brandishing Republican flags and emblems, now seemed to be everywhere. Then suddenly two or three succeeded in scrambling up on to the principal balcony of the Palace. The moment of which the Queen had been terrified seemed now to have arrived. But all that the men wanted to do was to plant the Republican flag on the balcony. Having done this they got down again.

The shouting, however, went on and the royal family's fear increased with the knowledge that they were by now completely at the mercy of the crowd should any of their number wish to make a concerted attack on any of the doors or windows. The Officer in charge of the remnant of the Hussars felt that any confrontation with the crowd would be unduly provocative. A telephone call was therefore put through to the Home Office where the new Home Secretary, Miguel Maura, was already at his desk. He, though a Republican supporter, was, like the new Prime Minister, Alcala Zamora, a Catholic and a Conservative. He assured the Palace authorities that reinforcements would immediately be sent to guard the Palace and protect the royal family. 'Guards' were thus sent round forthwith. They turned out to be working-class men in ordinary clothes with red arm bands. But they seemed to know what was expected of them and acted with immediate despatch. They quickly inserted themselves between the Palace façade and the front row of the crowd. Joining hands, they set up a shouted chorus of 'five metres back!' The crowd relayed the command through its ranks and then, like an ebbing sea, gradually fell back by the required distance. Soon after this, most of the crowd dispersed to let off steam in other parts of the city. This eye-witness account reproduced in a book about, and approved by, Queen Ena[6] puts into perspective the story of what happened outside the Palace on that historic night. The assembled con-course of people were shouting not for blood but for joy. They were concerned not with death but with life as they celebrated the birth of the Republic, an event for which many of them had waited all their lives.

The 'civilian guards' sent by the Home Office stayed for the rest of the night and took over the function of 'sentries'. Not unnaturally, however, little sleep came to the inmates of the Palace. The night 'seemed endless,' said the Queen in retrospect. 'I packed no bag, sorted out no belongings. As I was forced to go, I would leave with nothing . . .'[7] But she had been asked to bring certain things which were precious to the King. These she collected up, being surprised to find that, when coming across once treasured objects of her own, she now looked at them with complete indifference.[8] But she did bring whatever jewellery she could, including that which had belonged to her mother-in-law as Alfonso wanted to keep it.

Her main concern was over the safety and well-being of the children, particularly that of the Prince of Asturias who was in a very low condition at the time and could not get out of bed. Over-exertion during a recent bird-spotting excursion had brought on some painful haematomas in the shoulder. His three principal doctors, Elosegui, Pascual and Emilio Larru were staying the night with him at the Palace. He nevertheless managed to speak to all the Palace servants who filed into his room one by one to say goodbye to him. Tears could not be held back. The rest of the royal family also said goodbye individually to each of the servants all of whom received mementoes from members of the family as farewell presents.

The noise outside died down gradually but intermittent shouting and disturbances continued. Inside the building the children's pet canaries sang all night long, something that had never happened before. Ena tried to write some letters but could not concentrate and had to give up the effort. She did not go to bed in her usual room but in the children's sitting-room. She had instructed two beds to be made up there, one for herself and one for her younger daughter Christina who was particularly nervous.

In adjoining rooms in the same part of the Palace were the Queen's sister-in-law, Lady Carisbrooke, Ena's clinging companion the Duchess of Lecera, another old friend and collaborator the Duchess de la Victoria and also the Countess del Puerto, as well as certain other Court ladies. The menfolk were accommodated downstairs and included the Prince of Asturias' suite; the ADC of Don Jaime; Don Gonzalo's tutor; and, perhaps surprisingly in view of past events, the King's companion of former days the Marquis of Someruelos. Some but not all of these were due to travel to France with the Queen the next day.

Such sleep as was possible was interrupted by a call at five o'clock the next morning. Ena was told that a friend of the King's had arrived at the Palace and wished to see her urgently. He had apparently managed to persuade the Republican guards that he meant no harm to the royal family and had therefore been admitted. The Queen put on her dressing gown and received him in her sitting-room. It was Joaquin Santos Suarez who lost no time with formalities and said immediately to the Queen 'The Revolution has come.' He told her it would be impossible to go, as originally planned, to Madrid's North Station as the streets in that area were crowded with people waiting for the return from exile of the 'terrible men' who were the Republican heroes. The Queen and her party would therefore have to leave by the so-called 'secret door' on the garden side of the Palace and be driven to the Escorial Station outside Madrid from which they could pick up the express that would take them across the frontier into France. Suarez was in a state of some panic and was convinced that any other course of action would endanger the lives of the royal family. Shortly afterwards the others were awakened and at seven o'clock the Royal Chaplain, Father Urriza, said Mass for everyone who was there that night. His Mass was served by Don Gonzalo. After breakfast the Queen said a final farewell to the servants and thanked them for their loyalty over so many years. But they did not want to delay their departure. The crowds were beginning to swell again and the morning papers were already on sale extolling the birth of the Republic and rejoicing in the flight of the King. A group of youths tried to batter down the main door of the Palace with a lorry but did not succeed. By eight o'clock the Queen and her family were in the four cars which were waiting to take them to the Escorial Station. She had managed to persuade several people not to risk coming on the journey with them. Among those who did go, apart from the boys' tutors and attendants, were the Duke and Duchess of Lecera and, again of all people, Princess Beatrice of Saxe-Coburg whose husband, the Infante Alfonso of Orleans, had accompanied the King the day before.

The Home Secretary in the last Government, the Marquis of Hoyos, was with them and he was intending to accompany them to the frontier. The Queen, he said, made no reproachful remarks about anyone of whatever political allegiance. All she said was that 'The Spaniards are very vehement and passionate.' The caravan of cars stopped on the way to the Escorial as it was realized that they would be too early for the train and they wanted to limit the time of waiting at the station as much as possible. The whole party got out of the cars and the Queen sat on a large boulder by the side of the road smoking a cigarette. The spot they stopped at was called Galapagar. They were soon joined by the group of people who were waiting to see them off at the Escorial who had heard that the Queen had stopped on the way. The group was headed by Count Romanones and the Queen spoke earnestly to him and the others, urging them to go back to Madrid in case of danger when they reached the Escorial. The occasion at Galapagar was remembered as Queen Ena's 'last court' held on Spanish soil.

At a given signal the royal fugitives returned to their respective cars, the last of which was occupied by civil guards. Those who had joined the party at Galapagar could hardly believe their eyes when seeing that the Queen and her family were travelling under the official protection of the armed forces of the Second Spanish Republic.

The health of the Prince of Asturias was a great worry at every stage of this journey. He was suffering acutely and had to be carried, either in the arms of the chauffeur or on a stretcher, as he could not walk even a step. When they reached the Escorial Station he remained slumped in the car, a pathetic figure asking in a small voice if someone would kindly go and buy him some cigarettes from the news stand.

The Queen and the rest of the family went into the waiting-room where Ena was approached by a tall figure. It was Sir George Graham who had succeeded Sir Esmé Howard as British Ambassador. Graham was much criticized for his failure to do anything for Ena. When he asked her now if there were any service he could perfom she said, 'It's too late now.' Graham was an indecisive man who could not make up his mind how to act in such rapidly changing circumstances as those which had overtaken Spain in the previous forty-eight hours. It was said of him that 'He put off the old man and put on the old woman.' The period of waiting for the train was embarrassing as well as sad. No one knew what to say. Mercifully the arrival of the train was eventually announced and they filed out to the platform. There was muffled silence although, by now, large crowds—of well-wishers and others—had gathered within the precincts of the station. A tall grey-haired man pierced the silence with a cry of 'Viva La Reina!' He was told to stay silent for fear of provoking disorder. It seemed as if he was English and many thought that he was Searle, who had once stood behind the Queen's chair in those far off days of her early marriage and who had eventually 'deserted to the enemy camp' for the employment of Dõna Sol.

There were some curious human touches to the whole drama which, to Ena, did not seem in any way real. She had yet to take in what was really happening to her and passed most of the journey in a stunned daze. As each hour passed, it became more obvious that the royal family was in little real danger. The crowds were strangely indifferent. The plans for an orderly escape had been made in consultation with the new government. But there was great scope for drama and royalist supporters actually on the

[228]

Ena holding her 'last court' on Spanish soil at Galapagar

scene were determined to make the best of it. They fluttered about the Queen and busied themselves with numerous superfluous tasks. They fumed, fretted and fussed, cursed 'those filthy reds', and expressed undying loyalty to the throne. How they would have loved the Queen to enter into the spirit of the thing! If only she had burst into tears, screamed, and sobbingly kissed everyone in sight, they would then have got their money's worth. But—not for the first time—she disappointed her Spanish audience. She appears to have remained impassive at every stage. While some of the 'passionate and vehement' Spaniards were on the verge of hysteria, the Queen remained British—all too British—to the last!

The royalists nevertheless tried not to be discouraged. A Ruritanian touch was injected by the presence on the scene of the Duke of Zaragoza in his capacity as honorary 'engine driver' to the royal family. He had got permission to ride on the footplate and the story has been handed down that he actually drove the train out of the Escorial Station. But this little adventure did not unfortunately last for long. The royal coach suddenly caught fire and had to be evacuated by the royal family, complete with all attendants and friends, at Avila. More pandemonium ensued.

The Queen was very annoyed at having to squash into an adjoining coach and travel 'like an ordinary person'. The incident, however, highlighted the anomaly and possible provocation of letting a very grand-looking coach, with the Royal Coat of Arms emblazoned on its exterior, be seen travelling through Spain on the first day of the country's life as a Republic. It was thus realized that the coach would be better abandoned and it was duly disconnected. The Queen was much safer in the less dignified surroundings of a plain carriage where she was given the seat courteously vacated by a young English nobleman who happened to be travelling that day on the Hendaye Express. But she was extremely cross at having to do so. (This at least produced some show of emotion at long last on her part.)

It is sometimes small things that can upset people most, even in times of tragedy, whose very magnitude compels maximum emotional resistance by way of response. The trivial by-products can often prove to be the last straw. Ena's unhappiness during her journey to France increased with her mounting discomfort and irritation. They were at least spared the embarrassment of meeting, head-on, any of the Republican stalwarts now pouring south after being in exile to take up their places in the life and administration of the new Spain. Most of these were travelling by train but they had been carefully diverted onto branch lines so that the express carrying the royal family could go straight through. Groups of the returning exiles, however, were seen on sidings from time to time when the express stopped at certain stations. The Queen could hear their cries of jubilation and the occasional strains of the Internationale. She became intensely melancholy having been saying to herself so very recently, 'I thought I had done well.'[9] Very different thoughts now crowded in on her and she could do nothing to dispel them. She dwelt on the fall of the monarchy and the obsessive feeling that this event would be for ever associated in many minds with a personal failure of her own. She was intensely relieved when they finally left Spanish territory and had no time to ponder on how pitifully different was her exit from the country compared to her triumphal entry into it a quarter of a century earlier.

It was a dispirited and exhausted group that arrived in Paris late that evening. They were scarcely in a mood to face the clamorous representatives of the Spanish colony in the city who had swarmed into the station to greet them, prompted by morbid curiosity as much as anything else. The Prince of Asturias was brought out to his car by a side entrance so as to avoid the public as far as possible. Even now the pitiable extent of his illness was far from generally known. The Queen and her daughters faced their welcomers with brave smiles. Don Jaime, of course, could barely speak, but he could lip-read extraordinarily well. He smiled charmingly and bravely at all those who approached him. It was left to the young Don Gonzalo to answer most of the questions fired at them from all sides. He showed himself to be surprisingly mature and dealt with it all with admirable courtesy and composure.

Exhausted though she was, Ena insisted that her intended bedroom should be properly prepared and her retiring toilette observed with its usual minute care. Never, in fact, during her adult life, had she undressed at night or dressed in the morning without the help of two maids. And never, to the end of her life, was she to do so. The first days of exile, otherwise so unreal, so eerie and so humiliating, were to see no exception to this routine. Such comforts and niceties were always of great importance to Ena and proved to be a prop to her in moments of stress. But nothing could quell the nagging question which was uppermost in her mind: To what kind of life with Alfonso could she now look forward? At some point soon they would once again have to face each other alone and at the same time face the truth, however bitter.

One ordeal—that of getting her family safely out of Spain—was over. But Ena knew that a far more punishing personal ordeal now awaited her.

[12]

Exile

ALFONSO'S and Ena's first 'home' in exile was the Hotel Meurice in Paris. The purely external facts—where they lived, what their daily routine was, whom they met, and so forth—form the main part of all available written accounts of the weeks and months that followed. These facts, though they give no hint of the intense drama that was being enacted behind the scenes, can be quickly described.

The sojourn at the Hotel Meurice was obviously not meant to be permanent. It provided merely breathing space while future plans could be clarified. The Spanish Government, moreover, made clear to the French Foreign Office that it desired the King to live outside Paris even if he kept an office there for 'private' purposes. Villas at Chantilly and Compiègne were considered but it was finally decided that the family should make its home, at least for the foreseeable future, in a virtually private wing of the Hotel Savoy in Fontainebleau.

The arrival in Paris had been a tumultuous one and the first day spent by King Alfonso in the French capital had been described as 'triumphal'.[1] The King, despite the trauma of what had happened to him, was stimulated by the excitement of suddenly being the centre of renewed interest. He lost as little time as possible in setting up a 'Secretariat' and began granting audiences to certain notabilities. Nothing that Alfonso did at this stage was expected to have any fundamental effect on the actual situation in Spain. But it was a heady moment for him personally. He needed something, above all some urgent sort of activity, to

[233]

hold onto, still being convinced in his own mind that his absence from Spain would only be temporary. He thus plunged himself into a busy quasi-official routine of work, being not, indeed, the 'pretender' to the Spanish throne, as he has often been called, but its immediate claimant having never abdicated any of his prerogatives.

Paris, on the other hand, had nothing at this moment to offer Ena in the way of consolations. The shops and theatres that she had visited with such pleasure in former times now held out few charms. Bottled up though she felt in the hotel, there was little or no incentive to venture far afield. It was an unhappy period lasting several weeks during which time she saw little of her husband. He seemed to be occupied or in demand at all times and there were few chances to discuss family matters or future plans. But eventually these had to be faced up to. Relations between the King and Queen had reached a point of almost intolerable strain. Even before they had had to leave Spain they had begun to consider separating. But for reasons of state no moment had been found to be opportune at which any such announcement could possibly have been made without damaging the throne. Even now the King's advisers were terrified of what the Press would make of news that the King and Queen intended to part company. But that last, sad and almost silent tête-à-tête in the Queen's boudoir had convinced both parties, if any doubts still lingered, that the end of the road had been reached.

What had happened to Alfonso and Ena was the reverse of what had happened to other famous royal couples in similar circumstances, notably Nicholas and Alexandra of Russia. In their case tragedy was also caused by haemophilia transmitted by descent from Queen Victoria (through her second daughter, Princess Alice). But this fact had brought them closer together. With Alfonso and Ena it had driven them apart, never more so than at this moment when they had not even got a proper home of their own. A final confrontation seems to have been put off until the move to Fontainebleau had been completed. By June the Queen

[234]

was settled there, at the Hotel Savoy, with Don Jaime, Don Gonzalo and her two daughters, Beatrice and Christina. The Prince of Asturias did not move in with them. His illness made it impossible for him to be looked after properly in such surroundings and he was sent to a clinic in Switzerland. Their other son, Don Juan, had meanwhile resumed his naval career and been accepted as a cadet at Dartmouth. He was greatly to enjoy his days in the British Navy and speaks of them proudly and happily to this day.

The part of the hotel at Fontainebleau occupied by the royal family was really an annexe to the main building, consisting of a not unattractive virtually self-contained house. This enabled privacy to be maintained and all meals were served in a private dining-room in this house. The King, however, did not at first move in himself but stayed on for the time being at the Hotel Meurice. Accommodation was nevertheless prepared for him and his retinue at Fontainebleau. The retinue consisted of the Duke of Miranda, the King's private secretary, Don Emilio Maria de Torres, the Duchess of Victoria and Don Jesus Corcho, a legal adviser to the King. But what of Queen Ena's friends, notably the Duke and Duchess of Lecera, who had, throughout, stuck to her like leeches? They and the King's friends had nothing in common. There was now no room under one so small a roof for enemies to live together in harmony. Thus was the stage set for the most dramatic and tragic event in the whole of Ena's life—an event which has always been described up to now in misleadingly bland terms. The full horror of the truth was only revealed by Ena to certain close friends many years after the Second World War.

The story told to the world at the time, and still, as it were, the 'official' version, has been similarly treated by all the authors of the period and the biographers of King Alfonso. It is a very short version since this whole interlude in the life of the Spanish royal family has invariably been skated over with the minimum of detail. Indeed the whole dark decade after the royal family's departure

The Spanish royal family in exile. *Left to right*: Queen Ena, Don Jaime, King Alfonso, Don Juan, the Infanta Christina, the Princess Manuela (wife of Don Jaime), the Infanta Beatrice

from Spain has been carefully glossed over in all written accounts of the period. In the guarded words of one author[2] 'The royal family reassembled at the Hotel Meurice in Paris and after a few weeks there they went to live more quietly at Fontainebleau. Unfortunately the shock of what had happened caused an estrangement between the King and Queen, and for a time they separated, not to come together again until a few years later in Rome.' In the book which gives short biographies of every Spanish queen from Isabel the Catholic to Queen Sofia, it is said discreetly that, with the entry into exile, 'patriotic sentiment induced her [Ena] to suspend her royal prerogatives and, now that he was away from Spain, Alfonso XIII sought solace in amorous adventures from the sadness caused by his being driven from the country. In Madrid Doña Victoria Eugenia had been forced by dynastic reasons to be tolerant. But now, as a mere wife, bereft of her throne, she was in no position to engage in heroics. The royal couple therefore decided to separate amicably, without mutual recriminations, without provoking scandal, knowing full well that the press would be interested.'[3] Frank though it is up to a point this version is, to say the least of it, incomplete.

The sad truth is that the separation of Alfonso and Ena was far from amicable. The final explosion had roots extending deep into the past. The rift in Court and society already mentioned had one particularly damaging result for Ena. It may originally have been triggered off by the King's callous behaviour, for which all due allowance must be made in view of his suffering over his son's haemophilia. But when Ena began losing the battle for the friendship of those in and around the court, her own circle of friends started to shrink. Many of the 'elegantes' turned out to be the most superficial of friends. In the final stages Ena's base had, as already mentioned, become dangerously narrow. It was dominated, almost monopolized, at the end by the Leceras. They poured poison in her ears about Alfonso and his friends. The latter's faults and alleged 'evil' ways became greatly exaggerated in the Queen's mind. But she had suffered so much that, just as Alfonso had become predisposed for his own reasons to move irrevocably in one direction, Ena seemed to be drawn, with no hope of escape, in quite another. The Queen's sufferings, moreover, naturally made her listen more attentively to the advice and reactions of those who remained closest to her.

It was one of those immensely sad situations in which two people, with so many good qualities as individuals, had become totally incompatible with each other. Alfonso may have been politically immature and irresponsible. But most people found him warm and charming as a man. Winston Churchill called him the finest gentleman he had ever met. However, almost everything Ena did, and the way in which she did it, rubbed Alfonso up the wrong way. It may have been partly his subconscious desire to justify his indifference, not to say cruelty, towards her. But he found himself a victim of his tempestuous nature. The beautiful girl he had fallen in love with as a boy was not in the least like the woman he had had to live with as a man. Ena's nature, on the other hand, impelled her—as was said of her—to do many things 'al revés' as far as Spaniards were concerned. That is to say, her actions went 'against the grain'. In no area was this more true than in her relationship with Alfonso. When the exhausted and disillusioned couple had reached Paris and Fontainebleau they were plunged into a strange and unreal world. The props of royalty had been removed. Their new surroundings were humdrum and humble.

They would be forced, if they stayed there together, to live in a state of close proximity and forced intimacy such as they had not known for years—if ever. Whose fault was it primarily that their marriage had failed? The most objective view generally taken was that they had been drawn into a vicious circle from which neither had been able to escape: the haemophilia drama; the humiliations and private agonies; Alfonso's infidelities; Ena's cold response at moments of tenderness; the mischievous interference of 'friends' on either side; a second haemophilic son; more recriminations; more infidelities; more coldness; more callousness; more interference; finally, a point of no return. A psychological block now separated Alfonso from his wife and this block was never to be removed.

Each party dreaded a final confrontation. When it came, things were said that may not have been intended but which, once uttered, affected everything that happened thereafter. Alfonso demanded that Ena should end her alleged affair with the Duke of Lecera. Ena was shocked to the core and vehemently denied that any such affair had ever taken place. Almost certainly it hadn't. But just as certainly the Duke had long been in love with her. It will be remembered that Lecera had been sent to El Pardo to perform the duty of honorary bodyguard to the princess the night before her marriage. They had been friends ever since but never, as Ena insisted, and most onlookers averred, lovers. The balance of the evidence, not least that supplied by Ena's own temperament, is strongly against any such possibility. Unfortunately the situation was much more complicated—more sinister even—than most people imagined. For many years before 1931 the Duke of Lecera's relationship with his own wife had been a distinctly flawed one. For not only was *he* in love with the Queen, but the Duchess of Lecera was in love with her as well. There was no question at any time of Ena's having responded to this love on the part of Rosario Lecera in any physical way. Ena had no such proclivities although those of the Duchess were fairly well known. Over the years a number of governesses and maids had been dismissed from her service in mysterious circumstances. But the chief object of Rosario's affection had always been the Queen. Ena not only did not reciprocate but managed to put this aspect of their relationship out of her mind. She did not let it enter into her daily life, chiefly because she so desperately needed, or thought she needed, the continuing support and friendship of the Leceras. They had never deserted her, even in the darkest hours, and had of late made themselves indispensable to her. She could not imagine existing without them, especially now that the nightmare of exile had become a reality. It was for this reason that, in an unguarded and possibly hysterical moment, she said something to Alfonso that was to change both of their lives for ever.

The King persisted in his accusations about the Duke and his wife and tempers rose to an ugly pitch. The scene, described by Ena to friends years later, remained engraved on her mind forever. She chose to tell them the story feeling that one day it was right that the truth should be known; anything short of the whole truth—finally revealed when enough time had passed—would have been less than just to all concerned. Alfonso repeated his demand that she should choose between him and Lecera. But for Ena no such choice existed. The King, however, was intending to dismiss both the Leceras, and Ena was terrified at the thought of not seeing them again. She needed them now more than ever and the prospect of losing them at a moment when everything else had been lost was too terrible for her to contemplate. It opened up prospects of a void in her life which she thought, at that moment, could never be filled. It was not an appropriate moment, however, for thinking straight. With all too little consideration for what she was saying, Ena flung back at Alfonso the retort: 'I choose them and never want to see your ugly face again.' Alfonso was aghast. He could hardly believe his ears. Ena had so seldom spoken to him with such violence. This was a side of her nature of which he had seen little. Perhaps she should have exhibited more of it much earlier in their married life. Now it was too late to do anything except irreparable harm.

It must be noted that Ena said, 'I choose *them*.' She did not say, 'I choose *him*.' For her there was no question of choosing between Alfonso and Jaime Lecera. Her conscience was clear with regard to the latter despite interpretations to the contrary of some people privy to these events. Such interpretations gained ground as the years passed which was why Ena was so anxious that the truth should one day be revealed. But for many years she had to live with the thought that those in Alfonso's world believed that he had been forced to leave her because she had refused to give up her lover. Not all of them, by any means, knew that the Duchess of Lecera was also in love with Ena and that, though the Queen herself was equally blameless in this regard, her only desire was to keep near to herself, at a time of great trial, the two people whom she considered, rightly or wrongly, to be her best friends. She came to realize her mistake later on. But by that time matters had gone beyond recall. The Leceras were eventually dismissed and they returned to their beautiful house in Andalucia. There, Rosario continued her preferred way of life and the Queen was, at long last, freed from a friendship which had once meant so much but had brought tragedy in its train.

The immediate effect on the Queen of the showdown with

Alfonso was, as could be expected, traumatic. She entered a twilight period in her life from which she did not fully emerge for over a year. The first few months were particularly agonizing. She would not allow the subject of Spain to be mentioned. It was as if she were in mourning for her whole life. But the shock of realizing that her life with Alfonso was definitely over could not dispose of the necessity for making immediate and practical decisions. First of all she had to decide where to live. She had considered leaving Fontainebleau immediately and going to the Riviera or to England, in both of which places houses had been offered to her. But the prospect of making the necessary plans for such a move overpowered her now that she realized she was to be left entirely to her own devices. To stay for the time being at Fontainebleau, though far from ideal, would at least give breathing space and time to think. But what of her 'life' with Alfonso if they were in fact to be living separately from now on?

The decision was taken out of her hands in practice by the fact that, though Fontainebleau remained their nominal joint home for the sake of appearances, they were practically never there together. Ena began moving about quite a lot while Alfonso embarked on a programme of almost non-stop travelling. The Queen, recovering very slowly from the impact of what had befallen her, managed to fend off often mischievous enquiries with dignity and a latent sense of loyalty which was never to desert her. When people asked after the King—which they often did— she merely said he was undertaking a journey.

Alfonso, indeed, scarcely stopped. He had only been in Paris for a week when he decided to go to London. This he had done on the very day that the Queen and the rest of the family transferred themselves to Fontainebleau. The King made several other visits to England in the course of the year as well as to various European capitals. 'Such journeys were undertaken in connection with "work". But it was work that could not hope to achieve anything. The journeys were undertaken only to fill in, to some degree, the emptiness which had now invaded Alfonso's spirit since his absence from Spain.'[4] The cynics noted that female company was always a prominent feature of these excursions on the King's part. Almost the whole of 1932 was spent travelling, more extensively than ever, around Europe and also as far afield as India and the Holy Land. He kept on the look-out for a permanent home that would be more to his liking than Fontainebleau which was a home in name only. It began to look as if his final choice would fall on Rome where he spent long periods during 1933. It was now ten years since he had been there with 'his Mussolini', Primo de Rivera. But that poor man was now dead and buried and so was everything that he had stood for. But the real Mussolini was still going from strength to strength and Alfonso, who had never lost his admiration for Fascism, began to look with favour on the Italian capital.

Ena recovered much less quickly from her separation from Alfonso than he seemed to from his separation from Spain. (His separation from *her* hardly came within his consciousness at all.) Only in 1933 did Ena begin to take any genuinely renewed interest in the life around her and to plan for the future. Up until then, though she had not been inactive, she had gone through the motions of social and family visits without escaping from the haze of unreality by which she still felt surrounded. She has put on record[5] the thoughts which accompanied her determination at this point to make a new beginning of things. The former facing up to royal duties had been 'everyday work', and she had in general greatly enjoyed it. But it was only now, in fact, that she realized how much she missed being Queen of Spain. Ironically, she had often wished at the time to be free of the burdens it had imposed. Nowadays all was different. The trappings were gone, the surroundings were dull, the entertainments few and the prospects bleak. Sometimes, to cheer herself up she would wake to a new morning and say to herself 'I am still Queen.' But it was said without conviction for she then inevitably reflected that 'the scenery is lacking.' She thus began to organize her life in such a way that those around her could at last smile if laughter was impossible. Her motto became 'laugh and the world laughs with you; weep and you weep alone.'

She was philosophic even about the King whose virtues and vices she summed up with surprisingly little rancour: 'He was as gay as a Latin, as zealous as a Habsburg, as sport loving and poetic as a Spaniard . . .', but, she added, as if obliquely to describe her own life in one phrase, 'He was also as selfish as a man.' She knew that whatever happened he would never change in this respect. But even at this late date she did not give up hope of some sort of reconciliation. As long as Alfonso lived—faults and all—Ena knew that her life would never be quite complete without him.

The Dark Decade

ENA, by this time, was alone quite often as far as members of the family were concerned. Don Jaime had gone off to make what life for himself he could despite his handicap. Don Juan remained for five years in the British Navy, rising to the rank of Lieutenant. The girls divided their time, theoretically, between Alfonso and Ena, according to the terms of the legal agreement. In practice Alfonso was not always willing or able to have them with him and they spent long periods of time with friends in London or Switzerland. The youngest son, Don Gonzalo, was studying engineering at the University of Louvain. He was now nearly twenty and had so far suffered much less from the effects of haemophilia than his unfortunate elder brother.

All this time Alfonso, Prince of Asturias, was leading a dreary and lonely life at his clinic in Switzerland. It was clear that his passionate nature, come what may, would not let him waste away without his making some bid for happiness based on the kind of loving companionship which he had so greatly lacked in the past. It was thus that he announced, in the spring of 1933, that he had fallen in love. Could this event conceivably bring Alfonso and Ena any closer together, if only for a while? Any hopes that Ena may have had were quickly dashed. The Prince, for whom none of the usual type of marriage plans had been made, had fallen in love with a girl who was also undergoing treatment at the same clinic. She was a young Cuban whose name was Edelmira Sampedro-Ocejo y Robato, who is still alive and living in Florida. But the match met with the complete disapproval of the King. The girl was a commoner who could never be considered an appropriate wife for the man who was still heir apparent to the Spanish throne. The Prince was adamant, however, and to his father's intense annoyance insisted on going through with the intended marriage. It was held in church, on 21 June 1933, and was attended by the Queen and his sisters.[1] But it was a lacklustre affair and the bridegroom was deeply hurt by the attitude of his father. It seemed that as an innocent cause of so much heartbreak for Alfonso he himself had had to undergo more than his due share of mental suffering. Ten days before the wedding he had been obliged to renounce all rights of succession to the Spanish throne as well as to his title. Henceforth he would be known as the Count of Covadonga. After the wedding he left for the United States in search of a new life in a new world. He seemed to have lost his father's affection and knew he would never see him again.

By 1933 Alfonso was travelling less and spent more and more time in Rome, much of it in the company of his daughters, Beatrice and Christina. His spirits got a boost from meeting a lot of Spaniards that year in Rome as it was 'Holy Year', a year which, every quarter of a century, was considered a Jubilee year. Pilgrims came from many parts of the world but particularly from the Catholic countries to gain the special 'indulgence' available by saying prescribed prayers in Rome's four major basilicas. During his own visits to these churches, Alfonso was often recognized by Spanish groups and it was rather pathetic to see how thrilled he was by their greetings and cheers. A flash of his old spirit would return to him on such occasions. His daughters were meanwhile beginning to enjoy the social life of Rome and were attracting the attention of gallant young Italians. 'But the shadow of that same haemophilia—which had been responsible for Alfonso's plunge into love affairs and killed his adolescent and reckless love for Victoria Eugenia after the birth of his first son—now hovered like a black cloud over the future of the Princesses Doña Beatrice and Doña Maria Christina.'[2] They were called 'the nice girls of Europe' and widely admired—one a brunette, the other a

blonde—for their chic and beauty. But they were potential transmitters of the blood disease and Alfonso, mindful of the bitter
results of his own lack of caution thirty years earlier, felt obliged
to warn all would-be suitors of the possible consequences of
marriage with his daughters. The two girls felt condemned to a
life of spinsterhood.

Ena was now more frequently in England and in the course of
1934, while Alfonso seemed to be looking increasingly toward
Rome as his probable future home, she began to think of trying to
find a life for herself in London. She now felt she could face her
friends and family with greater equanimity. In the first two years
of exile their well meant enquiries and expressions of sympathy
had gone through her heart like daggers. But in 1934 tragedy
once more visited the family. The curse, in which more and more
people now believed, seemed destined never to leave its victims in
peace for long. During the summer of that year Alfonso was
holidaying in Austria and was joined by Gonzalo and Beatrice.
Ena, now left for long periods on her own, was staying at the time
at Divone-les-Bains in the Ain department of France near the
border with Switzerland.

On 13 August, young Gonzalo, not yet quite twenty, was out
driving with his sister Beatrice who was at the wheel. They were
returning to the villa at Portschach which Alfonso had rented on
the northern shore of Lake Worther in Carinthia. Beatrice
suddenly had to swerve to avoid an oncoming bicycle being ridden
by a certain Baron von Neinmann. The car crashed into the wall
of Krumpendorf Castle. Neither of them was badly hurt but the
collision brought on a bad attack of bleeding in the case of
Gonzalo. He died two days later. 'This was the first heavy blow
suffered by Alfonso XIII and Victoria Eugenia since leaving
Spain, but it was not enough to restore the bonds of conjugal
affection which had been destroyed years before.'[3] The royal pair
were reunited in their son's death but only for a brief moment.
They stood together as his coffin was lowered into the ground at
the local village cemetery. The order of the Golden Fleece was

borne on a cushion as the single symbol of Bourbon mourning. Gonzalo's body was later transferred to the grave next to his mother's at Lausanne. After the funeral Ena hurried back to London while Alfonso with his other sons and daughters went to Rome where the King had now decided definitely to live. He bought a villa outside the city belonging to the famous singer, Titta Ruffo. But the expense of this eventually necessitated his moving into the Grand Hotel in Rome itself.

Ena, for her part, acquired an extremely nice house in London at 34 Porchester Terrace off Bayswater Road. She was there at intervals from 1935 onwards and began to enjoy social life as much as circumstances would permit. But she made several memorable trips abroad as 1935, for the Spanish royal family, saw a sudden rush of weddings in the younger generation. The first to marry was Beatrice, King Alfonso having changed his mind and agreed to give his permission. In January, in Rome, she married Alexander Torlonia, Prince of Civitella-Cesi. Three months later, also in Rome, Don Jaime, who had, at the time of his elder brother's marriage, renounced his own rights of succession and taken the title of Duke of Segovia, married Manuela Dampierre Ruspoli, daughter of Viscount Roger de Dampierre, a Papal Duke, and the Roman Princess Victoria Ruspoli. By Don Jaime's renunciation, the third living son, Don Juan, had now become heir to the Spanish throne. And it was he, again in Rome, who, as the new Prince of Asturias, married his cousin Doña Maria Mercedes of Bourbon-Orléans. Their daughter, Princess Pilar, born in July of the following year (1936) was Alfonso's and Ena's first grandchild. The grandparents met in Cannes where the baby had been born and speculation soon began that now, surely, they would be reconciled. For on 18 July, the Civil War in Spain had broken out.

Alfonso, however, had no thoughts of reconciliation with his wife and his mind was entirely engrossed as to what might happen to and for him as a result of war in his country. The monarchists joined with the Falangists and Traditionalists under the banner of the Nationalist leader General Franco. Don Juan attempted to join up on the Nationalist side but was not allowed to. The expected immediate fall of the Republican Government did not occur, as planned, and it became clear that there would be a long and bitter struggle. Alfonso, on first leaving Spain, had proclaimed his desire to do nothing to unseat any Spanish government of whatever complexion. This had not stopped him associating himself later on with the 'Acción Española' which met periodically in Paris to discuss the possibility of a rising against the Republic. But now that a war had actually started, Alfonso found himself in a quandary. It was natural to suppose that he would be helped by a Nationalist victory. But what were the views of the enigmatic and personally ambitious Nationalist leader himself? In July 1937, Franco dashed any hopes Alfonso may have begun to harbour by asserting that 'Should the moment for a restoration arrive the new monarchy would be very different from that of 1931, different in constitution and in the person who should incarnate it.'[4]

Few statements could have been more crushing or humiliating to Alfonso. The poor man had little alternative but to remain strictly aloof from the conflict for the time being. He thus sought consolation as much if not more than ever with his favourite (particularly lady) friends and his rounds of travel. He started going quite frequently to Lausanne as a change from Rome since the former was a centre of international social life specially during the summer season. Ena started going there as well. The café society atmosphere, centring on social functions given at such places as the famous Hotel Beau Rivage on the lake front at Ouchy, appealed to both of them. So did the opportunities for golf and the numerous invitations to lunch and dinner from rich English, French and other seasonal occupiers of the surrounding villas. The occasional presence of such notabilities as the newly married Duke and Duchess of Windsor added spice to life. Surely Alfonso and Ena must eventually meet face to face if they were both there at the same time?

The King, however, annoyed by the thought that Ena appeared to be pursuing him, was determined that they should not meet if it could be avoided. Before arranging to play golf he would telephone to the club to ask when the Queen would be playing. If she was due to play in the morning he would make a point of playing in the afternoon, or vice versa. But Ena seemed endlessly prepared to pocket her pride particularly when she found on one occasion that Alfonso was staying at the Hotel Royal in Lausanne with none other than his old friend Doña Sol. Ena proposed that she should come and join them there, but Alfonso said it would be quite impossible because of the 'scandal' it would cause. Quite what type of 'scandal' he had in mind was not explained. When Ena persisted, he sent her a message through an intermediary reminding Ena that she had said to him at Fontainebleau that she never wanted to see his 'ugly face' again.

On another occasion a celebrated Lausanne hostess invited both the King and Queen to lunch. Alfonso accepted with great reluctance. Twelve people sat down to lunch with Alfonso and Ena at opposite ends of the table. Alfonso insisted on the seating being changed as he said he didn't like seeing women having to sit next to each other. He then shouted across at Ena, 'What a ridiculous telegram you sent me from Balmoral!' The telegram in question had concerned the possibility of a romance between their daughter Christina and Prince Napoleon. A supposedly confidential matter had thus become public knowledge. Ena was uncomfortably reminded of Alfonso's indiscretions during meals in the old days in Madrid. The lunch was of course an embarrassing failure.

People in fact found it surprising that Ena should so obviously want to re-establish a more intimate relationship with Alfonso after all the slights and insults that had been and still were piling up. One of the reasons was that, though she occasionally stayed with her children, particularly Beatrice, in Rome, she felt something of an outsider by not being somehow on an equal footing with Alfonso. He had so often overshadowed her in the past. His

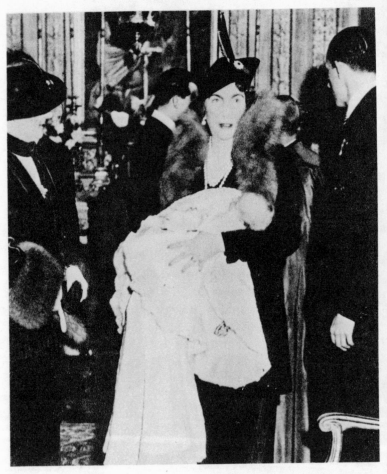

Ena with her grandson Juan Carlos at his christening

complexes had not vanished with the years. He was still upstaging her but she lived in hope that something more like a normal relationship could come back into their lives. In the late thirties she went quite often to Rome and the whole family were reunited for the baptism of the eldest son of Don Juan and Doña Maria. He was christened Juan Carlos with the proud Ena acting as his godmother. The ceremony was performed on 5 January 1938, at the chapel of the Knights of Malta, by Cardinal Pacelli, later Pope Pius XII. The infant was himself to become famous one day—as Juan Carlos I, the present King of Spain.

Ena stayed on for a little time in Rome after this baptism. She divided her time between friends just outside the city, her daughter Princess Beatrice at the Palazzo Torlonia, or the Excelsior Hotel. One day a certain Spanish lady—now living in England—arrived in Rome having been released from a Spanish Republican prison through action taken on her behalf by Queen Ena. What happened next she herself described to the author. In London during the previous year (1937) Ena had, it appears, obtained the ear of the British Prime Minister at the behest of the Duke of Alba, a strong Nationalist supporter. He had persuaded the Prime Minister that without British intervention the Spanish fleet would fall into the hands of the 'Spanish Reds' and be sold to Russia. Ena felt, afterwards,[5] that this rare intervention on her part into the politics of the Spanish war helped to prevent large funds from Russia reaching the Spanish government. Following up her success in this sphere she had managed to bring pressure to bear for the release of the lady who was imprisoned in Spain. She had done so at the request of an unlikely person, namely her cousin Princess Beatrice of Saxe-Coburg, a friend of the imprisoned lady. The latter had been in a cell with Franco's niece and they hoped, because of this, that they might eventually be released. The Republicans, or Loyalists as some called them, were willing to effect exchanges of prisoners. But it was Franco's firm policy never to allow such exchanges. For this many prisoners, including Franco's niece, never forgave him. But Franco, already styling himself 'Caudillo', or Leader, of Spain, held life, including, if necessary, his own, to be cheap compared with the glory of the cause for which he was fighting.

This particular release therefore was extremely unusual and would not have come about had it not been negotiated at such high levels. After it had taken place the lady in question arrived finally in Rome where she went immediately to see Alfonso who was a very old friend. From him she learned that Ena was also in Rome but the King seemed strangely nervous when he talked about her. He confessed that he did not himself wish to see her but that this was through something more akin to dread than hatred. The lady thus learned something which she was able to pass on to Ena, much to the latter's consolation. Alfonso, in fact, was keen that she should go to see his wife and as he put it 'be kind to her'. Why could he not do this himself? The reason, as it gradually came out, was that Alfonso, in his heart of hearts, had a guilty conscience toward Ena. But he could never bring himself to ask her forgiveness face to face. He still felt there was too much for which *he* had to forgive *her*, and in one way or another any tender words that he might, in the back of his mind, wish to speak to her would, he knew, stick in his throat if he ever tried to utter them. When Ena discovered this, which she had long suspected, her heart softened toward him even more. At the same time she realized that it was now hopeless ever to try to meet or be with him unless it should miraculously become clear that this was what *he* wished. This lady thus served as a useful intermediary between the two even if not in the cause of complete reconciliation. In the course of their conversation together Ena told the Spanish lady that she longed to return one day to Spain and have a farm there. It seemed, somehow, a strange thing to say at that particular juncture.

Ena's children also suffered from the continued estrangement of their parents. One day in Rome the queen went to a certain cinema accompanied by her son Don Juan. Suddenly, hardly by coincidence, Alfonso was seen entering the auditorium of the same cinema with his daughter Beatrice. For the sake of form but not without some embarrassment the King and Queen sat together. Nothing however came of this attempt to bring the two closer together. Soon Ena was back in London and grew to like her house very much. She had been able to furnish it to her taste, as, just before the Civil War, the Spanish Republican Government had returned to her most of her personal possessions and many treasured objects which she had spurned taking away with her on that last night at the Palace in 1931. It was thus that Ena now began to think that England might be the best place for her to settle permanently. She began in fact during these days in the British capital to know something of that contentment which often, in life, has to replace true happiness. Her resilience as Princess Alice had called it—others have called it superficiality— enabled her to put unpleasant things out of her mind. She was frequently seen in royal and other social circles in London, as well as at the fashionable Catholic church of Farm Street in Mayfair. As her work for the Spanish Red Cross was so well known, she had been asked to become chairman of the Ladies' Committee of a Catholic Hospital in London called St John's and St Elizabeth's. But many of the other ladies found her 'rather German' in her appearance and behaviour.

Unfortunately the Queen's new-found contentment, super- ficial though it may have been, was short-lived. Toward the end of 1938 tragedy struck again. She had seen very little over the past five years of her eldest son Alfonso whom she loved with particu- lar tenderness. He had never come back from America and, in the autumn of 1936, had had a particularly bad attack of his illness in New York. Ena had sailed over on the *Queen Mary* to see him and only returned when he was on the road to recovery. She had been saddened, however, to discover that his marriage was turning out unhappily. Young Alfonso, she grimly realized, had inherited not only her father's hot blood but also his roving eye. The marriage was dissolved in May 1937 and that same summer the Count of Cavadonga married a young Cuban model called Marta Racaforte y Alturraza. But this union lasted only six months, ending in divorce in January 1938. A few weeks later the girl married a rich American called Atkins while the Count embarked on a reckless and madcap career hoping, in fair company and escapist surroundings, to forget the misery with which he had been cursed by life. One of his love affairs was with a night club girl in Miami called Mildred Gaydon, known as the 'happy one' in the club where she worked. He was thinking of marrying her and they talked of it each night when he visited the club. One particular night, when he was driving her home, he crashed his car. The haemophilia did the rest, though 'Alfonsito' did not die straight away. He was rushed to hospital and news was sent to Ena. King Alfonso, long out of touch with his eldest son, did not hear about the accident at first and Ena had no idea where to contact him. It took her a full twenty-four hours to find her husband and give him the news. She then took the first available steamer to New York. The former Prince of Asturias meanwhile lay slowly bleeding to death. He had been told that Queen Ena was on her way and, from time to time, could be heard murmuring 'mother, mother'. But he was dead before she arrived. This was in September 1938. Ena was unable, as winter turned to spring in 1939, to recapture the feeling of contentedness that had just been emerging the previous year. Nor did anything any longer seem substantial or permanent. The Spanish War came to an end but signs of world war were now unmistakable. Mr Anthony Eden visited the Spanish Queen at Porchester Terrace to warn her that in the event of war the British Government could not guarantee her safety if she stayed in England. Technically she was no longer a member of the British royal family and there could be various complications for her, including financial ones, should she get caught in London by the war.

Ena became convinced by the end of the summer that she must leave England as soon as possible. In any event the land of her birth had only managed to provide in recent years the semblance of a permanent home. She had had no real home since leaving Spain and now she was torn with conflicting emotions. She knew she must leave Britain but she realized very forcibly, particularly in view of the uncertainties ahead, how much she would miss her English friends, her visits to such places as Balmoral, which she had always particularly loved, and the calm pleasures of English life which basically suited her nature so well. Most of all she would miss her mother who was now old and frail. But there seemed to be no other options open to her and at the end of August she prepared to leave Porchester Terrace, perhaps forever.

She decided to go back to Lausanne where she had various friends, one in particular. This was Mary, the daughter of Sir John and Lady Latta, who had now become Marchioness of Craymayel and who had a beautiful villa in Lausanne. They had first met in London, Mary having previously been a friend of Alfonso's. She had danced with the Spanish King in Lausanne. But there was no question of their ever having been lovers and Mary ultimately became one of Ena's closest friends, a principal confidante and a main prop and stay of her life.

It was hurriedly arranged that she should stay with her friend Mary and she arrived in Lausanne only a few days before war was declared. She brought with her two German maids. The nationality of the maids greatly alarmed Mary's husband the Marquis and the maids had to be boarded out, a circumstance which did not trouble Ena provided they were able to get her up in the morning and be waiting for her when she went to bed at night at whatever time that might be. Ena had never been one for letting crises, wars and domestic upheavals interrupt her personal comforts.

The Craymayels' house in Lausanne was called L'Elysée, a very fine eighteenth-century villa originally bought by Sir John Latta and today the property of the town of Lausanne. The Queen was intensely relieved to be with Mary in her spacious house at this moment when everything else in her fragile world seemed to have been plunged back into uncertainty. In fact Ena's ability to throw off adversity and adapt herself to new surroundings, particularly luxurious ones, seemed to some people almost offensively well-developed. She was not a crier over spilt milk. She would never have felt that the world was coming to an end unless she had suddenly had to do without meals or maids. In this respect she was a thorough representative of the cosseted upper-class ladies of her generation. She was very little more spoilt than most of them were. She had moreover come from a London where, in the best social circles, the idea of war had been laughed at. Life had gone on as usual as if nothing would ever change. The German Ambassador, Count von Ribbentrop, was often to be seen dining at the best houses. The 'Cliveden Set' were not alone in feeling that war with Hitler was unnecessary. Even King George VI seemed to think, a week before war was declared that it could still be avoided by negotiation. He said as much in a letter to Ena which she read out to her hostess as they were sitting in the drawing room at L'Elysée. Having read it, she was about to tear it up and throw it away when Mary Craymayel restrained her. The letter she said would be worth keeping so Ena handed it to her and she has kept it ever since. The letter reads as follows:

> BUCKINGHAM PALACE
> August 27th, 1939

My Dear Ena,

I was so sorry not to have spoken to you last night. We do live in very anxious days and from what I hear all hope is not (yet)* given up.

My Ambassador coming here at Hitler's request must show that H. has not really decided on War.

If only this can be avoided and that we can turn the *situation* onto negotiations instead of force with God's help we will.

I hope you will not be away long and that perhaps a visit to Balmoral will still be possible.

> Best Love to you,
> Yours very affectionate, (sic)
> BERTIE

---

* The word 'yet' had been added later by hand.

It is extraordinary to realize that these should have been the thoughts and beliefs of the King of Great Britain within a few days of the declaration of war. But such it appears they were.

Many indeed were still living in cloud-cuckoo-land and would continue to do so during the 'phoney war' which was to follow. Italy had not yet become a belligerent and Ena's thoughts turned to Rome. She wanted to be near her family for as long as circumstance permitted and knew that Alfonso's health had been deteriorating. After a few more weeks at L'Elysée and a brief stay at the Beau Rivage Hotel she therefore left for the Italian capital.

In Rome Ena and Alfonso appeared more together in public and carried this off well enough for some people to believe that there had been a true reconciliation at last. But unfortunately there was no great intimacy between them and they still did not live under the same roof. This was a source of frustration and sometimes of humiliation for Ena but she could not face the thought of leaving altogether to go and live alone in Lausanne. Her family life, severely fractured though it was, was based on Rome as far as it was based anywhere. But it was an embarrassment that, though both Alfonso and Ena received visiting Spaniards formally from time to time, they always gave separate audiences. The King and Queen, at the same time, were both very social. The Rome society of that day was still very small and exclusive. Naturally Ena and Alfonso were both invited to the same sort of parties and could hardly escape meeting occasionally. That they managed to carry off such occasions with dignity emerges from a description given by a French diplomat resident in Rome at that time, bearing in mind that he himself was (and still is) a passionate royalist: 'An important common point between King Alfonso and Queen Ena,' he says, 'was that they were both good society people. I mean by this that most royals are not all *gens du monde*, and that some fall prey to café society. Well, this was not the case with these two. They both appreciated and were appreciated by the international high society and the world of true elegance. They both felt at ease in the same set and had the same friends. In that regard they were very much like Prince Paul and Princess Olga of Yugoslavia. This is rare, for it more often happens among royals that only one is a society person. Such was the case with the Queen of Romania, Queen Margarita of Italy, and the late King of Sweden among others.' This description really says more for what might have been than for what actually was. But the royal couple played their part well on such occasions as the wedding in the summer of their youngest daughter Christina to Enrico Marone-Cinzano. His combined surnames were a combination of those of his father and mother, the latter having been Paula Cinzano of the Vermouth family. Enrico was therefore rich but untitled. Marone means Brown in English and it became a private joke in the Spanish royal family that the Infanta Christina could hardly, overnight, become plain Mrs Brown. Her bridegroom however, was ennobled and became the first Count Marone. Under this style he married the Infanta as his second wife, on 10 June 1940.

The entry of Italy into the war on the German side posed a new dilemma for Queen Ena. It was not certain how long, as a British-born Queen, she could go on residing in the capital of a country at war with her native land. Even when in the company of her close friend Queen Elena of Italy she sensed as time passed that there was growing tension in diplomatic circles. Eventually Ena was accused of being in touch with the British fleet but replied that 'In my family until now there have been no Mata Haris.' Ena nevertheless was forced to think about having to return to Lausanne. She was dissuaded from so doing chiefly by increasing worries over Alfonso's health. She decided to stay on in Italy but to live just outside Rome itself. This would ease the political delicacy caused by her presence there as well as avoiding the tension of living somewhere, such as the Excelsior Hotel, which was so near and yet so far from Alfonso, who was just up the road at the Grand. The King's health was observably worse by the end of this year and at the beginning of 1941 was giving serious cause for alarm. On one occasion he collapsed in a shop in the Via Veneto. Ena, still in her villa in the hills overlooking Rome, longed to get some news of him. Amazing as it may seem she did not dare to ring him up at his hotel. She wanted desperately to do so but the thought of actually ringing made her intensely nervous as she knew he would not welcome any such calls. The basic and brutal truth was that Ena was secretly frightened of Alfonso and always had been. He was ever the stronger character and it was this which had presented a continuing challenge to Ena. For this reason too, and despite everything, he had gone on fascinating her in a perverse and unsettling fashion. A proper reconciliation before Alfonso's death would go a long way to save honour on all sides. Even now Ena had not given up hope. Indeed she thought of little else as she waited nervously in the wings, wondering what part she would have, if any, in the final scene.

Alfonso's preoccupations, however, were with other matters. Realizing himself that death might be near he agreed to renounce his rights to the Spanish throne in favour of his son, Don Juan, who now became, in the eyes of his royalist supporters, King Juan III of Spain. By the same token Ena became, at least technically, 'Queen Mother'. Alfonso's act of renunciation was made on 15 January 1941. His paroxysms of pain were now becoming more frequent and alarming news kept reaching Ena by roundabout means. But no one seems to have sent for her or made any official attempt to contact her directly. At length, before the suspense and sense of exclusion became unbearable, she decided to ring the Grand Hotel to talk to her husband ostensibly about an everyday matter. She finally got through to him and in a voice which she hoped betrayed no tremble said, 'Don't forget it's Sandra's birthday in a couple of days.' She was referring to the fact that their granddaughter the eldest child of the Infanta Beatrice, would be five on 14 February. 'I'm going into town to buy her a small present,' the Queen Mother continued. 'On my way back I could drop in to see you.' Ena remembered this conversation and its aftermath so vividly that she was able to recount the words and

[259]

events in question in minute detail even twenty years later.[6] 'Come,' the King said in his reply. 'But not later than half past eleven as I must go out to lunch.'

Ena set out excitedly. But there was something rather uncanny, perhaps even telepathetic, about the timing of her telephone call. It had almost exactly coincided with Alfonso's first serious heart attack. When she was shown into Alfonso's room at the Grand Hotel she was appalled by what she saw. Alfonso was sitting up in a large straight-backed chair. 'Forgive me if I don't rise,' he said to Ena with the grave courtesy more appropriate to the receiving of a relative stranger. 'I'm suffering like mad.' Ena could not hide the shock she felt at his appearance. Even as she stood there, there was a doctor at his side 'stuffing him with pills'. As soon as he recovered somewhat he sent for his chaplain, Father Ulpiano Lopez, who heard his confession. The King's doctors, Cesare Frugoni, Cloazza and Raddu, could only give the worried priest a depressing diagnosis. And the King was afraid that, were he to try to receive Holy Communion, his nausea would make him choke over the host. Alfonso told his chaplain, with that famous smile which had broken many a heart and disarmed so many would-be critics, 'I don't think I'll die tonight!'

His condition was nevertheless grave. Ena and her children moved into the Grand Hotel to be as near as possible to her husband. She would have liked to spend the whole night at his bedside. But this task fell to Sister Teresa, the nursing nun who, along with her companion Sister Inés, were to be on twenty-four hour duty from now on. The King talked far into the night to Sister Teresa about Spain despite her protestation that he should be quiet and rest. It did him no good, she said, to talk about his country. Ena, though close at hand, felt almost more hopeless and cut off than ever. She was living in closer proximity to him that she had for years. But in all the most important respects she had seldom if ever, been further away. For even now, on his death bed, Alfonso made it clear that he did not want to see his wife. Day after day she waited, hoping not only for his improvement but also for some breakthrough at the eleventh hour in that barrier that still separated them. It never came.

There was, it is true, an official story that the estranged pair were fully reconciled at the end. Ena herself, for public consumption, gave credence to this story by saying, 'All that had kept us apart during the difficulties of his reign or the disappointments of exile had passed. We found again unchanged the great tenderness we had known at the beginning of our married life.'[7] This was the first admission in print that Ena and Alfonso had been driven 'apart' before 1931 and had lived under 'difficulties' ever since. It was a diplomatic way of saying that their marriage had been dead for thirty years. In the fullest series of interviews ever given by Queen Ena, however, there is no evidence of any reconciliation before the end. In the book based on these interviews, moreover,[8] the entire period from the departure from Madrid to the King's last illness is passed over in silence. The reason for this was that this period contained incidents and tragedies, and an overall sense of darkness, which she never wished to mention in public. In private, however, Ena revealed to a number of close friends that her unguarded words to Alfonso in 1931 had changed the course of her life. She nevertheless strove as hard for some sort of reconciliation after 1931 as she had striven for a measure of happiness, despite the enmities and infidelities, in the period before. In both endeavours she had failed. She thus went on to recount to the same friends what actually happened when Alfonso lay dying in Rome in February 1941. She had, on one occasion, to force her way into the sick-room when she thought that the end was near. Alfonso had given orders that she was not to be admitted. She had destroyed his life and possibly his throne. This was the conviction with which Alfonso had lived for a decade. He was no hypocrite and was not now going to pretend to sentiments that he did not feel. It would be better in his eyes for Ena to stay away rather than for him to die with a lie on his lips, the lie that he loved her despite everything and that all was forgiven.

The Queen Mother of Spain thus had no option but to watch

[261]

from a distance while her husband's life slowly ebbed away. She bore no malice. She seemed to understand. She was tortured by the physical agonies which she knew the King was undergoing and bore with bravery. She was with him at the very end but how much did he comprehend of what was happening and of who was in the room? The only detailed written account conflicts with what Ena told her friends in her declining years. According to the former[9] she actually slept in the sick-room on the last night and was holding his hands as he said to her 'It's all over, Ena'. These are the only words he spoke to her according to this account, and his very last words were, 'My God! My God!'

He died at two o'clock in the afternoon of 28 February 1941. His 'life' with the Queen had come to an end ten years earlier. His love for her had perished twenty years before that. But Ena remained faithful to the end, not only of Alfonso's life but to the end of her own as well. This steadfastness on her part helped to perpetuate a myth about herself in relation to her husband that still remains current in some circles and has never been corrected.

[14]

'Queen Mother'

THE myth about Ena, Spain's English Queen, was based on the theory of a virtual British plot to marry her to Alfonso XIII. The Spanish King, according to this theory, was not properly warned of the danger of haemophilia. In later years he thus had reason for a legitimate grievance against Ena's family and Ena herself when she proved to be an unresponsive wife who consorted chiefly with his friends' enemies. With one of such enemies, as the theory continued, she was having a love affair at the time of their exile, and he was therefore justified in leaving her. *He*, nevertheless, behaved at all times with the utmost courtesy and correctness towards her and bore his cross, for which she was largely if unintentionally responsible, with cheerful courage to the end. His unfailing charm captivated everyone he met and it was his lasting tragedy that Ena had failed him as a wife, a mother and a Queen. They were nevertheless reconciled in their later years.

This is to summarize the heart of the myth in a form more succinct and brutal than that adopted by many who actually believe in it. They invariably dress it up with expressions that are complimentary to Queen Ena in the sense of implying that she could not help herself. She was too young to realize all that was being planned behind her back in 1905 and 1906 and unable, through no fault of her own, to win back her husband's love after tragedy had struck. She was the victim of her own nature and this she could never change.

To straighten the record it is not necessary to blacken Alfonso's name. It is merely necessary to tell the whole truth. And this does no ultimate damage to Alfonso's reputation for it is quite true that, although he was not deceived about the haemophilia, he may well have deceived himself. Thereafter he became a largely innocent creature of circumstances. He too was a captive of his personality. Ena and Alfonso therefore by following their respective natures inevitably drifted into separate worlds. But Ena had an incredible ability to make the best of things at all times and to throw off tragedy as if casting aside a cloak. This very fact, taken as evidence of insensitivity, had the effect of strengthening the myth described above. Her Anglo-Saxon stoicism was, it is true, a perpetual source of mystery to her Latin friends. But it helped her to survive the years immediately following Alfonso's death during which there was no one place which she could call her real home. The war made impossible any decision as to where she could permanently settle. She hoped it would be in London but that could not be until after the fighting was over.

She stayed on in Rome for nearly a year after the King's death. It was not easy but the effort was worth it, in order, for as long as possible, to be near to her own family. The diplomatic problem posed by the presence in wartime of the British born Queen on 'enemy' soil was mitigated by her living a discreet and secluded life with her daughter and son-in-law at the Palazzo Torlonia. Her daughter, the Infanta Beatrice, has related[1] how her mother—gradually getting over the shock of Alfonso's death— managed to feel relaxed and at home in the Palazzo Torlonia. So true was this, in fact, that the Queen was soon observed breaking some of her own strict domestic rules. During the mornings she would sometimes sit at her open bedroom window overlooking the Via Condotti (Rome's Bond Street) wearing her dressing gown and curlers. She could occasionally be seen cheerfully conversing with Count Chigi, still in his pyjamas, who lived in a house opposite. Normally Ena disapproved strongly of such conversations being conducted across streets and courtyards. But the exception she made in her own case became quite a family joke. But life at this time was not easy. There were 'unpleasant restrictions of all sorts', as Ena was subsequently to explain (to the British Queen Mother when writing from Lausanne in April 1942) and Rome was full of 'Germans in uniform swarming everywhere'.[2] The Germans, in fact, were billeted at the Hotel D'Angleterre immediately opposite the main door of the Palazzo Torlonia. Restrictions meant shortages and the Torlonias managed secretly to keep an illegal cow to supply them with milk. Their efforts to smuggle the cow off the premises so that she could be impregnated were, however, frustrated by the watchful proximity of the Germans.

By the end of that first summer, in 1941, Ena had decided to leave Rome and return to Switzerland. She arrived in Lausanne on 30 January 1942, and made her home for the time being at the Hotel Royal. She had only stayed in Italy, 'so as to be near my children', she explained[3] but now no longer intended to go back there. She mentioned in the same letter to Queen Mary that 'This is the fourth time in eleven years that I have had to start life afresh in another country which is rather unsettling to say the least.' But her arrival in Lausanne, as the senior member of the Spanish royal family, turned out to have a decisive influence on its other members, notably Don Juan. He, as Ena reported, still in the same letter, would be arriving in May 'To stay for six months in the charming little house they have taken which is quite close to this hotel. It has a nice garden and hot house full of flowers with which I fill my room during their absence.' In the event Don Juan and his family stayed much longer than six months having elected Switzerland, because of its neutrality, as their country of residence for the balance of the war.[4] Lausanne became their principle base for the duration of hostilities and beyond. It marked, in more ways than one, an entirely new phase in the life of Ena, the Queen Mother of Spain. Two interests in particular were to absorb her attention from now on. One was the forwarding of Don Juan's claims to the throne of Spain. The other was her ever growing group of grandchildren who were to bring such pleasure and delight into her life.

Ena thus became the source of unity and hope for the Spanish royal family. After Alfonso's death she came into her own. She was bereaved but free. Alfonso, in the last ten years of his life, had cast an unhappy shadow over her life reminding her that though he was there she could not reach him. Death had removed this shadow. Ena now tried to remember the good things that had gone before and to rely on her capacity for romanticizing. She began again to be content if not completely happy. Her grandchildren came to play in the garden of her hotel: Juan Carlos, Spain's future king; Alfonsito, his younger brother, who was still only a toddler; Margarita, Don Juan's daughter whose blindness she tried to mitigate by showing her certain tricks and useful habits. When Ena had first become aware that this little child, then about three, could not see, she completely broke down in grief. This was a very rare thing for her to do. It only happened when some particularly affecting family tragedy reminded her of the curse supposedly originating, in this case, not with the Habsburgs, but with herself. It was the long-nursed fear, arising from what people had said to her, that a curse had been laid on her by her English Protestant friends for having abandoned the religion of her birth.

Little Margarita had an unhappy childhood because of her blindness but achieved fulfilment and satisfaction years later and is now happily married to a charming and talented doctor, Don Carlos Zurita y Delgado. Princess Margarita's memories of her grandmother[5] are vivid and enthusiastic: 'We adored her. She knew us all like the palm of her hand. She treated us all the same. She always spoke Spanish to us rather than English saying that it was bad enough to have to learn French and German ... We were more inclined to open our hearts to her—on some occasions—than to our own parents. She was extremely realistic in her outlook ... she loved our visits and pretended not to notice when we sneaked third helpings of the delicious chocolate cake she often had for us for the wonderful teas ...'

The young Prince, Juan Carlos, now King of Spain, had equally vivid memories of his grandmother at this period—the

early to middle forties—in Switzerland.[6] She took a detailed
interest in his life and education and came to visit him regularly
when he started to go to school in Fribourg. The Prince greatly
looked forward to such visits. A hitherto dormant side of Queen
Ena's nature now came out very strongly. Her rapport with
children and young people turned out to be remarkable. Their
mutual relationships were more relaxed than was the case as
between Ena and her own children. The Queen Mother had a
particularly important formative influence on King Juan Carlos in
his early days. It continued even after Don Juan and his family had
left Lausanne for Estoril, since Ena often saw them during visits
to Portugal. Ena and the future King were helped by being in a
sense 'equals' when approaching the study of the Spanish language. Don Juan Carlos spent most of his childhood among
non-Spanish speakers. Ena knew what a handicap it would be for
him to return as heir to the throne of Spain speaking Spanish with
a foreign accent. For she herself 'had suffered much in Spain
because of her English accent, particularly in Palace circles. For
this very reason she was anxious that her grandson would not
suffer the embarrassment of a foreign accent.' She thus dedicated
quite a long period each day to giving him phonetic exercises to
improve his Spanish pronunciation, especially when pronouncing
the 'r' in any word. She knew how disagreeable it was in Spanish
ears to hear this pronounced in the French manner. The lessons
were unsuccessful at first but the Queen refused to relax her
efforts. She knew how vital, linguistically and practically, this
apparently small point in fact was. Finally there was a breakthrough somewhat like the scene made famous in *My Fair Lady*
when the professor says 'I think she's got it!' From that magic
moment onwards the Infante Juan Carlos always pronounced
every 'r' in the trilling Spanish rather than in the rasping French
style. In its own way this was a major triumph and the Queen's
satisfaction was equalled by that of her grateful and enthusiastic
grandson who at this time in his life took so much after her in
looks. All in all Ena's role as a grandmother was both rewarding

and fruitful. 'She was a tremendous influence in all our lives' said Doña Olympia, the second daughter of the Infanta Beatrice.[7] To be with her grandchildren was indeed the major interest in Queen Ena's life during the forties and thereafter. They formed a central part of the new and very different world that became hers after Alfonso's death. She hoped her grandchildren would find a future as full of promise as her past life had been of disappointment. She was determined moreover to share their hopeful expectations now that she had emerged from the shadow of a dark decade. She had fourteen grandchildren in all of whom, mercifully, none was a haemophilic victim. The Infantas Beatrice and Christina who were potentially transmitters never actually had to face the horror of producing children who were sufferers. They were spared the agony which induced their mother to say, when looking back on her own life, 'The burdens of State, the difficulty of living with a King whose faults were as extreme as his duties were little compared with my grief in losing two sons, the eldest and the youngest. Love rarely dies a sudden death, especially when it is maternal love. And today I am obliged to close my eyes sometimes and try not to remember . . .'[8]

Apart from the presence of Don Juan and his wife and children in Lausanne, there were many welcome visits by Don Jaime and his children as well as by the Infanta Christina and hers. Ena was seldom alone or left without pleasant distractions. But she could not avoid having distractions of a less agreeable kind. She was worried about her family and friends in wartime England. The international mails were slow and unreliable. Ena's letter to Queen Mary of 12 April 1942, mentioned earlier, was brought to England by Mr (later Sir) David Kelly, then *en poste* at the British Legation in Berne who visited Queen Ena from time to time. The British royal family at least gathered from this letter, a long one, that the Spanish Queen Mother's life in Lausanne was, materially speaking, as comfortable as could be expected. She had managed to hire a small car which enabled her to visit such nearby spots as Montreux and Vevey where she had friends. There were also lovely walks to be enjoyed along the lake front. English newspapers could be obtained and Ena followed the war news with daily anxiety. But her biggest private worry about the family in England concerned her mother, now nearing the end of her life. With the death, in January 1942, of the Duke of Connaught—whose daughter's lack of interest in Alfonso had paved the way for Ena—Princess Beatrice was the last survivor of her generation. Later that year she went to live with the Athlones at Brantbridge Park in Sussex and became seriously ill in October 1944. Ena was desperately worried as to whether and how she would be able to get to England. The British Government arranged to send a partially converted bomber to bring her to London. She was thus just in time to see her mother before she died. She stayed on for a time at Claridges in order to be present at the funeral which was held at St George's Chapel, Windsor, on 3 November.

Back in London, Ena visited her old house in Porchester Terrace. It had been damaged by fire bombs but she was still, at this stage, planning to restore it and settle down there when the war was finally over. She thus returned to her hotel in Lousanne very much as to a temporary home. She did not expect to be there much longer. The grandchildren were still a central interest, particularly the sons of Don Jaime and Don Juan. The former was, of all Ena's own children, the one who was closest to her and always sought out her company. She was never as close to him as he was to her. His life, as the forties took their course, became increasingly troubled and troublesome. He had his full share of hot Bourbon blood and his susceptibility toward women was complicated by the psychological effects of his illness. In the course of a conversation with an attractive woman at a party he would become plainly disturbed and angry at his inability to communicate properly. He would resort to mouthing the word 'cuarto', meaning room, and pointing meaningfully to the upstairs region of the house. His marriage, which inevitably suffered, was eventually dissolved by a Romanian court in May 1947. His wife, who was known as the Duchess of Segovia, later married an

Italian economist called Dr Antonio Sozzani. Don Jaime also remarried but disastrously. His second wife was Charlotte Tiedermann, a German night club singer, and their marriage was stormy and unhappy. Charlotte was a mischief maker who went on causing havoc for many years to the Spanish royal family even after Don Jaime's death in 1975. One of the many embarrassments was the fact that Charlotte's daughter by a previous marriage, Helga Hippler, liked to call herself Helga de Borbon to create the impression in French social circles that she was a genuine member of that family. The sadness produced by all this was often mentioned by Don Jaime to his mother as it was to her that he always went when possible for consolation and advice.

For her part, unfortunately, Ena had a blind spot where Don Jaime was concerned. Her second son was tall, dark and good looking with much of Alfonso's charm. But whereas the Queen seemed able to make endless allowances for the irregularities of her husband's behaviour, she had less patience in the case of Don Jaime. Her indifference toward him amounted, in many eyes, to positive neglect. On the other hand she became very close to his two sons, Alfonso and Gonzalo. When subsequent family trouble threatened to isolate the two boys she referred to them as 'orphans in a storm' and tried to protect them. Their father meanwhile was left mostly to his own devices and his later life was unhappy. Jaime did not endear himself to his mother when in 1964 he rescinded his thirty-year-old renunciation and laid claim once more to the Spanish throne.

Much, however, was to happen meanwhile of which the 'Queen Mother' was to be at the centre. As far as her children were concerned she was chiefly interested, particularly from 1945 onwards, in the plans and prospects of her third son, Don Juan. Had she not curtsied deeply to him at the moment when he had received from his father the right of succession to the Spanish throne? The significance of this had ever since remained very much present in her mind. She was passionately keen that Don Juan, Count of Barcelona, Prince of Asturias should be universally recognized as head of the Spanish royal family. The latter, in April 1945, issued a manifesto to the Spanish people saying boldly, 'I have resolved, in order to free my conscience from the increasing burden of responsibility that afflicts it, to raise my voice and solemnly require General Franco that he should recognize the failure of his conception of a totalitarian state.' Don Juan proposed the return of 'a monarch' who 'would, by contast, favour reconciliation, justice and tolerance. Many reforms will be necessary in the interests of the nation. Its foremost duties will be: the immediate approval by popular vote of a political constitution which shall recognize the natural rights of the individual and guarantee political liberties . . .' Don Juan, however, was snubbed by Franco when they subsequently met and Queen Ena quietly but firmly made up her mind that this slight against her son would at all costs be removed before she died. Would she, one day, prove a match for the otherwise impregnable General Franco? In one way or another she was determined that the score should be settled. With the European war not yet over, however, a long waiting game might prove necessary.

Ena's first practical task when the war finally ended was to settle her domestic situation and find a permanent home. She wanted this to be in Great Britain where she spent many months in the course of several visits during 1946 and 1947. On one of these, in April 1946, she took the young Prince Juan Carlos with her. It was his first visit to England. When he returned to the continent it was not to Lausanne but to Estoril, near Lisbon, where Don Juan had now decided to make his home. In London Ena stayed mostly at Claridges as her house was not yet ready for occupation. She too, when returning to Europe, went more often to Lisbon than to Lausanne. She wanted to be in touch with Don Juan who, in turn, wanted to be as close as possible to Spain.

Ena, in London, was not being as successful as she had hoped in re-establishing her residence there. She was told she would have to pay British income tax as there were no grounds on which she could claim immunity. She had long had financial troubles

Ena with Don Juan, Count of Barcelona, his wife Doña Maria Mercedes and their son Juan Carlos

[272]

and this seemed to be a final blow. Her first step was to move out of Claridges where, in any event the food was 'very nasty if one gets away from chicken and fresh fruit'.[9] It was for making such remarks as this that Ena gained a reputation for being concerned with superficial things in the midst of more serious events. She was lucky enough to be able to stay quite often with Princess Alice, Countess of Athlone, at Kensington Palace though the servants there eventually rebelled, though discreetly, at the Queen's untidiness and lack of consideration and felt she was acting rather as a prima donna. Princess Alice was, as ever, patient and charming, even when Ena hinted about food of which, of course, she was very fond. Dining out on a recent evening, she remarked to her cousin Princess Alice, there had been some delicious salmon. 'Yes, but salmon's very expensive, dear,' the more practical Alice had replied. Ena never thought about money, or affected not to. Her original allowance from the Spanish Government had been suspended because of the Civil War but Franco later reinstated it. But she tended to be improvident and was lucky so frequently to have people in the offing to pick up her bills. One of these was the Duke of Mora who would remark, on seeing some particularly large bill from Claridges, that Ena had been 'very naughty'. He also felt that she was careless in such matters as taking large amounts of jewellery with her when travelling. She had amassed a considerable quantity of this over the years and, in the early days, Alfonso had been very generous with his gifts. She had been able to get most of her possessions out of Spain during the Republic, and of this the jewellery was what concerned her most. She hated to be parted from it even to the extent of putting it in a safe deposit box when staying at Claridges. Instead she left it in her room in the charge of her maid Evelina whose melancholy task was to stay there all day looking after the jewellery. Ena was lucky never to have any stolen but from time to time it was necessary to sell some piece or other.

It was a blow to her to find that financially she would be unable to live in London. She had no house anywhere else and there was little money to be got out of relinquishing her lease of the Porchester Terrace house. This was in due course acquired by the Peruvian Government as the residence for that country's Ambassador in London. But Ena was lucky. At just the right moment she received a legacy of £30,000 from the will of Mrs Ronnie Greville. She had always understood that she would receive something from this rich and generous old friend. She had thought it would be jewellery as well as money. When it turned out to be the latter she said she would have preferred the jewellery and implied that she did not really need the cash. Such affectations were typical of her and wholly transparent to her friends.

Ena's choice of a permanent home now seemed to lie between Portugal and Switzerland. In the former she could be nearer to her son Don Juan but in the latter she would feel much more at home and could still keep in close touch with the claimant to the Spanish throne. She had made up her mind—in favour of Switzerland—by the end of 1947 and wrote to Queen Mary, the Queen Mother, on 3 December, that 'I am very sorry that my happy stay here is drawing to a close. It has been so lovely being with you all again as it is a real grief to have had to let my house here for financial reasons as needless to say it is here where I would wish to live.'[10] In Lausanne, where she now intended to go, she would see a lot of Prince Juan Carlos who was still going to school nearby. Some said he was her favourite grandchild. His ultimate political—indeed dynastic—prospects appealed to her romantic optimism. She felt that whatever should happen meanwhile Don Juan Carlos's destiny and that of Spain would be identical. She confided as much to an elderly Spanish diplomat who listened with polite scepticism.

Her plan was to devote Mrs Greville's legacy to the purchase of a house in Lausanne. For practical purposes she enlisted the help of her old friend, the former Mary Craymayel. Her first husband had died and she was now the Countess Chevreu D'Antraigues. She was still living in the same house in Lausanne. Just next to the

Chevreu house, L'Elysée, it so happened that a charming villa was for sale. It was called Vieille Fontaine. It was considerably smaller than L'Elysée but would be big enough for Queen Ena and her retinue of servants, who numbered half a dozen. By July 1948, she was thus able to write enthusiastically to the Queen Mother that she had bought a new house in Lausanne and had been over it three times. 'Thank goodness the former inhabitants with their hideous furniture left on the 24th,' she wrote. 'Now I can visualize where I shall place the furniture and pictures I have kept; and it seems to me I have made the right decision.'[11] Ena's furniture came mostly from storage in London after she had 'closed down' Porchester Terrace and her mother's former house at Kensington Palace. Much had also been saved, particularly in the way of pictures and ornaments, from Spain, and was to come trickling through as time went on. Ena's firm re-establishment of a proper base was something for which she now longed more than anything. She was excitedly absorbed during the rest of the summer and autumn with moving in to Vieille Fontaine. When most of the task was completed there was a slight feeling of let-down and anti-climax. Would life in Lausanne be too quiet and cut off? At first, she complained, she felt it to be so after all the moving about and the adventures of the previous years. But a whole new routine which suited her soon began to fall into place.

The villa at Lausanne was to be her home for the rest of her life. Many now wrote her off as the retired and comparatively unimportant dowager member of a deposed royal house. But Ena, only just over sixty, had no intention of disappearing completely from the public eye. She was free to romanticize to her heart's desire about her days as Queen of Spain. The bad memories were successfully stifled. And though life might be dull at times in a bourgeois centre like Lausanne, Ena was determined to surprise the world yet. For the time being she could only watch and wait on world events. General Franco could not last for ever. And one day—such was her dream—she would surely go back to Spain.

[15]

A Final Triumph

VIEILLE FONTAINE, Queen Ena's house in Lausanne and her home for the last twenty years of her life, exactly suited her means and her needs. The Queen took a good year to settle in properly. Her next door neighbour, Mary Chevreu, was invaluable to her. They met three or four times a week and spoke every day on the telephone. Mary Chevreu was flattered to think she was one of the closest friends and confidantes of the Queen while Ena, for her part, found the friendship socially and personally useful. The Queen would ring up her friend every morning and they would discuss plans for the next few days. Bridge or canasta in the house of one or the other became the staple afternoon activity. Luncheon and dinner parties were frequent. Ena loved being asked out and would accept invitations from almost anyone. The rather middle-class locals never quite realized how easy it would have been to meet Ena if they had wanted to. They would only have had to ask her to lunch or dinner and she would have come like a shot—provided they had not expected to be asked back.

Ena, in fact, was considerably more relaxed in the presence of social inferiors and continued to meet the same sort of people she had got to know in her hotel days. Many of them were what the Spaniards would have called 'rastacueros'. These were the social climbers from the rich international set who spent long periods of the year in Lausanne. They flattered and entertained the often bored Queen and she would let her hair down in their company. This was something she liked doing despite her reputation for standing on her royal dignity. The same was to happen, when, at

Vieille Fontaine, she entertained such celebrities as Noel Coward and Marlene Dietrich. She would visibly unfreeze as the conversation opened up and give vent to her famous raucous laugh. Then, suddenly and rather disconcertingly, she was inclined to freeze up as if realizing that everyone had gone a bit too far. She would stiffen herself and sit bolt upright so as to signify that the merriment was over. One of her tragedies was in not being more easily able to relax in a natural fashion and behave in much the same way with everyone. But, whatever happened, the thing she dreaded most was boredom.

Not all of her activity was by any means superficial and frivolous. Politically it was a frustrating period and there seemed no hope, in the course of the fifties, of furthering the monarchist cause in a Spain in which Franco was still fighting an isolated and lonely battle for economic survival. Relations between the 'Caudillo' and Ena's son Don Juan were, much to her annoyance, very bad all this time. The Count of Barcelona was not only too liberal for Franco but also too emphatic—some said tactless—in his manner of making known his alternative policy for Spain. The royal family therefore had to take a very long term view of things. Hence the importance of young Juan Carlos's education and outlook. In the direction and formation of these Ena played a major part as already seen. During the first part of her life at Vieille Fontaine, Queen Ena saw the heir to the Spanish throne, as he technically then was, more than any other member of the family. He was brought over to visit her every weekend and on Sunday evening they would both go back to his school in Fribourg, the Ville Saint Jean College run by the Marist Brothers. On Thursdays Ena would visit her grandson at his school. In the early days, as the King himself recalls, her main concern was to make sure he was 'properly scrubbed'. Later her influence extended to more grown up matters. It was from Queen Ena that the future King of Spain gained so keen a sense of loyalty and dedication. For the former English Princess had by now become intensely Spanish in her outlook. Her fondest wish for him was that he should grow up to love Spain and wish to serve his country. Her own first loyalty was also to Spain by now and, perhaps incredibly, to the memory of her husband. Such was the miraculous effect of her romantic imagination. She revelled in talking about the old days and of the wise things Alfonso had said and done. It was as if such days had been the happiest of her life. She would frequently preface statements with the phrase 'Alfonso always said . . .' Friends who remembered bygone times, but also knew that Queen Ena in fact forgot nothing, could only marvel at the ease with which Ena had outwardly abandoned all her former bitterness. With amazing ease she had assumed the role of the mellow widow contentedly looking back. Her willingness to discuss the past—guardedly with strangers, freely with intimates—gave all around her new insights into her life and character hitherto unsuspected. Her strengths and weaknesses became more readily apparent to those who saw her regularly.

Her main strength was her stoicism. Her main weakness, perhaps a corollary, was her aloofness. The latter was contributed to by psychological factors. The Queen had become accustomed during her life to a good deal of grandeur and deference. There was not much of either to be had in bourgeois Lausanne particularly on limited funds. But Ena wanted to go on living as if there were no such restrictions. Her son was still making her an allowance, but it was not until 1955 that Franco asked his 'Parliament' to approve an annual grant to Queen Ena of 250,000 pesetas a year. £7,000 of this was payable in Lausanne and £2,300 in London. Even so the Queen continued to overspend, never having had to count or handle money and anxious to make her escapist type of existence in Lausanne seem as carefree and effortlessly regal as possible. She had been annoyed and disappointed by the failure to reach a favourable settlement of the tax situation whereby she could have lived in England. Even in Switzerland she was touchy on the subject of taxes and when a licence fee was introduced for dogs she tried to insist that her two precious dachshunds should be exempt.

In the early fifties it even became necessary to sell the family emeralds which were a famous and treasured heirloom. Most of them dated from a priceless gift from her godmother, the Empress Eugénie. It consisted of a beautiful box containing a fan. But the box had had a false bottom containing emeralds. Alfonso had, for many years, given Ena a diamond each year. Even these had eventually to be sold. Ena's love of jewellery was affronted by the necessity for such sales. But she still managed to keep most of the pieces she really wanted. After her death they were divided between her sons, the most spectacular piece of all going to Don Jaime. This was the magnificent diamond necklace which had been Alfonso's wedding present to her. It was subsequently sold, after Don Jaime's death, by his widow, Charlotte Tiedermann, for eight million pesetas. Ena no doubt would have been horrified by the sale. The necklace was one of the many pieces of jewellery which, even when she wasn't wearing them, she liked to fondle, hold up to the light, twist and turn about in her hands, and take on and off so as to be able to admire them in the looking-glass. The very feel of precious jewels was a source of sensuous pleasure to the Queen. When people complimented her on her pearls or other jewellery she had a way of almost coyly tossing her head. This had the effect of calling people's attention to her hair of which she was extremely proud even in her old age. She took immense pains over it and always went to the best hairdressers. She never wore a hat if she could help it and often wore jewellery in her hair instead. She had an eagle eye for the jewellery of other women sometimes looking at them with open envy. The wearer might well be embarrassed and feel it necessary to admire whatever the Queen had on at that moment. Ena would make some such reply as 'well these are only small ones like yours', or 'just travelling pearls, dear'.

Though she eventually became known in Lausanne as '*the* Queen'—despite the presence of other royalty—she was conscious of the difficulty of being really grand or regal in a comparatively small house. She had a distinct complex about visiting

Ena in 1955

people who had larger ones but went just the same and as often as possible. She thrived on being the centre of attention and the recipient of hospitality and entertainment. If all else failed she would attend the local cinema with her lady-in-waiting and friends. But she did not like being jostled by the crowds who, she felt, should make way for her. She would get her own back by talking rather loudly during the film and ignoring efforts to keep her quiet. In the interval, while standing in the foyer smoking a cigarette through her long holder, she would survey her fellow cinema-goers and remark 'I don't think *we* know any of these people, do we?'

She had an unfortunate habit of trampling on those who were frightened of her, which was a sort of relief for her from so often having been frightened of other people. She tended, in the last years of her life, to have rather stupid ladies-in-waiting whom she would bully unmercifully. But they were too loyal to admit this later on. In the early days at Lausanne, however, she had one very brilliant lady-in-waiting, the late Marchioness of Campo Alegre whose company she greatly enjoyed. 'The Campo Alegre', as she was affectionately called by the Queen's friends, understood Ena's little foibles, most of which highly amused her. Ena, for one thing, was very impatient of the weaknesses, particularly the physical ones, of others. She walked a lot in her early days but later found this too tiring. She then made a virtue of necessity and went to the opposite extreme. She went everywhere in a car which was so hot inside that people felt sick when travelling with her in it especially as the chauffeur always drove very fast which she liked. She also kept her house so hot that people often felt faint in her drawing-room. The Queen affected not to notice and made it known that she thought fainting a sign of lack of breeding. '*We* don't faint,' she said to one person who had the temerity to remark that one might well do so in such an atmosphere. The men who visited the Queen regularly always wore their lightest weight suits even in the winter. One such gentleman startled his tailor by asking for a suit of the lightest material possible as he needed it 'for visiting the Queen of Spain'. The excessive heat of her drawing-room made people feel distinctly drowsy during the long afternoon sessions of bridge. On one occasion a guest fainted dead away on to the carpet. She happened to be someone whom

Ena disliked and considered common, namely Joana, Princess of Hohernzollern, the morganatic wife of Prince Nicholas of Romania. Ena surveyed the Princess as she lay on the carpet as if looking at the conclusion of a successful experiment. She then said, 'She even faints in a common way, doesn't she?'

Ena affected to like bridge even though she played it badly. The convention that royalty must always be allowed to win was not invariably easy to comply with. Ena had a disconcerting habit of looking at her cards and absent-mindedly giving away what she had in her hand by some such muttered remark as 'only two hearts', or, 'quite a nice lot of spades'. Princess Alice (Countess of Athlone) often came to stay with her and enjoyed her visits, except for the overheatedness of the house. She would take as many opportunities as possible to go for walks which, as Ena by this time had taken to travelling always by car, rather annoyed the Queen. 'My cousin's like a mountain goat,' she remarked rather crossly. Princess Alice however sometimes agreed to accompany Ena in her hot and fast car for shopping expeditions. Ena loved going to dressmakers. She had always adored clothes and could seldom curb her extravagance in this direction. Her Comptroller eventually warned her politely that she could not afford to buy so many clothes. She thus decided, by way of acceding to his warning, to do something she had never done before. She would make a habit, after choosing her material or dresses, of saying 'Now how much will all that be?' But before any proper answer had been given she would sweep out of the shop feeling she had done enough by merely asking. On returning to Vieille Fontaine, the car would give two hoots as it came through the gates. This was to warn the servants of the Queen's return and one of them would be at the door to take any parcels. Invariably it would be her faithful butler Aldo Corbani who was with her for many years and stayed on at Vieille Fontaine with the new owners. He still lives in Lausanne and has vivid memories of his time there with the Queen and of the many visitors that came and went.

A lot of these were Spaniards, some humble and some grand.

Ena was not always very good with the former. On one occasion a whole busload of Spaniards arrived and lustily cheered the Queen as they stood in the front garden. They very much hoped to be allowed to look in to the house but the Queen did no more than stand on the porch and wave to them. Eventually, somewhat crestfallen, they got back into the bus and drove off. She was told on another occasion that most of the Spaniards living in Lausanne went to Mass each Sunday at the same church. It was not the church which Ena herself habitually attended but on one Sunday she went. The Spaniards were delighted and crowded round the Queen who was gracious and charming. But she never went there again, preferring to attend the more conveniently placed church of the Sacred Heart at Ouchy.

Among the more grand Spaniards who visited, or wanted to visit Ena, was Doña Sol. The Queen reacted nervously to the news that she had turned up in Lausanne after all these years. It represented a threat to her escapist, almost make-believe, life in which the less pleasant aspects of the past had largely been blotted out. Ena was reminded most of all of the thirties and of the painful occasions when Alfonso had flaunted the companionship of Doña Sol to her own frequent embarrassment and even humiliation. Doña Sol was herself now living in Switzerland and came to Lausanne expressly to see Ena. Most people who did this used the excuse that they were coming to see doctors there and wished to take the opportunity of paying their respects to the Queen Mother of Spain. Sol made no such excuses and was most taken aback when Ena refused to see her. Ena, in a moment of pique, said 'I have suffered enough from the Albas never to want to see them again.' She ultimately relented however and agreed to see Doña Sol, who was anxious 'to let bygones be bygones'. The meeting however was a stiff and not very pleasant one. Dõna Sol, no doubt quite genuinely, could not understand Ena's attitude and protested before her death that 'We had always been such good friends'.

When the real past tended to intrude too much into the rather unreal present, Ena would redouble her efforts to seek diversion and entertainment. Her friend Mary Chevreu would help her to devise fancy dress parties and of these there were many as the years went by. Ena gave parties for theatre and film people in whose company she felt at an advantage. She greatly enjoyed the opportunity thus afforded of being thoroughly 'gracious' in return. The only theatrical celebrity who put her off guard was Marlene Dietrich to whom Ena only said, 'Oh, we all know *you*, don't we?' and passed on hurriedly to another guest. Noel Coward understood her perfectly. He combined a subtle touch of flattery with appropriate touches of wit. Ena would get quite carried away and, forgetting herself, roar with laughter. Then, as if she had done something wrong, would quickly check herself and become stiff and regal again. She felt she was conferring a great honour on these show business personalities and would no doubt have been somewhat affronted by Noel Coward's subsequent verdict on the Queen that she was 'delightful but a great bore, poor dear'.

In these years she craved more than ever the company of her grandchildren with whom she could relax and be more natural than with anyone else. She relished visits from the sons of Don Jaime, Alfonso and Gonzalo, and worried about their future. There was indeed much wisdom behind her description of them as 'orphans in a storm'. Though she maintained her outward calm during almost all crises and arrivals of bad news there was one occasion when her composure had been utterly shattered. On 29 March 1956, Juan Carlos and his younger brother, Alfonso, were playing in the garden of their parents' house, Villa Giralda, in Estoril. A loaded gun went off, accidentally killing Alfonso, a bright and friendly boy of whom his brother had always been particularly fond. Their happy companionship over many years had been one of the most consoling factors of life for a royal family in exile. The tragedy cast a black cloud over the family which took years to disappear. With all the disasters that had gone before, yet another one seemed almost too much to bear. Queen Ena, in Lausanne, took the news particularly badly. It brought about one of those rare occasions on which she broke down completely. As usual, in such circumstances, rare though they mercifully were, she would hark back to the supposed existence of a curse. 'When will such tragedies cease?' she cried. 'When will the curse be lifted? I know that my Protestant friends cursed me when I deserted them. I know it. I know it.' These were the exact words which she was overheard to utter. On this terrible occasion her friends at Vieille Fontaine, one in particular, found that it took much longer than was normally necessary to quieten down the distressed, almost demented, Queen.

In happier times Ena enjoyed all sorts of visits but, most of all, visits from her family, particularly from her son Don Juan. And she, in turn, made numerous trips to England and to other parts of Europe, especially to Lisbon and to Monte Carlo. She had become very friendly with the Rainiers who were extremely generous and hospitable to her. But the great question was when, if ever, would she be able to visit Spain again? Throughout the fifties, Franco was trying to settle the 'monarchist question' in his own way. For years, he 'bored his courtiers and his family with outbursts against Don Juan and his evil counsellors.'[1] He had nevertheless decided as early as 1947 that monarchy would be the best form of government for the country. He thus opted for Don Juan's son, Juan Carlos, who eventually went to be educated in Spain and fell very much at that time under Franco's influence. The young Prince swore allegiance to the 'Caudillo' and stood discreetly behind him on public occasions. The personal animosity between Franco and Don Juan increased particularly with the emergence in the Spain of the early fifties of a liberal, overtly anti-Franco, political group. In 1954 four monarchists contested local elections in Madrid but were severely defeated owing, at least in part, to official pressures. There was a succession of amateurish plots to overthrow Franco in favour of a monarchy. Don Juan was aware of many of these, and approved of them, but none came anywhere near to being successful. It seemed to be a question of waiting for a gradual movement within Spain toward a

Ena at Vieille Fontaine in 1964

liberal monarchy to gain ground by peaceful means. Ena's determination to visit Spain, if at all, in the company of her son Don
Juan therefore looked as if it might have to wait a long time.

Then, as the fifties gave way to the sixties, another cloud arose
on the horizon from the Queen's point of view. She was now
becoming an old woman and she was beginning to be troubled by
illness. As early as 1952 she had had to have a gall bladder
operation and she was even, eventually, persuaded to give up
smoking. She had been a heavy smoker since her youngest days
but when she gave it up she did so without a murmur and never
afterwards complained about missing cigarettes. She had a
further operation at the same clinic—the Clinique Cecil—in
Lausanne in 1960, her doctor being the leading Swiss surgeon of
the day Dr René Paschoud. Don Juan and both the Queen's
daughters came to Lausanne at the time of the operation over
which the Queen was 'very brave'. Her friend Mary Chevreu
could personally vouch for her 'no nonsense' attitude toward
medical problems and this helped her to recover well. But by the
middle sixties Ena knew that if she were to visit Spain it would
have to be soon or never.

The Infante Juan Carlos was meanwhile living at the Zarzuela
Palace outside Madrid, having, in May 1962, married the extremely attractive young Princess Sofia of Greece. The hopes of
the liberal monarchists had been strengthened by this popular
marriage. But Carlism, though officially 'dead', still had strong
support in parts of the country and was represented in the person
of Prince Hugo Carlos of Bourbon-Parma. He, in February
1964, married Princess Irene, the chic second daughter of Queen
Juliana of the Netherlands. The marriage had angered most
people in Holland chiefly because Carlism was hated as a reactionary remnant from an unwanted past. The Princess moreover
had had to become a Catholic for the sake of the marriage and the
reaction to this among some Dutch people had been no less
unfavourable than that of the majority of the English over
Princess Ena's change of religion nearly sixty years earlier.

The Carlist claim worried Queen Ena in her old age. She knew in her bones what a romantic appeal it still held out for many Spaniards. She knew that Franco, whom she deeply distrusted, was a wily opportunist who might conceivably clutch at the Carlist straw in an emergency. This was highly unlikely. But it was not impossible that if Franco were to find himself in real difficulties, and in danger of losing his grip on Spain the Carlists might seize the chance—almost certainly their last ever—to fill a sudden vacuum before other, more liberal, forces could mobilize. Ena therefore would have liked to make a peace of sorts with the Generalissimo. If they were to meet face to face she was confident that her intuition would give her a strong clue as to his ultimate intentions with regard to her beloved grandson on whom, by his own account, she had so strong an influence in his earlier years. Were he to succeed to the throne it would somehow be a recompense for the tragedy which had withheld it from someone whom Juan Carlos greatly resembled in looks, namely Alfonsito, her eldest son, the haemophilic former Prince of Asturias. Ena knew she would die peacefully only if she could foresee a happy outcome to this nagging conundrum. But, as things then were, she could only wait.

It was a time for reflection. The past was beginning to crowd in on the old Queen's life. The escapism and frivolities of the first decade or so at Lausanne were fading into their own nebulous limbo. More and more Spaniards from bygone days, themselves feeling the toll of the years, were turning up and expressing a wish to see the Queen. Ena affected to be wearied by the procession. She said, however, 'But I suppose one cannot stop the trains.'

Many visitors were very welcome. There were some stalwart supporters from the past including a particularly distinguished grandee and former Spanish diplomat who asserted that Ena was loyal to the last to her 'extremely disloyal husband'. The Queen, even now, would preface remarks about Alfonso with the words, 'The poor, poor King, always such a gentleman and so good'. She saw no inconsistency in also pointing out that he had been a very selfish man. She recognized this as somehow inevitable and the price to be paid for other compensations. In one of her last interviews she reflected that, looking back on her life, she had 'welcomed as little daily miracles all the honours and extraordinary adventures that my birth, my priviledged education and travels of my youth and crowned love brought me. But I knew that by the mysterious working of compensation I would one day have to pay for them in one way or the other.'[2]

In April 1966 Ena went to stay once again in the house in Monaco that the Rainiers lent her from time to time. The house had belonged to Prince Rainier's father, Prince Pierre, and this visit was a particularly happy one for the Queen. For, as she wrote to her friend Mary Chevreu in Lausanne, 'Sophie and Juanito (her nickname for Juan Carlos) and their two children are arriving' and Ena had decided to stay on in order to see as much of them as possible. Her grandson and Princess Sophie had had two girls since marrying four years earlier: Elena, born in 1963, and Christina, born in 1965. Also in the south of France at the time was her daughter-in-law, the Countess of Barcelona, who had been lent the villa near Cap Martin which the Empress Eugénie had left Ena's old friend and benefactor Fernando de Moro. The house was called Villa Pumpenia and now belonged to Mora's daughter Maria who was the second wife of Alfonso XIII's nephew, Prince Luis Alfonso of Bavaria. Such was the tangle of threads that united the various members of Europe's royal families, and the members of their inner circle, even at this late date. Ena revelled in such situations. She was delighted to get a rare glimpse of her grandson and his enchanting family and finished her letter to Mary Chevreu by saying 'My days here are very happy'. It was also in 1966 that an event occurred which made Queen Ena more determined than ever to make a visit to Spain if humanly possible. For in that year her son Don Juan made a private visit to his country which was, in his own words 'a hush-hush affair'.[3] This was a diplomatic way of saying that politically speaking the visit was a failure. It had fallen flat as far as creating any public stir was concerned. The responsibility for this, as Ena's intuition rightly told her, was that of General Franco himself. Don Juan, for his part, took it all fairly philosophically but as far as the 'Queen Mother' was concerned it was a humiliating experience for the head of the Spanish royal house. Ena still bided her time. But not for long. In the late summer of the following year, 1967, it became known that Juan Carlos's wife, Princess Sophie, was again pregnant. The couple had already had two children, but, as yet, no son. An idea began germinating in Ena's mind.

Plans were meanwhile being made for celebrating the old Queen's eightieth birthday which would occur on 24 October 1967. These plans resulted in a reunion of friends and family in Lausanne on a scale rarely seen since Alfonso and Ena had left Spain. The Queen dreaded the actual day as it approached. There had been so many quarrels within her family, particularly in their children's generation, that she was unsure how felicitous a reunion this one would turn out to be. She reflected sadly that many of the quarrels were over 'nothing more' than material possessions. But such factors often bring out greater enmities than anything else. Ena ruefully confided in an old friend that such quarrels would probably be even worse after she was dead and contrived to put the matter out of her mind for the time being.

Her birthday finally came. It started with Mass at ten-thirty at which the Queen gave thanks for the blessings of her life. Surely the greatest grace vouchsafed her had been that of her resilience in the face of adversity. Ena was back at her house just before one o'clock and was then motored down to the Hotel Beau Rivage, the huge hotel by the lakeside where Ena had so often lunched, dined and entertained in the past. An elaborate luncheon had been prepared for 150 guests. Some of them were disappointed that there was no *placement* except at the 'top table' at which sat the family and the most important guests. These sat in a long row on one side of the table only. They thus faced the array of smaller tables at which the other guests had to find themselves places. The Queen had made a point of asking all her most personal friends from Lausanne and was anxious, until the very last moment, as to whether she had left anyone out.

Towards the end of the luncheon, Don Juan rose to propose his mother's health. He spoke in English and, according to one guest present, attempted to be lighthearted. But his efforts in this direction were not wholly successful. Somehow what he said about the past and the present came across as sad and heavy and the Queen could be seen to be in tears. All present were moved but at the same time slightly embarrassed. There were so many things that the Count of Barcelona was not able to mention about his mother's life. Such things were nevertheless vividly present in the minds of many of those, sitting there that day, who had known her so well for many years.

There was some relief when the luncheon broke up. Many of the guests, to be joined by yet other friends and acquaintances, were to be meeting again later in the day. When they did, the Queen having meanwhile rested and composed herself, the atmosphere quickly became much gayer. The family had a private dinner at Vieille Fontaine after which a large amount of friends poured in for a late evening party. The champagne flowed and so did the conversation and general merriment. Students from Madrid, in picturesque costumes, serenaded the birthday Queen with songs on guitars from which flowed long and colourful ribbons. Ena, according to one of those present, got 'quite skittish'. The Duke of Alba acted as 'master of ceremonies' and had to ask a special favour of one of the guests who was a society photographer. The Duke explained that the Spanish Press had been excluded from the occasion so that no photographs would come out in any newspapers in Spain. He therefore had to ask this British photographer, even though he was a personal friend of the Queen's, not to take any pictures. He resisted the temptations to take some secretly, for the sake of posterity, and the Queen afterwards wrote to thank him for his forebearance. Finally, exhausted but happy, and long after her normal hour, the octogenarian Queen finally went to bed.

It had been an exciting and emotional day, but in the course of it something of great significance had happened of which most people were not yet aware. The Queen had made a dramatic decision. It was perhaps a calculated gamble. She had asked her grandson, the Infante Juan Carlos, and his wife, Princess Sophie, if she could be godmother to the child they were then expecting in the event of their having a son. The suggestion was accepted by them with alacrity despite the possible diplomatic hurdles to be overcome. For, if all went as hoped, it would mean that the Queen would have to be present in Madrid for the baptism. As soon as he was back in Madrid, Juan Carlos began undertaking the necessary spadework with General Franco. It was finally agreed that Ena would be welcome in Spain but it would not rank as a state or official visit. It would be a strictly family affair. Ena herself wanted nothing more but could not possibly have foreseen how spectacular her impact on the Spanish public would be. The Government was anxious to underplay the visit for all it was worth, particularly as the Queen had insisted for obvious reasons that Don Juan should be there at the same time. This was where the calculated gamble came in.

Don Juan, still smarting from the fact that his previous visit had not been allowed to excite any public interest, was nervous before his actual arrival in Madrid. But as soon as he was there he was cheered to the echo. The reason was clear and the circumstances were not unlike Ena's arrival in Madrid on returning from England in February 1931. On that previous occasion as will be remembered, the acclaim with which she was greeted rubbed off on her husband and he suddenly found himself the inheritor of such popularity as he had not known for years. Now, in 1968, another minor miracle was occurring. The main object of Queen Ena's visit was to rehabilitate her son in the eyes of 'his subjects' as she still insisted they were. She was wholly successful. Don Juan was thrilled by the reception which, in his own words[4] was 'not organized, because we didn't make the people go anywhere, but they just did, *spontaneously*. The Government was horrified.' Despite the official blackout on all news about the Queen's time of arrival and subsequent movements, word had got round and had spread rapidly. When on 7 February 1968, Ena stepped down from the Air France plane which had brought her from Lausanne via Nice, there were several thousand wildly cheering citizens of Madrid at Barajas airport to greet her. Even though the visit was a private one, Franco had obviously had to make some gesture to mark her arrival. He sent his Minister of Aviation, General José Lacalle, to meet her. There were some other government ministers at the airport as well but it was made clear that they were there strictly in a 'private capacity'. The excitement engendered by the dowager Queen's arrival spread like wild fire. Wherever she went during the three days of her visit, word had got about and the crowds were there ahead of her. It was, by any standards, a truly remarkable display of public sentiment but not one which was susceptible of facile explanation. Thirty-seven years had passed since Ena had been in Spain. Only a few had vivid personal memories of her. But her arrival now seemed to spark off a pent-up feeling of love for the house of Bourbon as personified by the young Prince (Juan Carlos) who had been winning all hearts—to say nothing of the effect made by his attractive bride—together with the living link with the past now represented by the former Queen.

Prince Juan Carlos's son, Felipe, was christened on the following day. The Queen held him in her arms as if holding, which was indeed the case, a possibly vital part of Spain's future. Few knew that the Queen had undertaken the journey very much against the advice of her doctor. She was not, at this stage, a healthy woman. Her gall bladder and liver complaints had been giving more pain and trouble. But she kept these as secret from as many people as possible and managed to conceal her proneness to exhaustion. In the nature of her visit she was not a guest of General Franco. Had she been she would have occupied the same building as she had done on her very first night in Madrid. For Franco and his wife now lived at the Pardo Palace, which is still maintained as something akin to a museum in the Caudillo's memory. The present King however, is hoping, as soon as it is politic to do so, to convert the Palace into a place of hospitality for his royal guests from abroad. He hopes that one of the first to come there may be the Queen of Great Britain.

Ena, while in Madrid, was a guest of the Alba family at their fabulous house in the heart of Madrid, the Liria Palace. She did, however, meet Franco. The protocol of the meeting presented some problems since strictly speaking it was not Franco who should be 'receiving' the Queen but the other way round. The meeting, therefore, took place unofficially and privately on the neutral ground of the Zarzuela Palace occupied by Prince Juan Carlos as his official residence. There was little love lost between the Caudillo and the Queen. Ena could not easily forgive Franco for his long standing enmity toward Don Juan. The two respected each other however and Franco, for once, was not wholly the master of the situation when they met. It had come to his notice that Ena, reacting to instinct rather than any sense of subtlety, refused to refer to his wife as 'La Señora' since to do so would seem to confer some sort of 'title' upon her. (The only title she ever received in fact—that of 'Señora de Meiras—had to be conferred by Franco himself some years later.) Thus the Queen addressed Franco's wife as 'Madame'. As for the Queen's meeting with Franco it was stiff but cordial and, from Ena's point of view, highly satisfactory. She had long known that she would get some confirmation, however oblique, as to Franco's state of mind over the monarchy. After her meeting with him she was sure that her grandson would one day be King of Spain. She was to die three months before Franco actually nominated Juan Carlos as his 'successor', an action which annoyed Don Juan at the time. And Spain had to wait until 1974 before Juan Carlos had become King in his own right, soon after which he plucked the mantle of Francoism off Spain's back for ever.

A Final Triumph

'Thus while there was no state reception for the Queen there *was* a reception of another and far more impressive kind. It was a reception given not *for* the visiting Queen, but *by* her. It was a remarkable and magnificent occasion held in the vast main reception room of the Liria Palace. Her host, the Duke of Alba, was the son-in-law of the famous 'Jimmy' Alba who had been so close to the royal family in the old days, albeit much associated in Ena's mind with the machinations of his sister Doña Sol. Almost more importantly the new Duke of Alba was the son of the Duke of Sottomayor, a former Jefé Superior of the Royal Palace and subsequently Ena's Comptroller and close friend after she had gone into exile. It was fitting that this, comparatively young, Duke of Alba should now be her host in Madrid just as he had acted as her master of ceremonies on the occasion of her recent eightieth birthday.

So many people wanted to be received by, or at least to see the Queen, that several thousand people actually passed through the doors of the Liria Palace in the course of an astonishing and historic afternoon. It could not be more than a glorified procession during which Queen Ena nodded and smiled at those who filed past bowing and curtseying. One person filing past could not restrain her emotion. This was the veteran opera singer Porta Imperio. Her breaking of ranks caused some consternation so she was ushered round to the back to join up eventually with those, such as the Duchesses of Pastrara and Durcal, and other old friends, who were due to be received privately.

Queen Ena's stay in Madrid was tantalizingly short but it was enough. While there, she insisted on being driven along the Calle Mayor, the street in which the attempt had been made on her life on the day of her wedding. She also made one very significant, strictly private, visit. This was a preprandial one to her grandson Alfonso, Duke of Cadiz, eldest son of Don Jaime. She was always very fond of him and some say that her influence on him was to bear important fruit later on. For Alfonso had dreams of succeeding to the Spanish throne as the eldest surviving son of his father, arguing that Don Jaime's renunciation should not apply to him. Such a possibility was strengthened when in 1972 Alfonso married Franco's favourite granddaughter, Maria del Carmen. It was generally thought at that time that Franco wanted to give the impression that such an eventuality was possible in case of opposition from Don Juan over the succession of Juan Carlos. Alfonso moreover was given a very large sum of money by Franco when he married his granddaughter from whom, however, he has since been divorced. In any event the scheme came to nothing— possibly because of the strong latent sense of duty on Alfonso's part which unquestionably, according to many, he had learnt from his grandmother, Queen Ena.

The large crowd which had come to the airport to great Queen Ena on her arrival was greatly exceeded by that which came to see her off. Don Juan estimated that there were 50,000. Queen Ena, moved to tears, left Spain for the last time with their vociferous cries ringing unforgettably in her ears. It was possibly the most moving moment of her life. Gone was any of that stiffness or fear which she had felt in the face of Madrid's crowds sixty years earlier. That had been her first test. This was her final triumph. 'Now', she said, 'I can die happily.'

A month later, in March 1968, she found herself once more at the house put at her disposal by the Rainiers. She was still exhilarated by her experience in Madrid, but it had taken its toll on her physically. To make matters worse she stumbled over one of her dogs while in her bedroom at the house in Monaco and hurt her head badly. Princess Grace personally supervised the care taken of her. The Infantas Beatrice and Christina and the Barcelonas flew to her side, but miraculously she was soon well enough to resume, at least briefly, her ordinary life after returning to Lausanne. But there were those who sensed that her death could not be far off. Old friends began to congregate in Lausanne. One who came (and is still alive) was a genuine friend from former days. He felt that some of the others who were hovering in the wings were only waiting to be 'in at the kill'. For some of them represented a remnant of that scattered 'Court' which was now harbouring hopes of a revived monarchy. To be seen to rally round the Queen, and thus to find favour with Don Juan, was thought by some to be politic. There were disquieting rumours of incompatibilities between Don Juan and his son merely because the former had had to return to Estoril, after visiting his mother, the very day that the latter arrived to see her. There was in fact no such situation but there was much confusion as to procedures and protocol in these last weeks of the old Queen's life.

Because the family had been scattered for so long, there had been grave lack of continuity in the administrative side of the Queen's affairs. With Ena's liver condition deteriorating daily, the Duke of Alba stepped into the breach to 'take command'. This was the description given to the author, along with much else, by a veteran Spanish grandee who was near at hand throughout the entire period of Queen Ena's last days. He got the uncomfortable impression that among those whom she called the 'watchers and waiters' who had come to Lausanne there still existed, not far below the surface, much of that latent intrigue, backbiting and jealousy which had so poisoned Ena's life a generation earlier. It made him nervous to think that the Queen, whom he had so long served and admired in various capacities, particularly as a friend and intimate confidant, might sense such an atmosphere among the tattered remnants of the former Court. This could only add immeasurably to the growing suffering she began to undergo as March dragged wearily into April in the year 1969. The decision had finally to be made as to whether the doctors should try to prolong the Queen's life by artificial means.

Ena herself had specifically stated that she wanted no such thing. The doctors were told to 'do what they could'. The end came on 15 April. It was intended that the Queen should be buried in the royal pantheon at the Escorial outside Madrid. But such an event could not occur at once and has not yet been brought about. The Queen was buried instead at the church of Sacred Heart at Ouchy, Lausanne, her body having been removed an hour after death to a clinic in Lausanne for embalming. At her own request before death, she lay in state in the chapel dressed in the blue gown given to her by her grandaughter, Maria del Pilar, Duchess of Bajadoz, eldest child of the Count of Barcelona. Her head was covered in a mantilla of white silk and the body was surrounded by the flag of Spain. As already mentioned, no face at the funeral was more wracked with grief than that of the luckless but tender-hearted and pathetic Don Jaime.

Modestly present at the funeral was someone who had known and admired the Queen for over fifty years. Almost certainly he knew more about her than any other living person; but he breathed none of the Queen's confidences or secrets during her lifetime. In his view she was 'an essentially noble woman, very loyal and therefore supremely just'. It was the epitaph of someone probably more fitted than any other person then living to make a final judgement on 'Her Majesty Victoria Eugenia of Battenberg, Queen of Spain, Wife of Alfonso XIII, King of Spain.' As such she was to have been styled in the original draft of the official notice to be sent out on her death. But at the suggestion of that same old, wise and faithful friend, a further title had been added: 'Royal Princess of Great Britain and Ireland.' For this was a title which she had never lost. It was appropriate that it should adhere in perpetuity to Victoria Eugenia of Battenberg, known to those who loved and understood her best as Ena, Spain's English Queen.

Notes and References

Books referred to in the notes that follow—whose titles are in some cases abbreviated—are fully listed in the bibliography. The abbreviation RA refers to the Royal Archives at Windsor. Entries reading 'Vilmorin, G. de', refer to interviews by Genevieve de Vilmorin with Queen Ena published in the *News of the World*. The roman numerals after each entry refer to the date of publication in that paper, i.e.: I—1.10.61; II—8.10.61; III—15.10.61; IV—22.10.61; V—29.10.61; VI—5.11.61; VII—12.11.61. The interviews were described by the *News of the World* as extracts from a 'forthcoming book' entitled 'The Chronicles of the First Half of the Century,' a work commissioned by Messrs Silvio Galardi in France but never actually published.

Chapter 1

1   RA Queen Victoria's Journal, 24 October 1887
2   Ibid.
3   Graham, E., *The Queen of Spain*, p. 20
4   RA Add. A15/4981, 16 November 1887
5   *Aberdeen Journal*, 24 November 1887
6   Graham, E., op. cit., p. 21
7   Gomez Santos, M., *La Reina Victoria Eugenia*, p. 18
8   Vilmorin, G. de, VI
9   Hibbert, C., *The Court at Windsor*, p. 228
10 Graham, E., *Alfonso XIII*, p. 203
11 RA Queen Victoria's Journal, 10 February 1894
12 Ibid., 16 February 1894
13 Vilmorin, G. de, VI

14 Gomez Santos, M., op. cit., p. 20
15 Vilmorin, G. de, VI
16 Graham, E., *The Queen of Spain*, p. 28
17 Jerrold, C., *The Widowhood of Queen Victoria*, p. 298
18 See Noel, G., *Princess Alice*
19 Duff, D., *The Shy Princess*, p. 351
20 Jerrold, C., op. cit., p. 351
21 Gomez Santos, M., op. cit., pp. 22–3

Chapter 2

1 Madariaga, S. de, *Spain*, p. 109
2 de Polnay, P., *A Queen of Spain*, p. 22
3 Aronson, T., *Royal Vendetta*, p. 16
4 Hills, G., *Spain*, p. 108
5 Brandt, J. A., *Towards the New Spain*, p. 368
6 Carr, R., *Spain*, pp. 368–9
7 Madariaga, S.de, op. cit., p. 212
8 Aronson, T., op. cit., p. 148
9 Pilar, Princess, and Chapman Huston, D., *Don Alfonso XIII*, p. 51
10 Brenan, G., *The Spanish Labyrinth*, p. 18
11 Ibid.
12 Reparaz, Gonzalo de, *Alfonso XIII y sus Cómplices*, p. 52
13 Aronson, T., op. cit., p. 131
14 de Polnay, P., op. cit., p. 3
15 *World Magazine*, 28 May 1911—Royal Archives, Madrid, Leg. 9886

Chapter 3

1 Graham, E., op. cit., p. 43
2 E.g., Azorin, J., of Madrid's *ABC* as relied on by Gomez Santos, M., op. cit., pp. 27–48
3 Vilmorin, G. de, II
4 Petrie, C., *King Alfonso XIII*, p. 79
5 Lee, S., *King Edward VII*, Vol. II, p. 512

6 ˙Gonzales-Doria, F., *Las Reinas de España*, p. 584
7 Vilmorin, G. de, II
8 Gomez Santos, M., op. cit., p. 41
9 Quick, A. J., *The Haemorraghic Diseases*, p. 192
10 Ibid.
11 Green, G. H., *A Royal Obstetric Tragedy*, p. 303
12 Ibid., p. 304
13 Gonzales-Doria, F., op. cit., p. 587
14 Vilmorin, G. de, II

Chapter 4

1 Graham, E., *The Queen of Spain*, op. cit.
2 Vilmorin, G. de, II
3 Gomez Santos, M., op. cit.
4 Graham, E., op. cit., p. 62
5 Pilar, Pss., op. cit., p. 98
6 Vilmorin, G. de, II
7 Ibid.
8 Graham, E., op. cit., p. 76
9 Pilar, Pss., op. cit. p. 99
10 Aronson, T., *Grandmama of Europe*, p. 166
11 Graham, E., op. cit., p. 86
12 Pilar, Pss., op. cit., p. 100
13 Gomez Santos, M., op. cit., p. 71
14 Lee, S., op. cit. Vol II, pp. 513–5
15 Graham, E., op. cit., p. 99
16 Aronson, T., op. cit., p. 164
17 Aronson, T., *Royal Vendetta*, p. 179
18 RA/W49/34, 25 May 1906
19 Pilar, Pss., op. cit., p. 109
20 Sencourt, R., *Alfonso XIII*, p. 91

Chapter 5

1 Petrie, C., op. cit., p. 88
2 Pilar, Pss., op. cit., p. 129 ff.

3   Gomez Santos, M., op. cit., p. 122
4   Duff, D., op. cit., p. 222
5   Ibid., p. 224
6   Erskine, Mrs S., *Twenty Years at Court*, pp. 99–100
7   Gomez Santos, M., op. cit., p. 130
8   Graham, E., op. cit., p. 145
9   Vilmorin, G. de, III
10 Gore, J., *King George V*, p. 212
11 Petrie, C., op. cit., p. 90
12 Duff, D., op. cit., p. 228
13 Vilmorin, G. de, III
14 *New York World*, 1 June 1906
15 Pilar, Pss., op. cit., p. 131
16 Ibid., p. 132
17 Ibid., p. 133
18 Vilmorin, G. de, III
19 Aronson, T., op. cit. p. 169

Chapter 6

1   Alonso, J. M., *Sucedio en Palacio*, p. 367
2   *New York Times*, 2 June 1906
3   *New York Herald*, 3 June 1906
4   Challice, R., *Secret History*, p. 317
5   Ibid., p. 318
6   Graham, E., op. cit., p. 155
7   Petrie, C., op. cit., p. 93
8   *New York World*, 2 June 1906
9   Herr, R., *Modern Spain*, p. 367
10 Carr., R., *Spain*, p. 367
11 Cf. Shaw, R., *Spain from Within*, p. 112 ff.
12 *Nuevo Ripalda*, 14th ed., 1927, quoted in Brenan, G., op. cit., p. 51,
    and at greater length, in Trend, J. B., *Origins of Modern Spain*, p. 61
13 Carr., R., op. cit., p. 483
14 Ibid.
15 Shaw, R., *Spain from within*
16 Ibid., p. 16

17 Ibid., p. 18
18 Challice, R., op. cit., pp. 335–6
19 Shaw, R., op. cit., pl. 115
20 Ibid., p. 116
21 Challice, R., op. cit., p. 324
22 Ibid., p. 322
23 Shaw, R., op. cit., p. 120
24 Ibid., p. 123
25 Ibid., p. 125
26 Gomez Santos, op. cit., p. 298
27 Aronson, T., op. cit., p. 187
28 Shaw, R., op. cit., p. 183
29 Ibid.

Chapter 7

1   Graham, E., op. cit., p. 127
2   RA/GV/CC/45/297, 7 November 1906
3   Vilmorin, G. de, IV
4   Gomez Santos, op. cit., p. 241
5   Duff, D., op. cit., p. 233
6   RA/GV/CC45/305, 14 June 1907
7   Shaw, R., op. cit., p. 121
8   Graham, E., p. 227
9   Gonzales-Doria, F., op. cit., p. 592
10 Balansó, Juan; quoted by Gonzales-Doria, F., op. cit., p. 592
11 Ibid.
12 Tavera, J. M. (in *The Last Days*) quoted by Gonzales-Doria, F., op. cit., p. 592
13 Royal Archives, Madrid, Leg. 9869
14 Royal Archives, Madrid, Leg. 9886
15 Gonzales-Doria, op. cit., p. 593

Chapter 8

1   Vilmorin, G. de, IV
2   Graham, E., op. cit., p. 272

3 Blasco Ibañez, V., *Por España*, p. 114
4 Erskine, Mrs S., *Twenty Years at Court*, p. 169
5 RA/GV/CC45/475, 21 February 1915
6 *The Sun*, Biarritz, 2 November 1911
7 RA/GV/CC45/573, 3 January 1917

Chapter 9

1 Graham, E., op. cit., p. 277
2 Aronson, T., op. cit., p. 200
3 Ibid.

Chapter 10

1 *New York Sun*, 16 January 1911, Royal Archives, Madrid, Leg. 9919
2 Brenan, G., op. cit., p. 73
3 Pilar, Pss., op. cit., p. 105
4 Herr, R., op. cit., pp. 149–50
5 Alvaro-Galiano, A., *The Fall of a Throne*, p. 137
6 Ibid., p. 138
7 Ibid.
8 Ibid., p. 32

Chapter 11

1 Vilmorin, G. de, V
2 Vilmorin, G. de, II
3 Gomez Santos, M., op. cit., p. 282
4 Vilmorin, G. de, I
5 Gomez Santos, M., op. cit., p. 281 (Quoting Madrid journalist Tomas Borras)
6 Gomez Santos, M., op. cit., pp. 280 ff.
7 Vilmorin, G. de, V
8 Gomez Santos, M., op. cit., p. 282
9 Vilmorin, G. de, V

Notes and References

Chapter 12

1 Alvaro-Galiano, A., op. cit., *The Fall of a Throne*, p. 248
2 Petrie, C., op. cit., p. 321
3 Gonzales-Doria, F., op. cit., p. 598
4 *Semana*, Madrid, January 1980, p. 86
5 Vilmorin, G. de, V

Chapter 13

1 Gonzales-Doria, F., op. cit., p. 598
2 Ibid., p. 599
3 Ibid.
4 Petrie, C., *The Spanish Royal House*, p. 257
5 Vilmorin, G. de, V
6 Ibid.
7 Ibid.
8 Gomez Santos, M., op. cit.
9 Ibid., p. 295

Chapter 14

1 In conversation with the author, Palazzo Torlonia, Rome, 8 August 1980
2 RA/GV/CC/45/1320, 12 April 1942
3 Ibid.
4 Perez Mateos, J. A., *Juan Carlos*, p. 47
5 As related to the author in conversation over lunch with HRH the Princess Margarita, at her house in Madrid, 13 November 1980
6 Related to the author in an audience graciously granted by His Majesty King Juan Carlos at Zarzuela Palace, Madrid, 11 November 1980
7 Information given to the author by Queen Ena's granddaughter, Doña Olympia, Madame Paul Annik Weiller; London, 16 June 1980
8 Vilmorin, G. de, VII

9 Letter to Countess Chrevreu-d'Antraigues
10 RA/GV/CC/45/1549, 3 December 1947
11 RA/GV/CC/45/1593, 3 July 1948

Chapter 15

1 Carr, R., *Spain: Dictatorship to Democracy*, p. 41
2 Vilmorin, G. de, VII
3 Curley, W. J. P., *Monarchs in Waiting*, p. 144
4 Ibid., p. 145

Bibliography

ALFONSO XIII, *Diario Intimo*, ed., by J. C. Castillo-Puce (Madrid: Biblioteca Nueva, 1961)

ALICE, PRINCESS, *For My Grandchildren* (London: Evans Bros, 1966)

ALONSO, JOSÉ MONTERO, *Sucedio in Palacio* (Madrid: Editorial Prensa Española, 1975)

ALVARO-GALIANO, ALCALA, *The Fall of a Throne* (London: Thornton-Butterworth, 1933)

ARCHER, WILLIAM, *The Life, Trial and Death of Francisco Ferrer* (London: Chapman & Hall, 1911)

ARONSON, THEO, *Grandmama of Europe* (London: Cassell, 1973)

ARONSON, THEO, *Royal Vendetta*, (London: Oldbourne, 1967)

BENSALSAN, SAMUEL LEVY, *Home Life in Spain* (New York: Macmillan, 1910)

BLASCO IBAÑEZ, VICENTE, *Por España y contra el rey* (Paris: Editorial Excelsior, 1925)

BOWERS, CLAUDE G., *My Mission to Spain* (London: Gollancz, 1954)

BRANDT, JOSEPH A., *Towards the New Spain* (Chicago: University of Chicago Press, 1933)

BRENAN, GERALD, *The Spanish Labyrinth* (Cambridge: Cambridge University Press, 1943)

CALVERT, ALBERTO F., *Don Alfonso XIII en Inglaterra* (London: George Philip & Son; Madrid: Adrian Romo, 1906)

CARDIGAN, Countess of, *My Recollections* (London: Eveleigh Nash, 1914)

CARR, RAYMOND, *Spain 1808–1939* (Oxford: Clarendon Press, 1966)

CARR, RAYMOND and FUSI AIZPURUA, JUAN PABLO, *Spain: Dictatorship to Democracy* (London: George Allen & Unwin, 1979)

CHALLICE, RACHEL, *The Secret History of the Court of Spain* (London: John Long, 1909)

CURLEY, WALTER J. P., *Monarchs in Waiting* (London: Hutchinson, 1975)

D'AUVERGNE, EDMUND B., *A Queen at Bay* (New York: John Long Co., 1910)

de POLNAY, PETER, *A Queen of Spain, Isabel II* (London: Hóllis & Carter, 1962)

DUFF, DAVID, *The Shy Princess* (London: Evans Bros., 1958)

DUFF-GORDON, LADY LUCIE, *Discretions and Indiscretions* (London: Jarrolds, 1932)

DUGDALE, EDGAR T. S. *Maurice de Bunsen: Diplomat and Friend* (London: John Murray, 1934)

ERBACH-SCHONBERG, PRINCESS MARIE ZU, *Reminiscences* (London: George Allen & Unwin, 1925)

ERSKINE, MRS STEUART (ed.), *Twenty Years at Court: From the Correspondence of the Hon. Eleanor Stanley* (London: Nisbet, 1916)

EULALIA, HRH THE INFANTA, *Court Life from Within* (London: Cassell, 1915)

— , *Courts and Countries After the War* (London: Hutchinson, 1925)

— , *Memoirs* (London: Hutchinson, 1936)

FERNSWORTH, LAWRENCE, *Spain's Struggle for Freedom* (Boston: Beacon Press, 1957)

GOMEZ SANTOS, MARIO, *La Reina Victoria Eugenia de Cerca* (Madrid: Afrodisio Aguado, SA, 1944)

GONZALES-DORIA, FERNANDO, *Las Reinas de España* (Madrid: Editorial Alce, 1978)

GORE, JOHN, *King George V* (London: John Murray, 1941)

GRAHAM, EVELYN, *The Life Story of King Alfonso XIII* (London: Herbert Jenkins, 1930)

GRAHAM, EVELYN, *The Queen of Spain* (London: Hutchinson, 1930)

GREEN, G. H., *A Royal Obstetric Tragedy and the Epitaph* (*New Zealand Medical Journal*, 69 (1969))

HERR, RICHARD, *Modern Spain* (Berkeley: University of California Press, 1971)

HIBBERT, CHRISTOPHER, *The Court at Windsor, A Domestic History* (London: Longmans Green, 1964)

HILLS, GEORGE, *Spain*, (London: Ernest Benn, 1970)

JERROLD, CLARE, *The Widowhood of Queen Victoria* (London: Eveleigh Nash, 1916)

Bibliography

KELLY, Sir DAVID, *The Ruling Few* (London: Hollis & Carter, 1952)

LEE, Sir SIDNEY, *King Edward VII* (London: Macmillan, 1925)

LIVERMORE, HAROLD, *A History of Spain* (New York: Grove Press, 1960)

MADARIAGA, SALVADOR DE, *Spain* (London: Jonathan Cape, 1942)

MAGNUS, PHILIP, *King Edward the Seventh* (London: John Murray, 1964)

MARIE, GRAND DUCHESS OF RUSSIA, *A Princess in Exile* (London: Cassell, 1932)

MEYNADIER, ROBERT, *Les Etapes de la Royauté d'Alphonse XIII* (Paris: Perrin, 1914)

NICOLSON, HAROLD, *King George V* (London: Constable, 1952)

NOEL, GERARD, *Princess Alice, Queen Victoria's Forgotten Daughter* (London: Constable, 1974)

OLMET, LUIS ANTON DEL and CARAFFA, ARTURO GARCIA, *Alfonso XIII* (Madrid: Alrededor del Mundo, 1913)

PEREZ-MATEOS, JUAN ANTONIO, *Juan Carlos: La Infancia Desconocida de un Rey* (Barcelona: Editorial Planeta, 1980)

PETRIE, Sir CHARLES, *Alfonso XIII and His Age* (London: Chapman & Hall, 1963)

— , *The Spanish Royal House* (London: Geoffrey Bles, 1958)

PILAR OF BAVARIA, HRH PRINCESS, and CHAPMAN-HUSTON, DESMOND, *Don Alfonso XIII* (London: John Murray, 1931)

PLESS, PRINCESS DAISY, *From My Private Diary* (London: John Murray, 1931)

— , *What I Left Unsaid* (London: Cassell, 1936)

POPE-HENNESSY, JAMES, *Queen Mary, 1867–1953* (London: George Allen & Unwin, 1959)

QUICK, A. J., *The Haemorraghic Diseases* (Springfield & Baltimore: Charles C. Thomas, 1942)

REPARAZ, GONZALO DE, *Alfonso XIII y sus complices* (Madrid: 1931)

RIDLEY, JASPER, *Napoleon III and Eugenie* (London: Constable, 1979)

ROMANONES, Conde de, *Reflexiones y Recuerdos* (Madrid: Espasa Calpe, 1940)

— , *Sagasta el Politico* (Bilbao, Barcelona, Madrid: 1912)

SARA, M. E., *The Life and Times of HRH Princess Beatrice* (London: Stanley Paul, 1945)

SENCOURT, ROBERT, *King Alfonso* (London: Faber & Faber, 1942)

—, *Spain's Uncertain Crown* (London: Ernest Benn, 1932)

SHAW, RAFAEL, *Spain from Within* (London: T. Fisher Unwin, 1910)

STEVENSON, R. SCOTT, *Famous Illnesses in History* (London: Eyre & Spottiswoode, 1962)

THOMAS, HUGH, *The Spanish Civil War* (London: Eyre & Spottiswoode, 1961)

TREND, J. B., *Origins of Modern Spain* (Cambridge: Cambridge University Press, 1934)

VARELA, BENIGUO, *Alfonso XIII* (Madrid: 1925)

VELASIO ZAZO, ANTONIO, *El Madrid de Alfonso XIII* (Madrid: 1918)

WELLS, WARRE BRADLEY, *The Last King: Don Alfonso XIII of Spain* (London: Frederick Muller, 1934)

Index

Index

Index

rumour of his prior marriage, 142;
succeeds to the throne (1910), 142;
reprimands Alfonso XIII for being away
from Spain (1931), 217

George VI, King of Great Britain and
Ireland, 256–7

Gibraltar, destruction of 'Our Lady of
Europe' (1713), 24–5

Gimpera, Père Bosch, 208

Giner de los Rios, Francisco, 111

Glendinning, Bryden, 135

Glyn, Elinor, 189

Godoy, Manuel de, 36

Gonzalo (son of Don Jaime), 270, 284

Gonzalo, Don (son of Alfonso XIII and
Queen Ena), 203; his birth (1914), 147;
as a sufferer from haemophilia, 147,
238, 244, 246, 268; leaves Spain
(1931), 226, 231–2; in exile, 235, 244;
studies engineering at the University of
Louvain, 244; his death (1934), 246–7,
268

Grace, Princess of Monaco, 285, 289,
296

Graham, Evelyn, 59

Grand Hotel, Rome, Alfonso XIII living
at the, 257–62

grandees desert Alfonso XIII (1931),
218–19

Green, Mrs. (a nurse), 137

Greville, Mrs. Ronnie, 189–90, 274

Grey, Sir Edward, 75, 76

Guerrero, Maria, 168

Guildhall, London, banquet for Alfonso
XIII at (1905), 50–1

Gutierrez, Dr. Eugenio (*later* Count of
San Diego), 135

Habsburg dynasty, 24, 31, 36, 38, 45, 59,
133, 266

haemophilia, 54–8; Princess Ena as a
carrier of, 3, 57–8, 138–9, 147, 149,
162, 168–9, 172, 193–4, 216, 234,
237, 238, 263, 268; in the Russian
Imperial family, 55, 56, 234; Queen
Victoria as the originator of, 55–7, 234;
Alfonso XIII warned about, 55, 57–8,
193–4, 263–4; Queen Victoria's
daughters as carriers of, 56–7, 234;
affects the Infante Alfonso, 138–9,
142–3, 159–60, 162, 172, 190, 193–4,
197–9, 213, 225, 227–8, 231, 235,
237, 238, 244–5, 251–2, 268, 288;
affects Don Gonzalo, 147, 238, 244,
246, 268; the Infantas Beatrice and
Christina not carriers of, 246, 268

Hamilton, Robert, 103–4, 108

Hanover, Princess Frederica of *see*
Frederica, Princess of Hanover

Hanoverian dynasty and haemophilia,
55–6

Hauke, Countess Julie Theresa von *see*
Julie, Princess of Battenberg

Helena, Princess (Princess Christian of
Schleswig-Holstein), 3, 42, 43, 48

Helena Victoria, Princess (daughter of
Princess Helena), 48

Henry, Prince of Battenberg, 12, 17, 70;
his marriage to Princess Beatrice
(1885), 1–2, 18, 62; and the birth of
Princess Ena (1887), 3; and his
children, 6–7, 12, 15, 18, 20; his
relationship with Queen Victoria, 4–5,
9, 18; as Governor of the Isle of Wight,
15, 19; his family history, 15–16, 18; at
the Lord Mayor's dinner (1887), 19;
hostility towards, 18–19; his character,
18; his travels, 19–20; prophesies
Princess Ena's journey to Spain, 20; his
death (1896), 20

Henry, Prince of Prussia, 83

Herr, Richard, 207

Hesse, Prince Alexander of *see* Alexander,
Prince of Hesse

Hesse, Alice, Grand Duchess of *see* Alice,
Princess, Grand Duchess of Hesse

Hesse, Louis, Grand Duke of *see* Louis,
Grand Duke of Hesse

Hesse, Princess Marie of *see* Marie,
Princess of Hesse

Hesse, Princess Victoria of *see* Milford
Haven, Victoria Mountbatten,
Marchioness of

Hijar, Duke of, 87

Hippler, Helga, 270

Hitler, Adolf, 256

Hohernzollern, Princess Joanna of *see*
Joanna, Princess of Hohernzollern

Holy Year (1933), 245

Horrachuelos, Duke of, 95

hospitals, Spanish, 151, 153, 178, 195; in
Morocco, 156, 177–8

Hotel Beau Rivage, Ouchy, 248, 257,
290–1

Hotel Meurice, Paris, Spanish royal
family in exile in the, 233–4, 235, 236,
238, 241

Hotel Royal, Lausanne, 249, 265

Hotel Savoy, Fontainebleau, Spanish
royal family in exile in the, 233,
234–43, 249

Howard, Sir Esmé, 189, 193, 228

Hoyos, Marquis of, 227

Index

Index